MW00723380

The
Eclectic
Gourmet
Guide to
Washington, D.C.

Also available from MENASHA RIDGE PRESS

The Eclectic Gourmet Guide to Washington, D.C.

Eve Zibart

MENASHA
RIDGE
PRESS

Every effort has been made to ensure the accuracy of information throughout this book. Bear in mind, however, that prices, schedules, etc., are constantly changing. Readers should always verify information before making final plans.

Menasha Ridge Press, Inc.
P.O. Box 43059
Birmingham, Alabama 35243

Cover and text design by Suzanne Holt
Cover art by Michele Natale

ISBN 0-89732-232-0
Library of Congress Catalog Card Number 97-11987

Manufactured in the United States of America

10 9 8 7 6 5 4 3 2 1

First Edition

CONTENTS

About the Author

Eve Zibart has written more about dining and entertainment than most people experience in a lifetime. Starting as a feature writer for the *Nashville Tennessean* at the age of 17, she moved to the *Washington Post* in 1977 as a temporary night city editor. Eve quickly exhibited prowess in her prose coupled with an aptitude for grammar and an extensive vocabulary and rapidly moved through the ranks of the *Post* as a "Style" feature writer, a "Weekend" assistant editor, a "Maryland" columnist, and the "TV" editor. Currently, Eve is the restaurant columnist for the *Washington Post's* "Weekend" section. Known to friends and fans as "Dr. Nightlife," Eve has enough experience and knowledge to advise the Joint Chiefs of Staff on national trends.

In addition to her responsibilities at the *Post*, Eve is a regular contributor to *USAir* inflight and *Four Seasons* magazines and has written for *Cosmopolitan*, *Book Page*, and *Playboy*. Given an amazing ability to turn 24 hours in to 30, Eve has found time to author several books, including *The Unofficial Guide to Ethnic Cuisine and Dining in America*, *The Unofficial Guide to Dining in Washington, D.C.*, *The Unofficial Guide to Branson, Missouri*, and *The Unofficial Disney Companion: The Inside Story of Walt Disney World and the Man Behind the Mouse*.

In addition to her marriage with the English language, Eve is also married to Don Tippman, known as "Dodger" for his National League Dickensian proclivities. Eve and he have no kids but choose to complement their lives with a fat cat and a sports car—just as temperamental as children, maybe more so.

⚵ GETTING IT
⚵ RIGHT

A lot of thought went into this guide. While producing a dining guide may appear to be a straightforward endeavor, I can assure you that it is fraught with peril. I have read dining guides by authors who turn up their noses at anything except four-star French restaurants (of which there are a whole lot fewer than people think). Likewise, I have seen a guide that totally omits Thai and Indian restaurants—among others—because the author did not understand those cuisines. I have read guides absolutely devoid of criticism, written by "experts" unwilling to risk offending the source of their free meals. Finally, I've seen those books that are based on surveys and write-ins from diners whose credentials for evaluating fine dining are mysterious at best and questionable at least.

How, then, do you go about developing a truly excellent dining guide? What is the best way to get it right?

If dining guides are among the most idiosyncratic of reference books, it is primarily because the background, taste, integrity, and personal agenda of each author are problematic. The authors of most dining guides are vocational or avocational restaurant or food critics. Some of these critics are schooled professionals, with palates refined by years of practical experience and culinary study; others are journalists, often with no background in food criticism or cooking, who are arbitrarily assigned the job of reviewing restaurants by their newspaper or magazine publisher. (Although it *is* occasionally possible to find journalists who are also culinary professionals.) The worst cases are the legions of self-proclaimed food critics who mooch their way from restaurant to restaurant, growing fat on free meals in exchange for writing glowing reviews.

Ignorance of ethnic cuisine or old assumptions about what makes for haute cuisine particularly plague authors in cities without much ethnic variety in restaurants, or authors who have been writing for years about the same old, white linen, expense-account tourist traps. Many years ago in Lexington, Kentucky, for example, there was only one Chinese restaurant in town and it was wildly successful—in spite of the fact that it was Chinese in name only. Its specialty dishes, which were essentially American vegetable casseroles smothered in corn starch, were happily gobbled up by loyal patrons who had never been exposed to real Chinese cooking. The food was not bad, but it was not Chinese either. Visitors from out of town, inquiring about a good local Chinese restaurant, were invariably directed to this place. As you would expect, they were routinely horrified by the fare.

And, while you might argue that American diners are more sophisticated and knowledgeable nowadays than at the time of the Lexington pavilion, the evidence suggests otherwise. In Las Vegas, for instance, a good restaurant town with a number of excellent Italian eateries, the local Olive Garden (a chain restaurant) is consistently voted the city's best Italian restaurant in a yearly newspaper poll. There is absolutely nothing wrong with the Las Vegas Olive Garden, but to suggest that it is the best Italian restaurant in the city is ludicrous. In point of fact, the annual survey says much more about the relative sophistication of Las Vegas diners than it does about the quality of local Italian restaurants.

But if you pick up a guide that reflects the views of many survey respondents, a *vox populi* or reader's choice compendium, that is exactly the problem. You are dependent upon the average restaurant-goer's capacity to make sound, qualitative judgments—judgments almost always impaired by extraneous variables. How many times have you had a wonderful experience at a restaurant, only to be disappointed on a subsequent visit? Trying to reconcile the inconsistency, you recall that on your previous visit, you were in the company of someone particularly stimulating, and that perhaps you had enjoyed a couple of drinks before eating. What I am getting at is that our reflections on restaurant experiences are often colored by variables having little or nothing to do with the restaurant itself. And while I am given to the democratic process in theory, I have my doubts about depending entirely on survey forms that reflect such experiences.

There are more pragmatic arguments to be made about such eaters' guides as well. If you cannot control or properly qualify your survey respondents, you cannot assure their independence, knowledge, or critical sensitivity. And, since literally anyone can participate in such surveys, the ratings can be easily slanted by those with vested interests. How many bogus responses would it take to dramatically upgrade a restaurant's rating in a survey-based, big-city dining guide? Forty or even fewer. Why? Because the publisher receives patron reports (survey responses, readers' calls) covering more restaurants than can be listed in the book. Thus the "voting" is distributed over such a large number of candidate restaurants that the median number of reports for the vast majority of establishments is 120 or fewer. A cunning restaurant proprietor who is willing to stuff the ballot box, therefore, could easily improve his own rating—or lower that of a competitor.

So my mission in the *Eclectic Gourmet Guides* is to provide you with the most meaningful, useful, and accessible restaurant evaluations possible. Weighing the alternatives, I have elected to work with culinary experts, augmenting their opinions with a carefully qualified survey population of totally independent local diners of demonstrated culinary sophistication. The experts I have sought to author the *Eclectic Gourmet Guides* are knowledgeable, seasoned professionals; they have studied around the world, written cookbooks or columns, and closely follow the development of restaurants in their cities. They are well versed in ethnic dining, many having studied cuisines in their native lands. And they have no prejudice about high or low cuisine. They are as at home in a Tupelo, Mississippi, catfish shack as in an exclusive French restaurant on New York's Upper East Side. Thus the name "Eclectic Gourmet."

Equally important, I have sought experts who make every effort to conduct their reviews anonymously, and who always pay full menu prices for their meals. We are credible not only because we are knowledgeable, but also because we are independent.

You, the reader of this *Eclectic Gourmet Guide,* are the inspiration for and, we hope, the beneficiary of our diligence and methodology. Though we cannot evaluate your credentials as a restaurant critic, your opinion as a consumer—of this guide and the restaurants within—is very important to us. A clip-out survey can be found at the back of the book; please tell us about your dining experiences and let us know whether you agree with our reviews.

Eat well. Be happy.

Bob Sehlinger

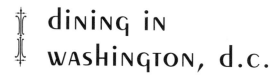

dining in
washington, d.c.

THE NEW WASHINGTON COOKERY

The great calorie inflation is over in Washington. Dollar for dollar (and pound for pound), dining in Washington has never been better: more varied, healthier, more affordable—and, when it is pricey, it's more apt to be worth the expense. And in addition, Washington restaurant patrons benefit from both "insider" trends and outside influences—from general trends in the restaurant business and from D.C.'s unique demographics.

ETHNIC INFLUENCE

This onetime cholesterol capital of the world has discovered not only its natural resources—its regional specialties and farm produce—but also its imported ones, the rainbow of immigrant chefs and cuisines and the even more intriguing pidgin cuisines that are constantly being created here. Consider the possibilities in a restaurant called "Cajun Bangkok" or "Thai Roma," or one that advertises Chinese-Mexican or Italian-Creole.

One of the most enjoyable aspects of dining out in Washington is exploring more exotic cuisines and new trends—even, for the newly watchful, haute health restaurants, where additives and chemicals are banned or heart-healthy cuisine is custom-tailored. What follows is not a list of the 200 "best" kitchens in the Washington area; it's a compendium of the best and the broadest, with an eye toward the unusual and even the mercurial.

NEW RESTAURANT districts

Along with the awakening of the Washington palate has come a rearrangement of the dining map. While Georgetown remains a busy shopping and night life area, it is no longer the dominant restaurant strip. The revitalized downtown arts district, particularly the hip/conspicuous strip of Seventh Street, NW between E and I streets; the ethnically mixed Adams-Morgan neighborhood; and the northwest suburbs—particularly the Asian polyglot neighborhoods of Wheaton and Bethesda with their "golden triangles" of restaurants—have all emerged as livelier locations, with Gaithersburg and Germantown hot on their heels. At the same time, restaurant dining has become so diversified that one no longer needs to go to the "Little Saigon" neighborhood around Clarendon for good Vietnamese cooking (although Adams-Morgan is still home to most of the Ethiopian restaurants); in fact, it's hard to imagine that anyone living in the Washington metropolitan area is more than a mile from three or four different ethnic restaurants.

SCOPING OUT THE lunch CROWD

In the old days the price of a Washington meal proved its importance—and by implication, the diners'. These days the appeal of a D.C. restaurant rests more on a kitchen's imagination, its beer selection, its service, even its bottled water. Half the fun of lunching out is scoping out the midday clientele: power lunchers (at the old standbys and some well-kept secret spots), hour lunchers (very often at ethnic restaurants, which are rather quicker on the uptake than traditional white-linen establishments), flower lunchers (the remnants of the leisure class), and shower lunchers (those roving bands of office workers who seem always to be celebrating someone's great occasion but who want individual checks).

If you're not sure which kind of restaurant you've just walked into, glance around at the beverage glasses. Power lunchers are more likely to order a cocktail, hour lunchers a beer, flower lunchers wine, and shower lunchers soft drinks or pitchers with paper fans.

Incidentally, there's a new "power meal" in Washington: afternoon tea. Over finger sandwiches and scones at the Four Seasons, Hay-Adams, and Jefferson hotels, you will see just as many pin-striped suits as flowered skirts—and a lot more briefcases than either. Lower-pressure than traditional conferences but still face-to-face, tea has become a very popular way for lawyers and lobbyists to take meetings. And it also fits the two-career-family lifestyle better than long, expensive dinners.

iNdusTRy TRENds

The end of price-padding inflation has had a rather more serious impact on the restaurant industry in Washington. Several of the finer establishments, caught between the pincers of exorbitant rent and declining expense-account business, have closed. A few have downscaled, and some of the most influential chefs in the area are opening what might be called "off-the-rack" restaurants (cafes and pizzerias) in addition to their designer rooms. More intriguing, some mixed-metaphor chefs are becoming partners: Galileo godfather Roberto Donna, who started the off-price trend with his Adams-Morgan kitchen I Matti, and Jean-Louis Palladin of the Watergate, arguably the two finest chefs in the city, created Pesce. Yannick Cam of Provence and Savio Racino of Primi Piatti founded Coco Loco and are about to open El Catalan, too. Donna also owns the retro-trendy spaghetti gardens Il Radicchio, Dolcetto, and Arucola; and with i Ricchi founder Francesco Ricchi, Cesco in Bethesda.

The 200 restaurant profiles that follow (we say 200, although it's closer to 250, since several profiles cover more than one location) are intended to give you a sense of the atmosphere and advantages of a particular establishment as well as its particular cuisine. None should be taken as gospel, because one drawback of Washington's new appetite for adventure is that restaurants open and close—and promising chefs play musical kitchens—with breathtaking speed. This also means that we have for the most part profiled only restaurants that have been in operation for at least a year, or that have chefs with such strong track records that they are of special interest.

And, blame it on yuppie consciousness, gourmet magazine proliferation, or real curiosity, the increased interest in the techniques of cooking has also produced a demand for variety, for constantly challenging presentations and guaranteed freshness. Consequently, many of the fancier restaurants change their menus or a portion thereof every day, and more change seasonally, so the specific dishes recommended at particular places may not be available on a given night. Use these critiques as a guide, an indication of the chef's interests and strengths—and weaknesses, too. We'll tell you what's not worth trying.

the new hotel dining

When it comes to hotel dining rooms, Washington contradicts the conventional wisdom that hotel restaurants are not worth seeking out. In D.C., many of the better chefs (including a dozen or so profiled in depth here) are working in hotels. This is a mutually beneficial arrangement, allowing the chefs to concentrate on managing a kitchen, not a business, and providing an extra attraction to potential clients. Since Washington's hotels count on a great deal of expense-account business, they generally offer menus on the expensive side. In addition to the restaurants listed, we recommend those at the George Washington Inn (**Zuki Moon**), Henley Park (**Coeur de Lion**), the Lansdowne Resort in Leesburgh (**Potomac Grille**), the Ritz-Carlton downtown (**Jockey Club**), The Stratford Motor Inn in Falls Church (**Cafe Rose**), the Westin (**Cafe on M**) and the Mayflower (**Cafe Promenade**), to name a few.

the inns and outs

The Washington area is also blessed with some very fine country inns within a couple of hours' drive. We have only actually profiled the **Inn at Little Washington** and **L'Auberge Provençal** in this edition (maybe we'll add a special category in the future), but in addition, we would recommend looking into such restaurants as **Antrim 1844** in Taneytown, **Willow Grove** in Orange, **Stone Manor** in Middleton, the **Turning Point Inn** in Urbana, **Four and Twenty Blackbirds** in Flint Hill, and the **Ashby Inn** in Paris.

diners' special needs

The following profiles attempt to address the special requirements of diners who use wheelchairs or leg braces. Because so many of Washington's restaurants occupy older buildings and row houses, options for wheelchair users are unfortunately limited. In most cases, wheelchair access is prevented right at the street, but many restaurants offering easy entrance to the dining room keep their rest rooms up or down a flight of stairs. In either case, we list them as having "no" disabled access. "Fair" access suggests that there is an initial step or small barrier to broach, or that passage may be a bit tight, but that once inside the establishment, dining is comfortable for the wheelchair user. Again, hotel dining rooms are good bets—the same wide halls and ramps used for baggage carts and deliveries serve wheelchair users as well. Newer office buildings and mixed shopping and entertainment complexes have ramps and elevators that make them wheelchair accessible; the ones above subway stations even have their own elevators.

Although there are only two restaurants categorized as vegetarian (and in fact one, Planet X, has recently added some meat dishes, although that is still not its focus), diners with restricted diets should peruse the comments; while almost all Washington restaurants now offer either vegetarian entrees on the menu or will make low-salt or low-fat dishes on request, some are particularly amenable to doing this, and we have said so. Use common sense: A big-ticket steakhouse is unlikely to have many nonmeat options (though even Morton's of Chicago has become accustomed to making veggie plates), but since few countries in the world eat as much meat as Americans, most ethnic cuisines are good bets for vegetarians.

plAces to see fAces

Washington may not really be Hollywood on the Potomac, but there are celebrity faces aplenty (so many movie stars come to town to lobby for their pet causes, it's getting close).

Consequently, out-of-towners often list "famous people" right after the Air & Space Museum on the required-viewing list. And since being seen is part of the scene—and getting star treatment is one of the perks of being famous—celebrities tend to be visible in dependable places, particularly at lunch.

The venerable steak-and-lobster **Palm**, with its wall-to-wall caricatures of famous customers and its bullying waiters, is still a popular media and legal-eagle hangout. Among its regulars: strange political bedfellows James Carville and Mary Matalin, who sometimes eat in and carry out simultaneously.

The Capital Grille is particularly well located in this expansive economy; only a short stroll from the Capitol grounds, it serves as both boardroom and back room for the GOP. After the party's gala in January 1995, a couple hundred of the black-tie guests dropped by the Grille for drinks and cigars; but only a few nights before, when a clutch of budget-crunching Republican senators had peeked in after last call, the general manager had rolled up his sleeves and grilled a dozen strategic burgers. Among those with preferred seats at the Grille are House Speaker Newt Gingrich and lawyer-turned-lobbyist-turned-actor-turned-populist Sen. Fred Thompson. But the Capital Grille gets its share of pairs, too: Right-Republican Sen. Lauch Faircloth and liberal intellectual Sen. Pat Moynihan once arrived for dinner, Faircloth announcing the pair to staff as "the redneck and the aristocrat."

Galileo, the flagship restaurant of Washington's *capo di tutti capi* chefs Roberto Donna, is a favorite of both Ted Kennedy and Bob Dole, as well as Treasury Secretary Robert Rubin. **Restaurant Nora** was an early favorite of the Clintons and Gores; its sibling **Asia Nora** draws Attorney General Janet Reno and other Cabinet shakers; and Energy Secretary Hazel O'Leary, Bosnian peacemeister Richard C. Holbrooke, and Clinton insider Vernon Jordan like **Melrose**. The old-clubby **Monocle** (107 D Street, NE; (202) 546-4488), the unofficial transfer point between the Senate and its office buildings, draws the Republican money men— Alfonse D'Amato and Pete Domenici, chairmen of the Senate banking and finance committees, respectively, and John Kasich, chairman of the House budget committee.

The elegant Raj-redux **Bombay Club** across the street from the White House attracts presidential advisor-cum-commentator George Stephanopoulos, Reno, and John Glenn. Sen. Frank Lautenberg of New Jersey (who wrote the bill banning smoking on airlines), Stephanopolous, D'Amato, and Bob Kerrey have taken the steak-and-stogie course at **Les Halles**.

Pol-watchers should also check out **Two Quail** for congresswomen or **La Colline** for committee staffers. **Bullfeathers** is full of national committee staffers from both parties (410 1st Street, NW; (202) 543-5005). **The Hay-Adams** is where the power breakfast was born, starring White House staff and federal bureaucrats, and the **Powerscourt** (under renovation at press time) is the branch office of Bostonian politicians. Behind-the-scenes power-wielders, "spouses of," and social arbiters congregate at the Ritz-Carlton's **Jockey Club** (2100 Massachusetts Avenue, NW; (202) 659-8000) and **Maison Blanche** (1725 F Street, NW; (202) 842-0070).

Treasury and White House staff crowd the neighboring **Old Ebbitt Grill**, the **Occidental Grill**, and **Georgia Brown's**. And, among the low-profile politicians and working press who frequent the **Market Inn**, especially in shad roe season, are rumored to be CIA and other professionals incognito (200 E Street, SW; (202) 554-2100).

World Bank and OAS suits lunch at **Taberna del Alabardero**; corporate write-offs go to the **Prime Rib** and the new midtown **Morton's**, which is also where Art Buchwald, who lost his longtime favorite table when Tiberio's closed, is imperially re-ensconced.

MORE RECOMMENDATIONS

◆ The Best Afternoon Teas

Four Seasons Hotel
2800 Pennsylvania Avenue, NW   (202) 342-0444
The Hay-Adams Hotel
16th and H streets, NW   (202) 638-6600
Henley Park Hotel
926 Massachusetts Avenue, NW   (202) 638-5200
Jefferson Hotel
1200 16th Street, NW   (202) 347-2200
Park Hyatt Hotel
24th and M streets, NW   (202) 955-3899
The Tea Cozy
119 South Royal Street, Alexandria   (703) 836-8181
Teaism
2009 R Street, NW   (202) 667-3827

◆ The Best Bagels

Bagel City
12119 Rockville Pike, Rockville   (301) 231-8080
Bethesda Bagel
4819 Bethesda Avenue, Bethesda   (301) 652-8990
Bruegger's Bagels
Many area locations
Chesapeake Bagel Bakery
Many area locations

◆ The Best Bar Food or Appetizers

Citronelle Latham Hotel
3000 M Street, NW   (202) 625-2150

Cottonwood Cafe
4844 Cordell Avenue, Bethesda   (301) 656-4844
Red Sage
605 14th Street, NW   (202) 638-4444

◆ The Freshest Beers (Brewed on Site)

Bardo Rodeo
2000 Wilson Boulevard, Arlington   (703) 527-9399
Blue-N-Gold Brewing Company
Corner of Washington Boulevard and Highland Street, Arlington
   (703) 908-4995
Brewer's Alley
124 N. Market Street, Frederick   (301) 631-0089
Capitol City Brewing Co.
1100 New York Avenue, NW   (202) 628-2222
2700 South Quincy Street, Arlington   (703) 578-3888
7735 Old Georgetown Road, Bethesda   (301) 652-2282
DuClaw Brewing Co.
16-A Bel-Air South Station Parkway, Bel Air   (410) 515-3222
John Harvard's Brewhouse
1299 Pennsylvania Avenue, NW   (202) 783-2739
Mount Airy Brewing Co.
223 South Main Street, Mount Airy   (410) 795-5557
Old Dominion Brewing Co.
44633 Guilford Drive, Ashburn   (703) 689-1225
Olde Towne Taverne & Brewing Co.
Summit and Diamond avenues, Gaithersburg   (301) 948-4200
Potomac River Brewing Co.
14141-A Parke Long Court, Chantilly   (703) 631-5430
Rock Bottom Restaurant & Brewery
7900 Norfolk Avenue, Bethesda   (301) 652-1311
Sweetwater Tavern
14250 Sweetwater Lane, Centreville   (703) 449-1100
Virginia Beverage Co.
607 King Street, Alexandria   (703) 684-5397

◆ The Best Burgers

Brewbaker's
6931 Arlington Road, Bethesda   (301) 907-2600
The Brickskeller
1523 22nd Street, NW   (202) 293-1885
Clyde's
3236 M Street, NW   (202) 333-9180
8332 Leesburg Pike, Tysons Corner   (703) 734-1901
Reston Town Center, Reston   (703) 787-6601
The Old Ebbitt Grill
675 15th Street, NW   (202) 347-4801
Union Street Public House
121 South Union Street, Alexandria   (703) 548-1785

◆ The Best Coffee

Dean & DeLuca
3276 M Street, NW   (202) 342-2500
1299 Pennsylvania Avenue, NW   (202) 628-8155
1919 Pennsylvania Avenue, NW   (202) 296-4327
Pop Shop
1513 17th Street, NW   (202) 328-0880
Puccini's
1620 L Street, NW   (202) 223-1975
Starbuck's
Many area locations

◆ The Best Desserts

Citronelle
3000 M Street, NW (Latham Hotel)   (202) 625-2150
Dean & DeLuca
3276 M Street, NW   (202) 342-2500
Dolci Finale
2653 Connecticut Avenue, NW (Pettito's)   (202) 667-5350
Patisserie Cafe Didier
3206 Grace Street, NW   (202) 342-9083
Lespinasse
16th and K streets, NW (Carlton Hotel)   (202) 879-6900

The Kennedy Center Roof Terrace
Virginia and New Hampshire avenues, NW   (202) 416-8555

◆ The Best Dining and Dancing

Brasil Sol e Mar
2519 Pennsylvania Avenue, NW   (202) 463-3025
Cafe Milano
3251 Prospect Street, NW   (202) 333-6183
Coeur de Lion
925 Massachusetts Avenue, NW (Henley Park Hotel)
    (202) 414-0500
Coco Loco
810 7th Street, NW   (202) 289-2626
Felix
2408 18th Street, NW   (202) 483-3549
Ritz-Carlton Hotel
1700 Tysons Boulevard, McLean   (703) 506-4300
Melrose
24th and M streets, NW (Park Hyatt Hotel)   (202) 955-3899
701
701 Pennsylvania Avenue, NW   (202) 393-0701

◆ The Most Entertaining Decor

Bangkok St. Grill and Noodles
5872 Leesburg Pike, Falls Church   (703) 379-6707
Busara
2340 Wisconsin Avenue, NW   (202) 337-2340
8142 Watson Street, McLean   (703) 356-2288
Clyde's of Chevy Chase
70 Wisconsin Circle, Chevy Chase   (301) 951-9600
Filomena's
1063 Wisconsin Avenue, NW   (202) 337-2782
Hibiscus Cafe
3401 K Street, NW   (202) 965-7170
Pizzeria Paradiso
2029 P Street, NW   (202) 223-1245
Planet Hollywood
1101 Pennsylvania Avenue, NW   (202) 783-7827

Provence

2401 Pennsylvania Avenue, NW   (202) 296-1166

Rain Forest Cafe

Routes 7 and 123 (Tysons Corner Center), Tysons Corner
(703) 821-1900

Raku: An Asian Diner

19th and Q streets, NW   (202) 265-7258

7240 Woodmont Avenue, Bethesda   (301) 718-8681

Red Sage

605 14th Street, NW   (202) 638-4444

Tara Thai

226 Maple Avenue West, Vienna   (703) 255-2467

4828 Bethesda Avenue, Bethesda   (301) 657-0488

◆ The Best Family Dining

Generous George's

7031 Little River Turnpike, Annandale   (703) 941-9600

6131 Backlick Road, Springfield   (703) 451-7111

3006 Duke Street, Alexandria   (703) 370-4303

Guapo's

4515 Wisconsin Avenue, NW   (202) 686-3588

9811 Washingtonian Boulevard (Rio Centre), Gaithersburg
(301) 977-5655

Hard Rock Cafe

999 E Street, NW   (202) 737-ROCK

Olney Ale House

2000 Sandy Spring Road (Route 108), Olney   (301) 774-6708

Oodles Noodles

1120 19th Street, NW   (202) 293-3138

4907 Cordell Avenue, Bethesda   (301) 986-8833

Radio Free Italy

5 Cameron Street (Torpedo Factory)   (703) 683-0361

Rain Forest Cafe

Routes 7 and 123 (Tysons Corner Center), Tysons Corner
(703) 821-1900

◆ The Best Pizza

Faccia Luna
2400 Wisconsin Avenue, NW   (202) 337-3132
23 Washington Boulevard, Alexandria   (703) 838-5998
2909 Wilson Boulevard, Arlington   (703) 276-3099
Pizza de Resistance
2300 Clarendon Boulevard, Arlington   (703) 351-5680
Pizzeria Paradiso
2029 P Street, NW   (202) 223-1245
Primi Piatti
2013 I Street, NW   (202) 223-3600
8045 Leesburg Pike, Tysons Corner   (703) 893-0300
Zio's
9083 Gaither Road, Gaithersburg   (301) 977-6300

◆ The Best Raw Bars

Blue Point Grill
600 Franklin Street, Alexandria   (703) 739-0404
Georgetown Seafood Grill
3063 M Street, NW   (202) 333-7038
1200 19th Street, NW   (202) 530-4430
The Old Ebbitt Grill
675 15th Street, NW   (202) 347-4801
Kinkead's
2000 Pennsylvania Avenue, NW   (202) 296-7700
The Sea Catch
1054 31st Street, NW, rear   (202) 337-8855

◆ The Most Romantic Dining

Asia Nora
2213 M Street, NW   (202) 797-4860
Iron Gate Inn
1734 N Street, NW   (202) 737-1370
L'Auberge Chez François
332 Springvale Road, Great Falls   (703) 759-3800
La Chaumière
2813 M Street, NW   (202) 338-1784

Lafayette

16th and H streets, NW (Hay-Adams Hotel)   (202) 638-2570

Lespinasse

16th and K streets, NW (Carlton Hotel)   (202) 879-6900

Old Angler's Inn

10801 MacArthur Boulevard, Potomac   (301) 299-9097

Provence

2401 Pennsylvania Avenue, NW   (202) 296-1166

Red Sage

605 14th Street, NW   (202) 638-4444

Sarinah Satay House

1338 Wisconsin Avenue, NW   (202) 337-2955

1789

1226 36th Street, NW   (202) 965-1789

Tabard Inn

1739 N Street, NW   (202) 833-2668

Two Quail

320 Massachusetts Avenue, NE   (202) 543-8030

◆ The Best Sunday Brunches

Clyde's

3236 M Street, NW   (202) 333-9180

8332 Leesburg Pike, Tysons Corner   (703) 734-1901

The Four Seasons Hotel Garden Terrace

2800 Pennsylvania Avenue, NW   (202) 342-0444

Gabriel

2121 P Street, NW, in Radisson Barcelo Hotel
   (202) 956-6690

The Inn at Glen Echo

MacArthur Boulevard and Clara Barton Parkway, Glen Echo
   (301) 229-2280

The Kennedy Center Roof Terrace

Virginia and New Hampshire avenues, NW   (202) 416-8555

The Old Ebbitt Grill

675 15th Street, NW   (202) 347-4801

◆ The Best Sushi Bars

Atami
3155 Wilson Boulevard, Arlington   (703) 522-4787
Blue Ocean
9440 Main Street, Fairfax   (703) 425-7555
Ginza
1009 21st Street, NW   (202) 833-1244
Matuba
2915 Columbia Pike, Arlington   (703) 521-2811
4918 Cordell Avenue, Bethesda   (301) 652-7449
Miyagi
6918 Curran Street, McLean   (703) 893-0116
Niwano Hana
887 Rockville Pike (Wintergreen Plaza)   (301) 294-0553
Sakana
2026 P Street, NW   (202) 887-0900
Shiro-Ya
2512 L Street, NW   (202) 659-9449
Sushi Kappo Kawasaki
1140 19th Street, NW   (202) 466-3798
Sushi-Ko
2309 Wisconsin Avenue, NW   (202) 333-4187
Tachibana
6715 Lowell Avenue, McLean   (703) 847-7771
Tako Grill
7756 Wisconsin Avenue, Bethesda   (301) 652-7030
Yosaku
4712 Wisconsin Avenue, NW   (202) 363-4453

◆ The Best Views

America
50 Massachusetts Avenue, NE (Union Station)   (202) 682-9555
Hotel Washington Roof
515 15th Street, NW   (202) 638-5900
Lafayette
16th and I streets, NW (Hay-Adams Hotel)   (202) 638-2570
New Heights
2317 Calvert Street, NW   (202) 234-4110

Sequoia

3000 K Street, NW   (202) 944-4200

Tony & Joe's

3000 K Street, NW   (202) 944-4545

J. W.'s View

1401 Lee Highway (Key Bridge Marriott), Arlington
   (703) 243-1745

Perry's

1811 Columbia Road, NW   (202) 234-6218

Potowmack Landing

Washington Marina, George Washington Parkway, Alexandria
   (703) 548-0001

◆ The Best Wee-Hours Service

Afterwords Cafe

1517 Connecticut Avenue, NW   (202) 387-1462

American City Diner

5532 Connecticut Avenue, NW   (202) 244-1949
Wisconsin Avenue at East-West Highway, Bethesda
   (301) 654-3287

Amphora

377 Maple Avenue West, Vienna   (703) 938-7877

Bistro Français

3128 M Street, NW   (202) 338-3830

Full Kee

509 H Street, NW   (202) 371-2233

Hunan Number One

3033 Wilson Avenue, Arlington   (703) 528-1177

Il Ritrovo

4838 Rugby Avenue, Bethesda   (301) 986-1447

Polly's Cafe

1342 U Street, NW   (202) 265-8385

Tastee Diner

7731 Woodmont Avenue, Bethesda   (301) 652-3970
8516 Georgia Avenue, Silver Spring   (301) 589-8171
10536 Lee Highway, Fairfax   (703) 591-6720

Thai Flavor

2605 Connecticut Avenue, NW   (202) 745-2000

◆ Dining Near the Convention Center

Cafe Atlantico
405 8th Street, NW   (202) 393-0812
Capitol City Brewing Co.
1100 New York Avenue, NW   (202) 628-2222
2700 South Quincy Street, Arlington   (703) 578-3888
7735 Old Georgetown Road, Bethesda   (301) 652-2282
China Inn
631 H Street, NW   (202) 842-0909
Coco Loco
810 7th Street, NW   (202) 289-2626
Jaleo
480 7th Street, NW   (202) 628-7949
Luigino
1100 New York Avenue, NW   (202) 371-0595
Metro Center Grill
775 12th Street, NW   (202) 737-2200
Mr. Yung's
740 6th Street, NW   (202) 628-1098
Red Sage
605 14th Street, NW   (202) 638-4444
Ruppert's
1017 7th Street, NW   (202) 783-0699
Tony Cheng's Mongolian Restaurant
619 H Street, NW   (202) 842-8669

◆ Tables in the Kitchen

Aquarelle
2650 Virginia Avenue, NW (Watergate Hotel)   (202) 298-4455
Bice
601 Pennsylvania Avenue, NW   (202) 638-2423
Citronelle
3000 M Street, NW (Latham Hotel)   (202) 625-2150
Galileo
1110 21st Street, NW   (202) 293-7191
Hibiscus Cafe
3401 K Street, NW   (202) 965-7170

Melrose

24th and M streets, NW (Park Hyatt Hotel)   (202) 955-3899

Restaurant Nora

R Street and Florida Avenue, NW   (202) 462-5143

The Kennedy Center Roof Terrace

Virginia and New Hampshire avenues, NW   (202) 416-8555

UNDERSTANDING THE RATINGS

We have developed detailed profiles for the best and most interesting restaurants (in our opinion) in town. Each profile features an easily scanned heading that allows you, in just a second, to check out the restaurant's name, cuisine, star rating, cost, quality rating, and value rating.

Cuisine. This is actually less straightforward than it sounds. A couple of years ago, for example, "pan–Asian" restaurants were generally serving what was then generally described as "fusion" food—Asian ingredients with European techniques, or vice versa. Since then, there has been a pan-Asian explosion in the area, but nearly all specialize in what would be street food back home: noodles, skewers, dumplings, and soups. Once-general categories have become subdivided—French into bistro fare and even Provençal; "new continental" into regional American and "eclectic"—while others have broadened and fused: Middle Eastern and Provençal into Mediterranean, Spanish and South American into nuevo Latino, and so on. In these cases, we have generally used the broader terms (i.e., "French"), but sometimes added a parenthetical phrase to give a clearer idea of the fare. Again, though, experimentation and "fusion" is ever more common, so don't hold us, or the chefs, to too strict a style.

Star Rating. The star rating is an overall rating that encompasses the entire dining experience, including style, service, and ambience in addition to the taste, presentation, and quality of the food. Five stars is the highest rating possible and connotes the best of everything. Four-star restaurants are exceptional and three-star restaurants are well above average. Two-star restaurants are good. One star is used to indicate an average restaurant that demonstrates an unusual capability in some area of specialization—for example, an otherwise unmemorable place that has great barbecued chicken.

Cost.   To the right of the star rating is an expense description that provides a comparative sense of how much a complete meal will cost. A complete meal for our purposes consists of an entree with vegetable or side dish and choice of soup or salad. Appetizers, desserts, drinks, and tips are excluded.

Inexpensive	$14 and less per person
Moderate	$15–30 per person
Expensive	Over $30 per person

Quality Rating.   On the far right of each heading appears a number and a letter. The number rates the food quality on a scale of 0–100, with 100 being the best rating attainable. It is based expressly on the taste, freshness of ingredients, preparation, presentation, and creativity of food served. There is no consideration of price. If you are a person who wants the best food available, and cost is not an issue, you need look no further than the quality ratings.

Value Rating.   If, on the other hand, you are looking for both quality and value, then you should check the value rating, expressed in letters. The value ratings are defined as follows:

A	Exceptional value, a real bargain
B	Good value
C	Fair value, you get exactly what you pay for
D	Somewhat overpriced
F	Significantly overpriced

locatiNq the restaurant

Just below the heading is a designation for geographic zone. This zone description will give you a general idea of where the restaurant described is located. We've divided Washington, D.C. into the following 11 geographic zones:

Zone 1.   The Mall
Zone 2.   Capitol Hill
Zone 3.   Downtown
Zone 4.   Foggy Bottom
Zone 5.   Georgetown
Zone 6.   Dupont Circle/Adams-Morgan
Zone 7.   Upper Northwest
Zone 8.   Northeast
Zone 9.   Southeast
Zone 10.   Maryland Suburbs
Zone 11.   Virginia Suburbs

The Maryland suburbs are divided into four smaller areas: Zones 10A (Bethesda) and 10B (Rockville-Gaithersburg) are bounded by the Potomac and Georgia Avenue and divided by the Beltway; Zone 10C is defined by 16th Street/Georgia Avenue, the District Line, New Hampshire Avenue and I-95 as a wedge that runs north from Silver Spring and which necessarily splits Wheaton down the middle; and Zone 10D reaches from the District Line up New Hampshire and I-95 around to the Virginia line.

The Virginia suburbs are marked off more cleanly along I-66 and I-95/395 into three slices: Zone 11A covers Tysons Corner, McLean, Vienna, and Reston; Zone 11B includes Arlington, Annandale, and Fairfax; and Zone 11C is Alexandria, Old and otherwise. See pages 23–35 for detailed zone maps.

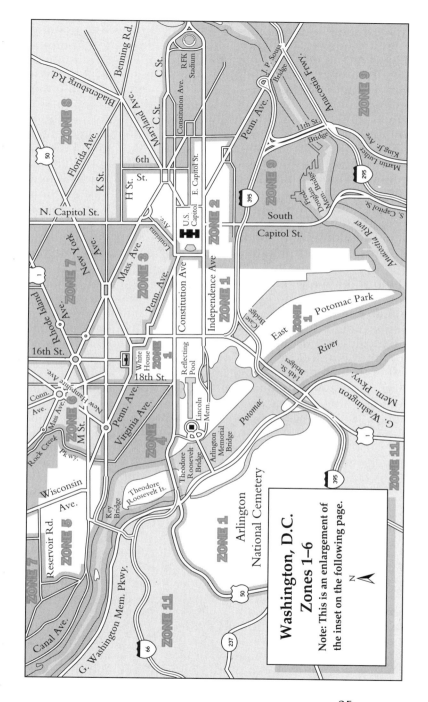

Washington, D.C.
Zones 1–6

Note: This is an enlargement of the inset on the following page.

N

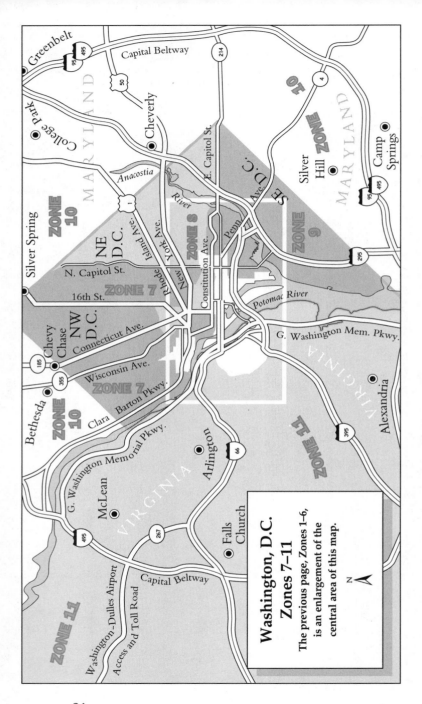

Washington, D.C.
Zones 7–11

The previous page, Zones 1–6, is an enlargement of the central area of this map.

N

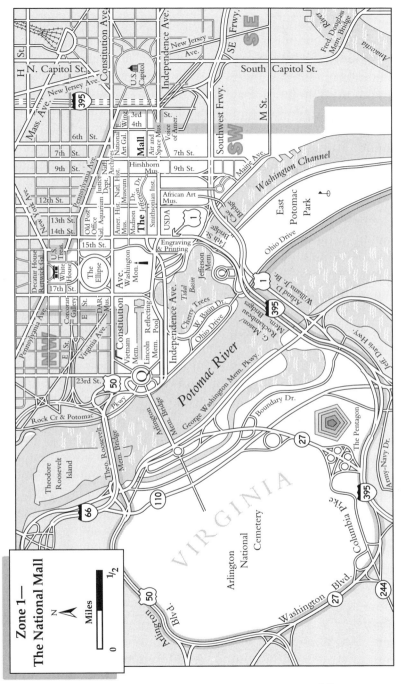

Zone 1—
The National Mall

N

Miles

0   1/2

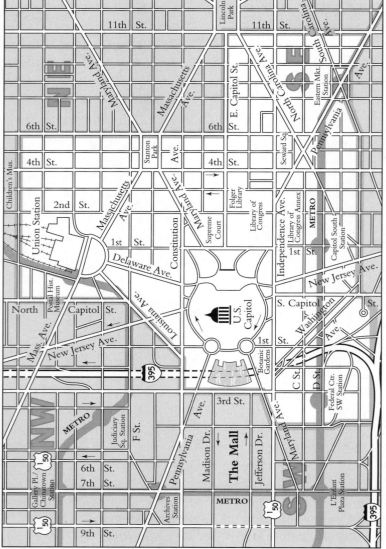

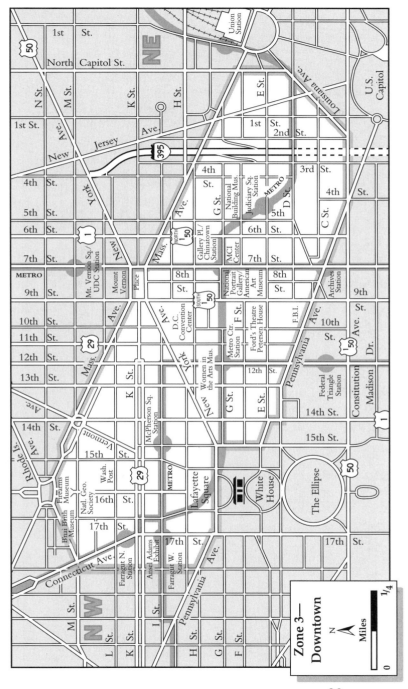

Zone 3—
Downtown

N

Miles

0   1/4

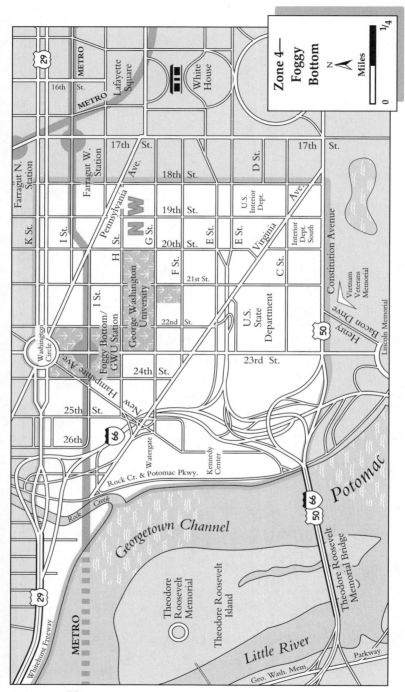

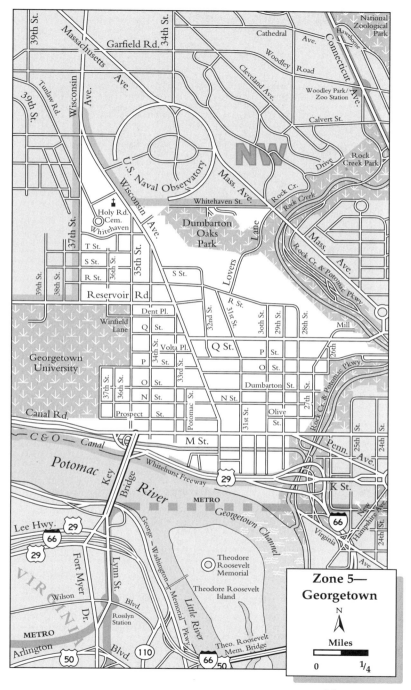

Zone 5—
Georgetown

N

Miles

0   1/4

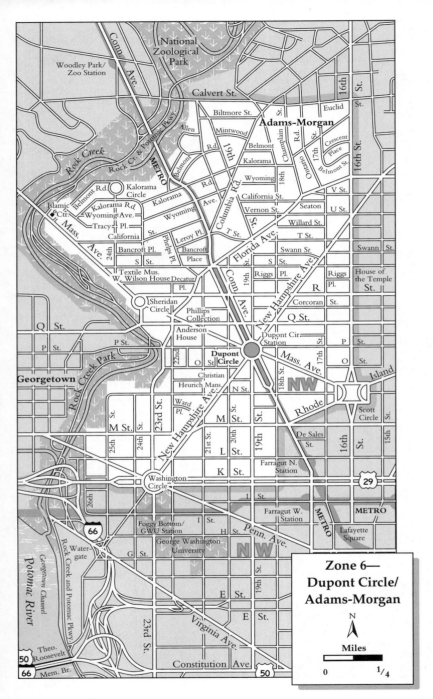

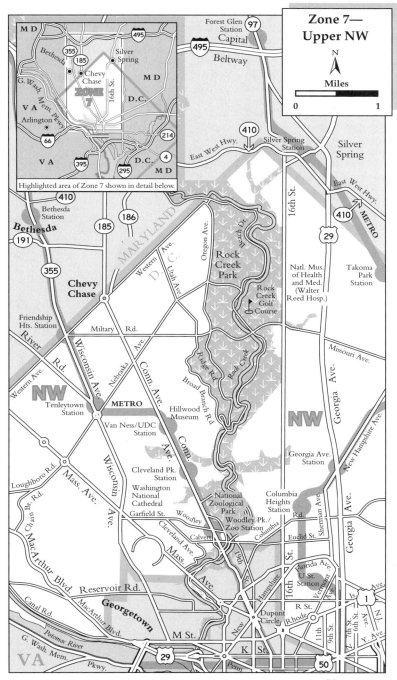

Zone 7—
Upper NW

N

Miles

0   1

MD
Bethesda 355
185
Silver Spring
Chevy Chase
MD
ZONE 7
16th St.
D.C.
G. Wash. Mem. Pkwy
VA
Arlington
66
214
VA
395 D.C.
295
MD

Highlighted area of Zone 7 shown in detail below.

Forest Glen Station 97
Capital
495
Beltway

410
Silver Spring Station
East West Hwy.
Silver Spring

East West Hwy.
410
METRO

410
Bethesda Station
185
186
16th St.
29

Bethesda
191

355

Chevy Chase

Rock Creek Park

Natl. Mus. of Health and Med. (Walter Reed Hosp.)

Takoma Park Station

Western Ave.
Utah Ave.
Oregon Ave.

Rock Creek Golf Course

Friendship Hts. Station

Miltary Rd.

River Rd.

Wisconsin Ave.

Nebraska Ave.

Conn. Ave.

Ridge Rd.

Broad Branch Rd

Rock Creek

Missouri Ave.

Georgia Ave.

New Hampshire Ave.

NW

Tenleytown Station

METRO

Van Ness/UDC Station

Hillwood Museum

NW

Georgia Ave. Station

Loughboro Rd.

Mass. Ave.

Wisconsin Ave.

Conn. Ave.

Cleveland Pk. Station

Washington National Cathedral

Garfield St.

Woodley

National Zoological Park

Woodley Pk./ Zoo Station

Columbia Heights Station

Columbia Rd.

Sherman Ave.

Georgia Ave.

Canal Rd.

Br. Rd.

MacArthur Blvd.

Reservoir Rd.

Georgetown

Cleveland Ave.

Mass. Ave.

Calvert

19th St.

Woodley

Hampshire

16th St.

Florida Ave.

U St. Station

Vermont Ave.

1

R St.

7th St.

6th St.

N.J. Ave.

MacArthur Blvd.

Potomac River

G. Wash. Mem. Pkwy.

VA

Canal Rd.

M St.

New

Dupont Circle

Rhode

11th

9th

K St.

29

50

Penn

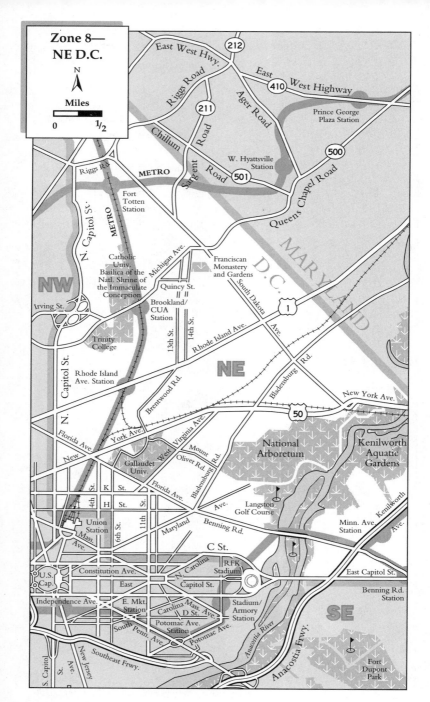

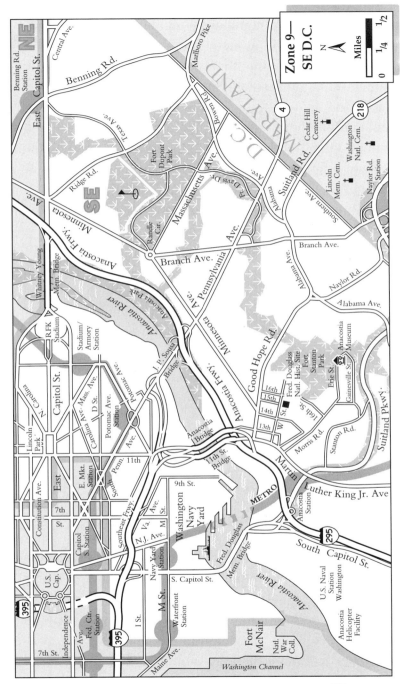

NE

Benning Rd.
Station

East Capitol St.

Central Ave.

Benning Rd.

Texas Ave.

Marlboro Pike

Bowen Rd.

4

MARYLAND

D.C.

218

Cedar Hill Cemetery

Washington Natl. Cem.

Lincoln Mem. Cem.

Naylor Rd. Station

Southern Ave.

Fort Dupont Park

Massachusetts Ave.

F.D. Davis Dr.

Alabama Ave.

Ridge Rd.

SE

Randle Cir.

Ave.

Branch Ave.

Branch Ave.

Minnesota Ave.

Anacosta Frwy.

Whitney Young Mem. Bridge

Pennsylvania Ave.

Alabama Ave.

Naylor Rd.

Alabama Ave.

Anacostia Park

Anacostia River

RFK Stadium

Stadium/ Armory Station

Potomac Ave.

J. P. Sousa Bridge

Minnesota

Good Hope Rd.

Anacosta Frwy.

Fred. Douglass Natl. Hist. Site

Fort Stanton Park

Anacostia Museum

Gainesville St.

Erie St.

16th

15th   W. St.

14th

13th   W.

16th St.

Morris Rd.

Stanton Rd.

Sutland Pkwy.

Lincoln Park

Capitol St.

Carolina Ave.

North

D St.

Mass. Ave.

Potomac Ave.

E. Mkt. Station

Ave.

Anacostia Bridge

11th

11th St. Bridge

Martin Luther King Jr. Ave

Constitution Ave.

East

7th St.

South Penn.

9th St.

Washington Navy Yard

METRO

Anacostia Station

Southeast Frwy.

Capitol S. Station

Ave.

N.J. Ave.

M.

V. Ave.

Navy Yard Station

Fred Douglass Mem. Bridge

South   Capitol St.

295

395

U.S. Cap.

Federal Ctr. Station

Independence

Waterfront Station

I St.

M St.

S. Capitol St.

U.S. Naval Station Washington

7th St.

Maine Ave.

Maine Ave.

Fort McNair

Natl. War Coll.

Anacostia Helicopter Facility

Anacostia River

Washington Channel

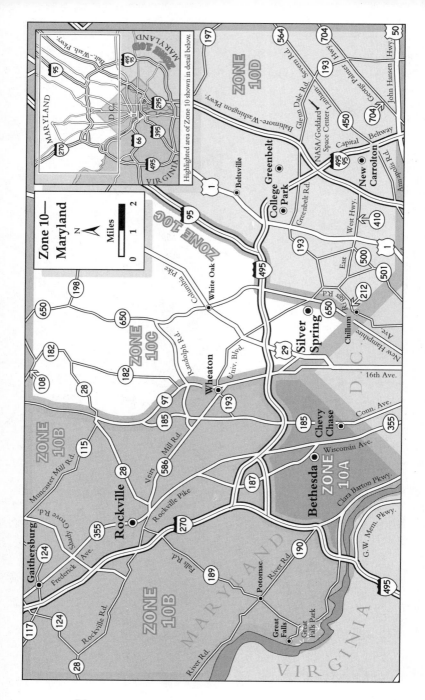

Zone 10—
Maryland

N

Miles
0   1   2

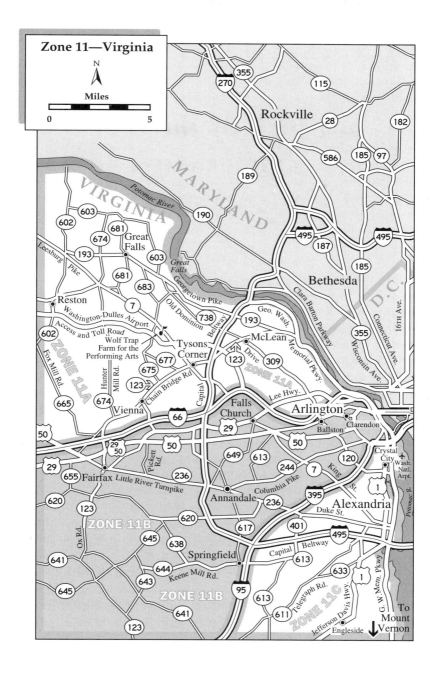

✝ OUR pick of the best
d.c. RESTAURANTS

who's included

Because restaurants are opening and closing all the time in Washington, we have tried to confine our list to establishments with a proven track record over a fairly long period of time. Franchises and national chains are not included, although local "chains," restaurant groups of three or four, may be. Newer restaurants (and older restaurants under new management) are listed but not profiled. Newer or changed establishments that demonstrate staying power and consistency will be profiled in subsequent editions. Also, the list is highly selective. Noninclusion of a particular place does not necessarily indicate that the restaurant is not good, but only that it was not ranked among the best in its genre.

Among the restaurants "just bubbling under" the Top 200, as *Billboard* magazine would say, are some new arrivals, some restaurants with new and promising chefs, a few who are just in already-crowded categories, and some who are on the verge of jelling into reliable favorites. Among them are B. Smith's (Southern), Blue Plate (American), Cafe New Dehli (Indian), El Caribe (Latin), Galaxy (Vietnamese), Hee Been (Korean), Il Borgo (Italian), Melati (Indonesian/Malay), Mendocino Grill (California pop), Moby Dick (kebabs), Nam Viet (Vietnamese), Nulbom (Korean), Oriental East (Chinese), Pho (Vietnamese), Ruppert's (American), Starke's Head Hog Barbecue, Stella's (American), Udupi Palace (Indian Vegetarian), Le Vieux Logis (French), Xing Kuba (eclectic/fusion), and Yosaku (Japanese).

Detailed profiles of individual restaurants follow in alphabetical order at the end of this chapter.

A NOTE About spelling

Most diners who enjoy ethnic restaurants have noticed subtle variations in the spellings of certain dishes and preparations from one menu to the next. A noodle dish found on almost all Thai menus, for example, appears in one restaurant as *pad thai*, in another as *Phat Thai,* and in a third as *Phad Thai*.

This and similar inconsistencies arise from attempts to derive a phonetic English spelling from the name of a dish as pronounced in its country of origin. While one particular English spelling might be more frequently used than others, there is usually no definitive correct spelling for the names of many dishes. In this guide, we have elected to use the spelling most commonly found in authoritative ethnic cookbooks and other reference works.

We call this to your attention because the spelling we use in this guide could differ from that which you encounter on the menu in a certain restaurant. We might say, for instance, that the *tabbouleh* is good at a particular Middle Eastern restaurant, while at the restaurant itself the dish is listed on the menu as *tabouli*.

Restaurants by Cuisine

Name	Star Rating	Price Rating	Quality Rating	Value Rating	Zone
Afghani					
Panjshir	★★½	Inexp	79	A	11A, 11B
American (See also Modern American)					
Clyde's	★★½	Mod	77	B	5, 10A, 11A, 11B
Old Ebbitt Grill	★★½	Mod	77	C	3
Olney Ale Hosue	★★½	Inexp	76	C	10C
Argentine					
Argentine Grill	★★½	Mod	75	B	6
Barbecue					
Rocklands	★★★	Inexp	80	C	5, 11B
Red Hot & Blue	★★½	Inexp	79	B	10B, 11B
Old Glory	★★½	Mod	78	B	5
Brazilian					
Grill from Ipanema	★★½	Mod	78	C	6
Burmese					
Burma	★★½	Inexp	79	B	3
Cajun					
Louisiana Express	★★½	Inexp	76	A	10A
R.T.'s	★★	Mod	73	B	11C
Cajun/Thai					
Cajun Bangkok	★★½	Inexp	77	B	11C
Cambodian					
Angkor Wat	★★½	Inexp	79	B	11A
Chili					
Hard Times Cafe	★★½	Inexp	75	A	10B, 11B, 11C, 11A
Chinese					
Seven Seas	★★★½	Mod	85	B	10B
China Inn	★★★	Inexp	83	B	3

Name	Star Rating	Price Rating	Quality Rating	Value Rating	Zone
Four Rivers	★★★	Mod	83	B	10B
City Lights of China	★★★	Mod	81	B	6
Hunan Palace	★★★	Inexp	81	B	10B
Good Fortune	★★★	Inexp	80	B	10B
Vegetable Garden	★★★	Mod	80	B	10B
Hope Key	★★½	Inexp	79	B	11B
Mr. Yung's	★★½	Inexp	79	B	3
Peking Eastern House	★★½	Inexp	79	A	10B
Hunan No. 1	★★½	Inexp	78	B	11B
Tony Cheng's Mongolian Restaurant	★★½	Inexp	75	A	3
Paul Kee	★★	Inexp	71	A	10C
Full Key	★½	Inexp	69	A	10C

Cuban

Name	Star Rating	Price Rating	Quality Rating	Value Rating	Zone
La Cantinita's Havana Cafe	★★	Inexp	73	B	11B

Ethiopian

Name	Star Rating	Price Rating	Quality Rating	Value Rating	Zone
Meskerem	★★★½	Inexp	86	A	6
Fasika's	★★★	Inexp	82	A	6
Zed's	★★½	Inexp	79	B	5

French

Name	Star Rating	Price Rating	Quality Rating	Value Rating	Zone
L'Auberge Chez François	★★★★	Mod	92	A	11A
Gerard's Place	★★★★	Exp	90	C	3
Le Lion d'Or	★★★½	Exp	86	C	6
La Bergerie	★★★	Mod	84	C	11C
La Colline	★★★	Mod	84	A	2
La Miche	★★★	Inexp	83	B	10A
La Chaumière	★★★	Mod	81	C	5
Le Caprice	★★★	Exp	81	C	5
Bistro Bistro	★★½	Inexp	79	B	11B
Bistro Français	★★½	Inexp	79	B	5
Bistrot Lepic	★★½	Mod	79	B	5
Le Gaulois	★★½	Mod	79	C	11A
Jean-Michel	★★½	Mod	78	C	10A

Name	Star Rating	Price Rating	Quality Rating	Value Rating	Zone
French *(continued)*					
La Ferme	★★½	Mod	78	B	10A
La Fourchette	★★	Inexp	74	B	6
Le Refuge	★★	Mod	73	B	11C
French (Provençal)					
L'Auberge Provençal	★★★★★	Exp	96	A	11A
Provence	★★★½	Mod	87	C	6
La Provence	★★★½	Inexp	85	B	11A
Le Paradis	★★★	Mod	83	B	10B
La Côte d'Or Cafe	★★½	Exp	78	C	11B
Lavandou	★★½	Inexp	78	B	7
Fusion					
Perry's	★★½	Mod	79	B	6
German					
Wurzburg Haus	★★★	Mod	80	B	10B
Cafe Berlin	★★½	Inexp	79	C	2
Greek					
Mykonos	★★★	Mod	80	B	4
Athenian Plaka	★★½	Mod	75	B	10A
Indian					
Bombay Club	★★★½	Exp	89	C	3
Aditi	★★★	Inexp	84	B	5
Bombay Bistro	★★★	Inexp	83	A	10B, 11B
Aarathi	★★½	Inexp	79	B	11B
Kashmir Palace	★★½	Inexp	79	B	10B
Aangan	★★½	Inexp	78	A	10A
Delhi Dhaba	★★½	Inexp	78	A	10B, 11A
Cafe Taj	★★½	Inexp	77	B	11A
Haandi	★★½	Inexp	77	B	10A, 11B
Indonesian					
Sarinah Satay House	★★½	Inexp	77	C	5
Sabang	★★½	Inexp	75	B	10B
Straits of Malaya	★★	Inexp	71	C	6

Name	Star Rating	Price Rating	Quality Rating	Value Rating	Zone
Italian					
Galileo	★★★★★	Exp	98	C	6
Obelisk	★★★½	Exp	89	B	6
Goldoni	★★★½	Inexp	85	C	6
I Matti	★★★	Mod	84	B	6
i Ricchi	★★★	Exp	84	B	6
Cafe Milano	★★★	Mod	82	C	5
Sesto Senso	★★★	Mod	82	B	6
Vincenzo al Sole	★★★	Exp	82	C	6
Bice	★★½	Mod	79	C	3
Filomena	★★½	Mod	79	B	5
Il Radicchio	★★½	Inexp	79	A	5, 6, 11B
Luigino	★★½	Mod	79	B	3
Il Pizzico	★★½	Inexp	77	A	10B
Primi Piatti	★★½	Exp	77	C	4, 11A
Paolo's	★★½	Mod	76	B	5, 11A
That's Amore	★★½	Mod	76	A	7, 10B, 11A
Cafe Oggi	★★½	Mod	75	B	11A
Jamaican					
Hibiscus Cafe	★★★½	Inexp	85	B	5
Japanese					
Sushi-Ko	★★★★	Mod	92	B	5
Tako Grill	★★★★	Mod	92	B	10A
Makoto	★★★½	Mod	89	A	7
Tachibana	★★★½	Mod	88	B	11A
Niwano Hana	★★★½	Inexp	87	B	10B
Matuba	★★★½	Inexp	85	B	10A, 11B
Sushi Kappo Kawasaki	★★★	Exp	84	D	6
Hinode	★★½	Inexp	75	B	10A, 10B
Atami	★★	Mod	74	A	11B
Korean					
Woo Lae Oak	★★★	Mod	82	A	11B
Sam Woo	★★★	Mod	81	B	10B
Jin-Ga	★★½	Mod	79	B	5
Yijo	★★½	Inexp	78	B	10D

Name	Star Rating	Price Rating	Quality Rating	Value Rating	Zone
Korean/Japanese					
Ichiban	★★★	Mod	83	B	10B
Yokohama	★★½	Mod	79	A	10B
Lebanese					
Bacchus	★★★	Mod	73	B	6, 10A
Lebanese Taverna	★★	Mod	74	B	6, 11B
Mediterranean					
George	★★★½	Mod	85	B	3
Il Ritrovo	★★★	Mod	80	B	10A
Isabella	★★★	Mod	80	B	3
The Bistro at the ANA	★★½	Mod	79	B	5
Mexican					
Los Chorros	★★★	Inexp	82	B	10B, 10C
Tia Queta	★★½	Mod	75	B	10A
Acajutla	★½	Inexp	68	A	10B
Modern American					
The Inn at Little Washington	★★★★★	Exp	98	B	11B
Seasons	★★★★	Exp	93	B	5
Vidalia	★★★★	Exp	93	B	6
Kinkead's	★★★★	Mod	91	C	4
Old Angler's Inn	★★★½	Exp	89	C	10B
New Heights	★★★½	Mod	88	C	6
Elysium	★★★½	Exp	87	B	11C
Melrose	★★★½	Mod	87	C	5
Greenwood	★★★	Mod	84	B	7
Lafayette	★★★	Mod	84	B	3
Morrison–Clark Inn	★★★	Mod	83	B	3
1789	★★★	Exp	83	C	5
Cashion's Eat Place	★★★	Mod	82	B	6
Carlyle Grand Café	★★★	Mod	81	C	11B
Citronelle	★★★	Exp	81	C	5
Aquarelle	★★★	Exp	80	B	4

Name	Star Rating	Price Rating	Quality Rating	Value Rating	Zone
Café Bethesda/Café Bethesda North	★★★	Exp	80	B	10A, 10B
Nora	★★★	Mod	80	C	6
Bistro Twenty-Fifteen	★★½	Inexp	79	B	6
Market Street Bar & Grill	★★½	Mod	79	C	11A
701	★★½	Mod	79	C	3
Trumpets	★★½	Mod	79	B	6
Two Quail	★★½	Mod	79	C	2
Tabard Inn	★★½	Mod	77	B	6
Mrs. Simpson's	★★½	Mod	76	C	6
Inn at Glen Echo	★★½	Mod	75	B	10A
Occidental Grill	★★½	Mod	75	B	3
Modern Continental					
Lespinasse	★★★★	Exp	92	B	3
Willard Room	★★★	Exp	82	B	3
Moroccan					
Dar es Salaam	★★½	Mod	79	B	5
Taste of Casablanca	★★½	Inexp	79	A	11B
New Southwestern					
Red Sage	★★★★	Exp	94	B	3
Cottonwood Cafe	★★★	Mod	80	B	10A
Santa Fe East	★★★	Mod	80	B	11C
Nuevo Latino					
Cafe Atlantico	★★★½	Inexp	85	B	3
Coco Loco	★★★	Mod	84	A	3
Gabriel	★★★	Mod	84	A	6
Jaleo	★★★	Mod	77	B	3
Pan Asian					
Asia Nora	★★★½	Mod	86	B	6
Raku: An Asian Grill	★★★½	Inexp	84	A	6, 10A
Germaine's	★★½	Mod	79	B	5
Oodles Noodles	★★½	Inexp	78	B	4, 10A
Cafe Asia	★½	Inexp	69	A	6

Name	Star Rating	Price Rating	Quality Rating	Value Rating	Zone
Persian					
Kabob Bazaar	★★½	Inexp	79	B	11B
Paradise	★★	Inexp	73	C	10A
Pizza					
Pizzeria Paradiso	★★★	Inexp	83	A	6
Zio's	★★½	Inexp	77	A	10B
Pizza de Resistance	★★½	Inexp	75	B	11B
Faccia Luna	★★	Inexp	73	B	5, 11A, 11C
Russian					
Serbian Crown	★★★	Exp	80	B	11A
Russia House	★★½	Mod	79	B	11B
Seafood					
Pesce	★★★½	Mod	86	B	6
Sea Catch	★★★	Mod	83	B	5
Georgetown Seafood Grill	★★½	Inexp	79	B	5
Legal Sea Foods	★★½	Mod	78	B	4, 11A
Blue Point Grill	★★½	Exp	77	B	11C
Southern					
Georgia Brown's	★★★	Mod	80	B	3
Music City Roadhouse	★★	Inexp	74	A	5
Spanish					
Taberna del Alabardero	★★★½	Exp	88	C	3
Andalucia	★★	Mod	74	B	10A, 10B
Lauriol Plaza	★★	Mod	72	B	6
Steak					
Morton's of Chicago	★★★½	Exp	89	B	3, 5, 11A
Prime Rib	★★★½	Exp	88	B	4
Les Halles	★★★	Mod	84	B	3
Sam & Harry's	★★★	Exp	84	C	6
The Palm	★★½	Exp	79	B	6
The Capital Grille	★★½	Exp	78	C	3
Tex-Mex					
Austin Grill	★★★	Inexp	83	A	5, 10A, 11B, 11C

Name	Star Rating	Price Rating	Quality Rating	Value Rating	Zone
Rio Grande Cafe	★★½	Mod	78	C	10A, 11B
Guapo's	★★½	Inexp	76	B	7, 10B
Thai					
Busara	★★★½	Mod	87	B	5, 11A
Benjarong	★★★½	Inexp	85	B	10B
Tara Thai	★★★½	Mod	85	A	10A, 11A
Star of Siam	★★★	Inexp	80	A	6
Bangkok Garden	★★½	Inexp	79	B	10A
Bangkok St. Grill and Noodles	★★½	Inexp	79	B	11B
Duangrat	★★½	Mod	79	C	11B
Rabieng	★★½	Inexp	79	B	11B
A Little Place Called Siam	★★½	Inexp	76	C	11A
Thai Tavern	★★½	Inexp	76	A	10B
Bangkok-Vientiane	★★½	Inexp	75	B	11B
Thai Sa-Mai	★★	Inexp	74	A	10B
Dusit	★★	Inexp	70	A	10C
Turkish					
Kazan	★★½	Inexp	79	B	11A
Nizam	★★	Mod	72	B	11A
Vietnamese					
Taste of Saigon	★★★½	Mod	86	A	10B, 11A
Cafe Saigon	★★★	Inexp	84	A	11B
Cafe Dalat	★★½	Inexp	79	B	11B
Miss Saigon	★★½	Inexp	79	B	5, 6
Pho Cali/The Seafood Place	★★½	Inexp	79	A	11B
Pho 75	★★½	Inexp	79	A	10B, 10D, 11B
Little Viet Garden	★★½	Inexp	77	A	11B
Queen Bee	★★½	Inexp	76	B	11B
West African					
Bukom	★★	Inexp	72	B	6

Restaurants by Star Rating

Name	Cuisine	Price Rating	Quality Rating	Value Rating	Zone
Five-Star Restaurants					
Galileo	Italian	Exp	98	C	6
The Inn at Little Washington	Modern American	Exp	98	B	11B
L'Auberge Provençal	French (Provençal)	Exp	96	A	11A
Four-Star Restaurants					
Red Sage	New Southwestern	Exp	94	B	3
Seasons	Modern American	Exp	93	B	5
Vidalia	Modern American	Exp	93	B	6
L'Auberge Chez François	French	Mod	92	A	11A
Lespinasse	Modern Continental	Exp	92	B	3
Sushi-Ko	Japanese	Mod	92	B	5
Tako Grill	Japanese	Mod	92	B	10A
Kinkead's	Modern American	Mod	91	C	4
Gerard's Place	French	Exp	90	C	3
Three-and-a-Half-Star Restaurants					
Bombay Club	Indian	Exp	89	C	3
Makoto	Japanese	Mod	89	A	7
Morton's of Chicago	Steak	Exp	89	B	3, 5, 11A
Obelisk	Italian	Exp	89	B	6
Old Angler's Inn	Modern American	Exp	89	C	10B
New Heights	Modern American	Mod	88	C	6
Prime Rib	Steak	Exp	88	B	4
Taberna del Alabardero	Spanish	Exp	88	C	3

Name	Cuisine	Price Rating	Quality Rating	Value Rating	Zone
Tachibana	Japanese	Mod	88	B	11A
Busara	Thai	Mod	87	B	5, 11A
Elysium	Modern American	Exp	87	B	11C
Melrose	Modern American	Mod	87	C	5
Niwano Hana	Japanese	Inexp	87	B	10B
Provence	French (Provençal)	Mod	87	C	6
Asia Nora	Pan Asian	Mod	86	B	6
Le Lion d'Or	French	Exp	86	C	6
Meskerem	Ethiopian	Inexp	86	A	6
Pesce	Seafood	Mod	86	B	6
Taste of Saigon	Vietnamese	Mod	86	A	10B, 11A
Benjarong	Thai	Inexp	85	B	10B
Cafe Atlantico	Nuevo Latino	Inexp	85	B	3
George	Mediterranean	Mod	85	B	3
Goldoni	Italian	Inexp	85	C	6
Hibiscus Cafe	Jamaican	Inexp	85	B	5
La Provence	French (Provençal)	Inexp	85	B	11A
Matuba	Japanese	Inexp	85	B	10A, 11B
Seven Seas	Chinese	Mod	85	B	10B
Tara Thai	Thai	Mod	85	A	10A, 11A
Raku: An Asian Grill	Pan Asian	Inexp	84	A	6, 10A

Three-Star Restaurants

Name	Cuisine	Price Rating	Quality Rating	Value Rating	Zone
Aditi	Indian	Inexp	84	B	5
Cafe Saigon	Vietnamese	Inexp	84	A	11B
Coco Loco	Nuevo Latino	Mod	84	A	3
Gabriel	Nuevo Latino	Mod	84	A	6
Greenwood	Modern American	Mod	84	B	7
I Matti	Italian	Mod	84	B	6
i Ricchi	Italian	Exp	84	B	6

Name	Cuisine	Price Rating	Quality Rating	Value Rating	Zone
Three-Star Restaurants (continued)					
La Bergerie	French	Mod	84	C	11C
La Colline	French	Mod	84	A	2
Lafayette	Modern American	Mod	84	B	3
Les Halles	Steak	Mod	84	B	3
Sam & Harry's	Steak	Exp	84	C	6
Sushi Kappo Kawasaki	Japanese	Exp	84	D	6
Austin Grill	Tex-Mex	Inexp	83	A	5, 10A, 11B, 11C
Bombay Bistro	Indian	Inexp	83	A	10B, 11B
China Inn	Chinese	Inexp	83	B	3
Four Rivers	Chinese	Mod	83	B	10B
Ichiban	Korean/ Japanese	Mod	83	B	10B
La Miche	French	Inexp	83	B	10A
Le Paradis	French (Provençal)	Mod	83	B	10B
Morrison-Clark Inn	Modern American	Mod	83	B	3
Pizzeria Paradiso	Pizza	Inexp	83	A	6
Sea Catch	Seafood	Mod	83	B	5
1789	Modern American	Exp	83	C	5
Cafe Milano	Italian	Mod	82	C	5
Cashion's Eat Place	Modern American	Mod	82	B	6
Fasika's	Ethiopian	Inexp	82	A	6
Los Chorros	Salvadoran/ Mexican	Inexp	82	B	10B, 10C
Sesto Senso	Italian	Mod	82	B	6
Vincenzo al Sole	Italian	Exp	82	C	6
Willard Room	Modern Continental	Exp	82	B	3

Restaurants by Star Rating (continued)

Name	Cuisine	Price Rating	Quality Rating	Value Rating	Zone
Woo Lae Oak	Korean	Mod	82	A	11B
Carlyle Grand Café	Modern American	Mod	81	C	11B
Citronelle	Modern American	Exp	81	C	5
City Lights of China	Chinese	Mod	81	B	6
Hunan Palace	Chinese	Inexp	81	B	10B
La Chaumière	French	Mod	81	C	5
Le Caprice	French (Alsatian)	Exp	81	C	5
Sam Woo	Korean	Mod	81	B	10B
Aquarelle	Modern American	Exp	80	B	4
Café Bethesda/ Café Bethesda North	Modern American	Exp	80	B	10A, 10B
Cottonwood Cafe	New Southwestern	Mod	80	B	10A
Georgia Brown's	Southern	Mod	80	B	3
Good Fortune	Chinese	Inexp	80	B	10B
Il Ritrovo	Mediterranean	Mod	80	B	10A
Isabella	Mediterranean	Mod	80	B	3
Mykonos	Greek	Mod	80	B	4
Nora	Modern American	Mod	80	C	6
Rocklands	Barbecue	Inexp	80	C	5, 11B
Santa Fe East	New Southwestern	Mod	80	B	11C
Serbian Crown	Russian	Exp	80	B	11A
Star of Siam	Thai	Inexp	80	A	6
Vegetable Garden	Chinese (vegetarian)	Mod	80	B	10B
Wurzburg Haus	German	Mod	80	B	10B
Jaleo	Nuevo Latino	Mod	77	B	3
Bacchus	Lebanese	Mod	73	B	6, 10A

Name	Cuisine	Price Rating	Quality Rating	Value Rating	Zone
Two-and-a-Half-Star Restaurants					
Aarathi	Indian	Inexp	79	B	11B
Angkor Wat	Cambodian	Inexp	79	B	11A
Bangkok Garden	Thai	Inexp	79	B	10A
Bangkok St. Grill and Noodles	Thai	Inexp	79	B	11B
Bice	Italian	Mod	79	C	3
The Bistro at the ANA	Mediterranean	Mod	79	B	5
Bistro Bistro	French	Inexp	79	B	11B
Bistro Français	French	Inexp	79	B	5
Bistro Twenty-Fifteen	Modern American	Inexp	79	B	6
Bistrot Lepic	French	Mod	79	B	5
Burma	Burmese	Inexp	79	B	3
Cafe Berlin	German	Inexp	79	C	2
Cafe Dalat	Vietnamese	Inexp	79	B	11B
Dar es Salaam	Moroccan	Mod	79	B	5
Duangrat	Thai	Mod	79	C	11B
Filomena	Italian	Mod	79	B	5
Georgetown Seafood Grill	Seafood	Inexp	79	B	5
Germaine's	Pan Asian	Mod	79	B	5
Hope Key	Chinese	Inexp	79	B	11B
Il Radicchio	Italian	Inexp	79	A	5, 6, 11B
Jin-Ga	Korean	Mod	79	B	5
Kabob Bazaar	Persian	Inexp	79	B	11B
Kashmir Palace	Indian	Inexp	79	B	10B
Kazan	Turkish	Inexp	79	B	11A
Le Gaulois	French	Mod	79	C	11A
Luigino	Italian	Mod	79	B	3
Market Street Bar & Grill	Modern American	Mod	79	C	11A
Miss Saigon	Vietnamese	Inexp	79	B	5, 6
Mr. Yung's	Chinese	Inexp	79	B	3
The Palm	Steak	Exp	79	B	6

Name	Cuisine	Price Rating	Quality Rating	Value Rating	Zone
Panjshir	Afghani	Inexp	79	A	11A, 11B
Peking Eastern House	Chinese	Inexp	79	A	10B
Perry's	Fusion	Mod	79	B	6
Pho 75	Vietnamese	Inexp	79	A	10B, 10D, 11B
Pho Cali/The Seafood Place	Vietnamese	Inexp	79	A	11B
Rabieng	Thai	Inexp	79	B	11B
Red Hot & Blue	Barbecue	Inexp	79	B	10B, 11B
Russia House	Russian	Mod	79	B	11B
701	Modern American	Mod	79	C	3
Taste of Casablanca	Moroccan	Inexp	79	A	11B
Trumpets	Modern American	Mod	79	B	6
Two Quail	Modern American	Mod	79	C	2
Yokohama	Korean/ Japanese	Mod	79	A	10B
Zed's	Ethiopian	Inexp	79	B	5
Aangan	Indian	Inexp	78	A	10A
The Capital Grille	Steak	Exp	78	C	3
Delhi Dhaba	Indian	Inexp	78	A	10B, 11A
Grill from Ipanema	Brazilian	Mod	78	C	6
Hunan No. 1	Chinese	Inexp	78	B	11B
Jean-Michel	French	Mod	78	C	10A
La Côte d'Or Cafe	French (Provençal)	Exp	78	C	11B
La Ferme	French	Mod	78	B	10A
Lavandou	French (Provençal)	Inexp	78	B	7
Legal Sea Foods	Seafood	Mod	78	B	4, 11A
Old Glory	Barbecue	Mod	78	B	5
Oodles Noodles	Pan Asian	Inexp	78	B	4, 10A
Rio Grande Cafe	Tex-Mex	Mod	78	C	10A, 11B

Name	Cuisine	Price Rating	Quality Rating	Value Rating	Zone
Two-and-a-Half-Star Restaurants *(continued)*					
Yijo	Korean	Inexp	78	B	10D
Blue Point Grill	Seafood	Exp	77	B	11C
Cafe Taj	Indian	Inexp	77	B	11A
Cajun Bangkok	Cajun/Thai	Inexp	77	B	11C
Clyde's	American	Mod	77	B	5, 10A, 11A
Haandi	Indian	Inexp	77	B	10A, 11B
Il Pizzico	Italian	Inexp	77	A	10B
Little Viet Garden	Vietnamese	Inexp	77	A	11B
Old Ebbitt Grill	American	Mod	77	C	3
Primi Piatti	Italian	Exp	77	C	4, 11A
Sarinah Satay House	Indonesian	Inexp	77	C	5
Tabard Inn	Modern American	Mod	77	B	6
Zio's	Pizza	Inexp	77	A	10B
Guapo's	Tex-Mex	Inexp	76	B	7, 10B
A Little Place Called Siam	Thai/Pan Asian	Inexp	76	C	11A
Louisiana Express	Cajun	Inexp	76	A	10A
Mrs. Simpson's	Modern American	Mod	76	C	6
Olney Ale House	American	Inexp	76	C	10C
Paolo's	Italian	Mod	76	B	5, 11A
Queen Bee	Vietnamese	Inexp	76	B	11B
Thai Tavern	Thai	Inexp	76	A	10B
That's Amore	Italian	Mod	76	A	7, 10B, 11A
Argentine Grill	Argentine	Mod	75	B	6
Athenian Plaka	Greek	Mod	75	B	10A
Bangkok-Vientiane	Thai-Laotian	Inexp	75	B	11B
Cafe Oggi	Italian	Mod	75	B	11A
Hard Times Cafe	Chili	Inexp	75	A	10B, 11B, 11C, 11A
Hinode	Japanese	Inexp	75	B	10A, 10B
Inn at Glen Echo	Modern American	Mod	75	B	10A

Name	Cuisine	Price Rating	Quality Rating	Value Rating	Zone
Occidental Grill	Modern American	Mod	75	B	3
Pizza de Resistance	Pizza	Inexp	75	B	11B
Sabang	Indonesian	Inexp	75	B	10B
Tia Queta	Mexican	Mod	75	B	10A
Tony Cheng's Mongolian Restaurant	Chinese	Inexp	75	A	3

Two-Star Restaurants

Name	Cuisine	Price Rating	Quality Rating	Value Rating	Zone
Andalucia	Spanish	Mod	74	B	10A, 10B
Atami	Japanese	Mod	74	A	11B
La Fourchette	French	Inexp	74	B	6
Lebanese Taverna	Lebanese	Mod	74	B	6, 11B
Music City Roadhouse	Southern	Inexp	74	A	5
Thai Sa-Mai	Thai	Inexp	74	A	10B
Faccia Luna	Pizza	Inexp	73	B	5, 11A, 11C
La Cantinita's Havana Cafe	Cuban	Inexp	73	B	11B
Le Refuge	French	Mod	73	B	11C
Paradise	Persian/ Afghani	Inexp	73	C	10A
R.T.'s	Cajun	Mod	73	B	11C
Bukom	West African	Inexp	72	B	6
Lauriol Plaza	Spanish/ Mexican	Mod	72	B	6
Nizam	Turkish	Mod	72	B	11A
Paul Kee	Chinese	Inexp	71	A	10C
Straits of Malaya	Indonesian	Inexp	71	C	6
Dusit	Thai	Inexp	70	A	10C

One-and-a-Half-Star Restaurants

Name	Cuisine	Price Rating	Quality Rating	Value Rating	Zone
Cafe Asia	Pan Asian	Inexp	69	A	6
Full Key	Chinese	Inexp	69	A	10C
Acajutla	Mexican/ Salvadoran	Inexp	68	A	10B

Restaurants by Zone

Name	Star Rating	Price Rating	Quality Rating	Value Rating
Zone 2 — Capitol Hill				
◆ *French*				
La Colline	★★★	Mod	84	A
◆ *German*				
Cafe Berlin	★★½	Inexp	79	C
◆ *Modern American*				
Two Quail	★★½	Mod	79	C
Zone 3 — Downtown				
◆ *American*				
Old Ebbitt Grill	★★½	Mod	77	C
◆ *Burmese*				
Burma	★★½	Inexp	79	B
◆ *Chinese*				
China Inn	★★★	Inexp	83	B
Mr. Yung's	★★½	Inexp	79	B
Tony Cheng's Mongolian Restaurant	★★½	Inexp	75	A
◆ *French*				
Gerard's Place	★★★★	Exp	90	C
◆ *Indian*				
Bombay Club	★★★½	Exp	89	C
◆ *Italian*				
Bice	★★½	Mod	79	C
Luigino	★★½	Mod	79	B
◆ *Mediterranean*				
George	★★★½	Mod	85	B
Isabella	★★★	Mod	80	B
◆ *Modern American*				
Lafayette	★★★	Mod	84	B
Morrison–Clark Inn	★★★	Mod	83	B

Name	Star Rating	Price Rating	Quality Rating	Value Rating
701	★★½	Mod	79	C
Occidental Grill	★★½	Mod	75	B
◆ *Modern Continental*				
Lespinasse	★★★★	Exp	92	B
Willard Room	★★★	Exp	82	B
◆ *New Southwestern*				
Red Sage	★★★★	Exp	94	B
◆ *Nuevo Latino*				
Cafe Atlantico	★★★½	Inexp	85	B
Coco Loco	★★★	Mod	84	A
Jaleo	★★★	Mod	77	B
◆ *Southern*				
Georgia Brown's	★★★	Mod	80	B
◆ *Spanish*				
Taberna del Alabardero	★★★½	Exp	88	C
◆ *Steak*				
Morton's of Chicago	★★★½	Exp	89	B
Les Halles	★★★	Mod	84	B
The Capital Grille	★★½	Exp	78	C

Zone 4—Foggy Bottom

Name	Star Rating	Price Rating	Quality Rating	Value Rating
◆ *Greek*				
Mykonos	★★★	Mod	80	B
◆ *Italian*				
Primi Piatti	★★½	Exp	77	C
◆ *Modern American*				
Kinkead's	★★★★	Mod	91	C
Aquarelle	★★★	Exp	80	B
◆ *Pan Asian*				
Oodles Noodles	★★½	Inexp	78	B

Name	Star Rating	Price Rating	Quality Rating	Value Rating
Zone 4—Foggy Bottom (continued)				
◆ *Seafood*				
Legal Sea Foods	★★½	Mod	78	B
◆ *Steak*				
Prime Rib	★★★½	Exp	88	B
Zone 5—Georgetown				
◆ *American*				
Clyde's	★★½	Mod	77	B
◆ *Barbecue*				
Rocklands	★★★	Inexp	80	C
Old Glory	★★½	Mod	78	B
◆ *Ethiopian*				
Zed's	★★½	Inexp	79	B
◆ *French*				
La Chaumière	★★★	Mod	81	C
Le Caprice	★★★	Exp	81	C
Bistro Français	★★½	Inexp	79	B
Bistrot Lepic	★★½	Mod	79	B
◆ *Indian*				
Aditi	★★★	Inexp	84	B
◆ *Indonesian*				
Sarinah Satay House	★★½	Inexp	77	C
◆ *Italian*				
Cafe Milano	★★★	Mod	82	C
Filomena	★★½	Mod	79	B
Il Radicchio	★★½	Inexp	79	A
Paolo's	★★½	Mod	76	B
◆ *Jamaican*				
Hibiscus Cafe	★★★½	Inexp	85	B
◆ *Japanese*				
Sushi-Ko	★★★★	Mod	92	B

Name	Star Rating	Price Rating	Quality Rating	Value Rating
◆ *Korean*				
Jin-Ga	★★½	Mod	79	B
◆ *Mediterranean*				
The Bistro at the ANA	★★½	Mod	79	B
◆ *Modern American*				
Seasons	★★★★	Exp	93	B
Melrose	★★★½	Mod	87	C
1789	★★★	Exp	83	C
Citronelle	★★★	Exp	81	C
◆ *Moroccan*				
Dar es Salaam	★★½	Mod	79	B
◆ *Pan Asian*				
Germaine's	★★½	Mod	79	B
◆ *Pizza*				
Faccia Luna	★★	Inexp	73	B
◆ *Seafood*				
Sea Catch	★★★	Mod	83	B
Georgetown Seafood Grill	★★½	Inexp	79	B
◆ *Southern*				
Music City Roadhouse	★★	Inexp	74	A
◆ *Steak*				
Morton's of Chicago	★★★½	Exp	89	B
◆ *Tex-Mex*				
Austin Grill	★★★	Inexp	83	A
◆ *Thai*				
Busara	★★★½	Mod	87	B
◆ *Vietnamese*				
Miss Saigon	★★½	Inexp	79	B

Name	Star Rating	Price Rating	Quality Rating	Value Rating
Zone 6 — Dupont Circle / Adams-Morgan				
◆ *Argentine*				
Argentine Grill	★★½	Mod	75	B
◆ *Brazilian*				
Grill from Ipanema	★★½	Mod	78	C
◆ *Chinese*				
City Lights of China	★★★	Mod	81	B
◆ *Ethiopian*				
Meskerem	★★★½	Inexp	86	A
Fasika's	★★★	Inexp	82	A
◆ *French*				
Provence	★★★½	Mod	87	C
Le Lion d'Or	★★★½	Exp	86	C
La Fourchette	★★	Inexp	74	B
◆ *Fusion*				
Perry's	★★½	Mod	79	B
◆ *Indonesian*				
Straits of Malaya	★★	Inexp	71	C
◆ *Italian*				
Galileo	★★★★★	Exp	98	C
Obelisk	★★★½	Exp	89	B
Goldoni	★★★½	Inexp	85	C
I Matti	★★★	Mod	84	B
i Ricchi	★★★	Exp	84	B
Sesto Senso	★★★	Mod	82	B
Vincenzo al Sole	★★★	Exp	82	C
Il Radicchio	★★½	Inexp	79	A
◆ *Japanese*				
Sushi Kappo Kawasaki	★★★	Exp	84	D
◆ *Lebanese*				
Lebanese Taverna	★★	Mod	74	B
Bacchus	★★★	Mod	73	B

Name	Star Rating	Price Rating	Quality Rating	Value Rating
◆ *Modern American*				
Vidalia	★★★★	Exp	93	B
New Heights	★★★½	Mod	88	C
Cashion's Eat Place	★★★	Mod	82	B
Nora	★★★	Mod	80	C
Bistro Twenty-Fifteen	★★½	Inexp	79	B
Trumpets	★★½	Mod	79	B
Tabard Inn	★★½	Mod	77	B
Mrs. Simpson's	★★½	Mod	76	C
◆ *Nuevo Latino*				
Gabriel	★★★	Mod	84	A
◆ *Pan Asian*				
Asia Nora	★★★½	Mod	86	B
Raku: An Asian Grill	★★★½	Inexp	84	A
Cafe Asia	★½	Inexp	69	A
◆ *Pizza*				
Pizzeria Paradiso	★★★	Inexp	83	A
◆ *Seafood*				
Pesce	★★★½	Mod	86	B
◆ *Spanish/Mexican*				
Lauriol Plaza	★★	Mod	72	B
◆ *Steak*				
Sam & Harry's	★★★	Exp	84	C
The Palm	★★½	Exp	79	B
◆ *Thai*				
Star of Siam	★★★	Inexp	80	A
◆ *Vietnamese*				
Miss Saigon	★★½	Inexp	79	B
◆ *West African*				
Bukom	★★	Inexp	72	B

Name	Star Rating	Price Rating	Quality Rating	Value Rating
Zone 7 — Upper Northwest				
◆ *French*				
Lavandou	★★½	Inexp	78	B
◆ *Italian*				
That's Amore	★★½	Mod	76	A
◆ *Japanese*				
Makoto	★★★½	Mod	89	A
◆ *Modern American*				
Greenwood	★★★	Mod	84	B
◆ *Tex-Mex*				
Guapo's	★★½	Inexp	76	B
Zone 10A — Maryland Suburbs				
◆ *American*				
Clyde's	★★½	Mod	77	B
◆ *Cajun*				
Louisiana Express	★★½	Inexp	76	A
◆ *French*				
La Miche	★★★	Inexp	83	B
Jean-Michel	★★½	Mod	78	C
La Ferme	★★½	Mod	78	B
◆ *Greek*				
Athenian Plaka	★★½	Mod	75	B
◆ *Indian*				
Aangan	★★½	Inexp	78	A
Haandi	★★½	Inexp	77	B
◆ *Japanese*				
Tako Grill	★★★★	Mod	92	B
Matuba	★★★½	Inexp	85	B
Hinode	★★½	Inexp	75	B

Name	Star Rating	Price Rating	Quality Rating	Value Rating
◆ *Lebanese*				
Bacchus	★★★	Mod	73	B
◆ *Mediterranean*				
Il Ritrovo	★★★	Mod	80	B
◆ *Mexican*				
Tia Queta	★★½	Mod	75	B
◆ *Modern American*				
Café Bethesda/Café Bethesda North	★★★	Exp	80	B
Inn at Glen Echo	★★½	Mod	75	B
◆ *New Southwestern*				
Cottonwood Cafe	★★★	Mod	80	B
◆ *Pan Asian*				
Raku: An Asian Grill	★★★½	Inexp	84	A
Oodles Noodles	★★½	Inexp	78	B
◆ *Persian/Afghani*				
Paradise	★★	Inexp	73	C
◆ *Spanish*				
Andalucia	★★	Mod	74	B
◆ *Tex-Mex*				
Austin Grill	★★★	Inexp	83	A
Rio Grande Cafe	★★½	Mod	78	C
◆ *Thai*				
Tara Thai	★★★½	Mod	85	A
Bangkok Garden	★★½	Inexp	79	B
Zone 10B—Maryland Suburbs				
◆ *Barbecue*				
Red Hot & Blue	★★½	Inexp	79	B
◆ *Chili*				
Hard Times Cafe	★★½	Inexp	75	A

Name	Star Rating	Price Rating	Quality Rating	Value Rating
Zone 10B—Maryland Suburbs *(continued)*				
◆ *Chinese*				
Seven Seas	★★★½	Mod	85	B
Four Rivers	★★★	Mod	83	B
Hunan Palace	★★★	Inexp	81	B
Good Fortune	★★★	Inexp	80	B
Vegetable Garden	★★★	Mod	80	B
Peking Eastern House	★★½	Inexp	79	A
◆ *French*				
Le Paradis	★★★	Mod	83	B
◆ *German*				
Wurzburg Haus	★★★	Mod	80	B
◆ *Indian*				
Bombay Bistro	★★★	Inexp	83	A
Kashmir Palace	★★½	Inexp	79	B
Delhi Dhaba	★★½	Inexp	78	A
◆ *Indonesian*				
Sabang	★★½	Inexp	75	B
◆ *Italian*				
Il Pizzico	★★½	Inexp	77	A
That's Amore	★★½	Mod	76	A
◆ *Korean*				
Sam Woo	★★★	Mod	81	B
◆ *Korean/Japanese*				
Ichiban	★★★	Mod	83	B
Yokohama	★★½	Mod	79	A
◆ *Japanese*				
Niwano Hana	★★★½	Inexp	87	B
Hinode	★★½	Inexp	75	B
◆ *Mexican/Salvadoran*				
Acajutla	★½	Inexp	68	A

Restaurants by Zone (continued)

Name	Star Rating	Price Rating	Quality Rating	Value Rating
◆ *Modern American*				
Old Angler's Inn	★★★½	Exp	89	C
Café Bethesda/Café Bethesda North	★★★	Exp	80	B
◆ *Pizza*				
Zio's	★★½	Inexp	77	A
◆ *Salvadoran/Mexican*				
Los Chorros	★★★	Inexp	82	B
◆ *Spanish*				
Andalucia	★★	Mod	74	B
◆ *Tex-Mex*				
Guapo's	★★½	Inexp	76	B
◆ *Thai*				
Benjarong	★★★½	Inexp	85	B
Thai Tavern	★★½	Inexp	76	A
Thai Sa-Mai	★★	Inexp	74	A
◆ *Vietnamese*				
Taste of Saigon	★★★½	Mod	86	A
Pho 75	★★½	Inexp	79	A
Zone 10C—Maryland Suburbs				
◆ *American*				
Olney Ale House	★★½	Inexp	76	C
◆ *Chinese*				
Paul Kee	★★	Inexp	71	A
Full Key	★½	Inexp	69	A
◆ *Salvadoran/Mexican*				
Los Chorros	★★★	Inexp	82	B
◆ *Thai*				
Dusit	★★	Inexp	70	A

Name	Star Rating	Price Rating	Quality Rating	Value Rating
Zone 10D — Maryland Suburbs				
◆ *Korean*				
Yijo	★★½	Inexp	78	B
◆ *Vietnamese*				
Pho 75	★★½	Inexp	79	A
Zone 11A — Virginia Suburbs				
◆ *Afghani*				
Panjshir	★★½	Inexp	79	A
◆ *American*				
Clyde's	★★½	Mod	77	B
◆ *Cambodian*				
Angkor Wat GONE	★★½	Inexp	79	B
◆ *Chili*				
Hard Times Cafe	★★½	Inexp	75	A
◆ *French*				
L'Auberge Provençal	★★★★★	Exp	96	A
L'Auberge Chez François	★★★★	Mod	92	A
La Provence	★★★½	Inexp	85	B
Le Gaulois	★★½	Mod	79	C
◆ *Indian*				
Delhi Dhaba	★★½	Inexp	78	A
Cafe Taj	★★½	Inexp	77	B
◆ *Italian*				
Primi Piatti	★★½	Exp	77	C
Paolo's	★★½	Mod	76	B
That's Amore	★★½	Mod	76	A
Cafe Oggi	★★½	Mod	75	B
◆ *Japanese*				
Tachibana	★★★½	Mod	88	B
◆ *Modern American*				
Market Street Bar & Grill	★★½	Mod	79	C

Name	Star Rating	Price Rating	Quality Rating	Value Rating
◆ Pizza				
Faccia Luna	★★	Inexp	73	B
◆ Russian				
Serbian Crown	★★★	Exp	80	B
◆ Seafood				
Legal Sea Foods	★★½	Mod	78	B
◆ Steak				
Morton's of Chicago	★★★½	Exp	89	B
◆ Thai				
Busara	★★★½	Mod	87	B
Tara Thai	★★★½	Mod	85	A
A Little Place Called Siam	★★½	Inexp	76	C
◆ Turkish				
Kazan	★★½	Inexp	79	B
Nizam	★★	Mod	72	B
◆ Vietnamese				
Taste of Saigon	★★★½	Mod	86	A

Zone 11B—Virginia Suburbs

Name	Star Rating	Price Rating	Quality Rating	Value Rating
◆ American				
Clyde's	★★½	Mod	77	B
◆ Afghani				
Panjshir	★★½	Inexp	79	A
◆ Barbecue				
Rocklands	★★★	Inexp	80	C
Red Hot & Blue	★★½	Inexp	79	B
◆ Chili				
Hard Times Cafe	★★½	Inexp	75	A
◆ Chinese				
Hope Key	★★½	Inexp	79	B
Hunan No. 1	★★½	Inexp	78	B

Name	Star Rating	Price Rating	Quality Rating	Value Rating
Zone 11B—Virginia Suburbs (continued)				
◆ *Cuban*				
La Cantinita's Havana Cafe	★★	Inexp	73	B
◆ *French*				
Bistro Bistro	★★½	Inexp	79	B
La Côte d'Or Cafe	★★½	Exp	78	C
◆ *Indian*				
Bombay Bistro	★★★	Inexp	83	A
Aarathi	★★½	Inexp	79	B
Haandi	★★½	Inexp	77	B
◆ *Italian*				
Il Radicchio	★★½	Inexp	79	A
◆ *Japanese*				
Matuba	★★★½	Inexp	85	B
Atami	★★	Mod	74	A
◆ *Korean*				
Woo Lae Oak	★★★	Mod	82	A
◆ *Lebanese*				
Lebanese Taverna	★★	Mod	74	B
◆ *Modern American*				
The Inn at Little Washington	★★★★★	Exp	98	B
Carlyle Grand Café	★★★	Mod	81	C
◆ *Moroccan*				
Taste of Casablanca	★★½	Inexp	79	A
◆ *Persian*				
Kabob Bazaar	★★½	Inexp	79	B
◆ *Pizza*				
Pizza de Resistance	★★½	Inexp	75	B
◆ *Russian*				
Russia House	★★½	Mod	79	B

Name	Star Rating	Price Rating	Quality Rating	Value Rating
◆ *Tex-Mex*				
Austin Grill	★★★	Inexp	83	A
Rio Grande Cafe	★★½	Mod	78	C
◆ *Thai*				
Bangkok St. Grill and Noodles	★★½	Inexp	79	B
Duangrat	★★½	Mod	79	C
Rabieng	★★½	Inexp	79	B
Bangkok–Vientiane	★★½	Inexp	75	B
◆ *Vietnamese*				
Cafe Saigon	★★★	Inexp	84	A
Cafe Dalat	★★½	Inexp	79	B
Pho Cali/The Seafood Place	★★½	Inexp	79	A
Pho 75	★★½	Inexp	79	A
Little Viet Garden	★★½	Inexp	77	A
Queen Bee	★★½	Inexp	76	B

Zone 11C—Virginia Suburbs

◆ *Cajun*				
R.T.'s	★★	Mod	73	B
◆ *Cajun/Thai*				
Cajun Bangkok	★★½	Inexp	77	B
◆ *Chili*				
Hard Times Cafe	★★½	Inexp	75	A
◆ *French*				
La Bergerie	★★★	Mod	84	C
Le Refuge	★★	Mod	73	B
◆ *Modern American*				
Elysium	★★★½	Exp	87	B
◆ *New Southwestern*				
Santa Fe East	★★★	Mod	80	B
◆ *Pizza*				
Faccia Luna	★★	Inexp	73	B

Restaurants by Zone (continued)

Name	Star Rating	Price Rating	Quality Rating	Value Rating
Zone 11C—Virginia Suburbs *(continued)*				
◆ *Seafood*				
Blue Point Grill	★★½	Exp	77	B
◆ *Tex-Mex*				
Austin Grill	★★★	Inexp	83	A

RESTAURANT
profiles

Aangan

Zone 10A   Maryland suburbs
4920 St. Elmo Avenue, Bethesda
(301) 657-1262

	Indian
	★★½
	Inexpensive
Quality 78	Value A

Reservations:	Accepted
When to go:	Any time
Entree range:	$6.95−12.95
Payment:	VISA, MC, AMEX
Service rating:	★★½
Friendliness rating:	★★★½
Parking:	Street meters, lot on weekends
Bar:	Full service
Wine selection:	House
Dress:	Casual
Disabled access:	Good
Customers:	Ethnic, local
Lunch:	Every day, 11:30 A.M.−2:30 P.M.
Dinner:	Sunday−Thursday, 5:30−10 P.M.;
	Friday and Saturday, 5:30−10:30 P.M.

Atmosphere/setting: Just a small room, but very placid.

House specialties: Shrimp in coconut, onion, and mustard-seed sauce (jheenga masala dakshini); a "robust" (as the menu puts it) Goan-style fish curry with coconut; a range of chicken and lamb dishes marinated in yogurt, tomato-curry sauce, and even pureed spinach; lamb in crushed almonds; ginger-rubbed lamb chops.

Other recommendations: Roasted eggplant curry; lightly marinated grilled fish for the novice diner.

Summary & comments: This restaurant is one of two very nice Indian restaurants in this neighborhood—the other is Haandi (see profile)—but this one is particularly popular with vegetarian customers because of its broader-than-usual range of veggie dishes, including paneer kadhai (fried cottage cheese "fingers" with coriander and tomatoes) and biryani with fresh vegetables, saffron, raisins, and almonds.

Aarathi

Zone 11B   Virginia suburbs
409 Maple Avenue East, Vienna
(703) 938-0100

Reservations:	Helpful
When to go:	Any time
Entree range:	$4.95−13.95
Payment:	VISA, MC, AMEX, D, DC
Service rating:	★★★
Friendliness rating:	★★★
Parking:	Free lot
Bar:	Full service
Wine selection:	House
Dress:	Casual
Disabled access:	Good
Customers:	Local, ethnic
Lunch:	Every day, 11:30 A.M.−2:30 P.M.
Dinner:	Sunday−Thursday, 5:30−10 P.M.;
	Friday and Saturday, 5:30−10:30 P.M.

Atmosphere/setting: A nice, albeit very simple, sit-down spot—no steam table buffet here.

House specialties: Curried fish; mixed vegetable curries; chicken Makhanwala, the buttery, tomato-sauce dish made popular at Aarathi's parent restaurant, Aditi.

Other recommendations: Pumpkin in coconut-milk curry.

Summary & comments: Like an increasing number of Indian restaurants (particularly in the office-complex suburbs, where both price and time are of the essence) Aarathi offers a hot buffet, but goes one better by making it vegetarian. This is less the sort of place that gets a lot of publicity than the type you find yourself heading to more and more often with confidence.

Acajutla

Mexican/Salvadoran
★ ½
Inexpensive

Quality 68   Value A

Zone 10B   Maryland suburbs
18554 Woodfield Road, Gaithersburg
(301) 670-1674

Reservations:	Accepted
When to go:	Any time
Entree range:	$5.95–11.95
Payment:	VISA, MC, AMEX
Service rating:	★★½
Friendliness rating:	★★★½
Parking:	Free lot
Bar:	Beer and wine
Wine selection:	House
Dress:	Casual
Disabled access:	Good
Customers:	Ethnic, local
Open:	Sunday–Thursday, 11:30 A.M.–10 P.M.;
	Friday and Saturday, 11:30 A.M.–11 P.M.

Atmosphere/setting: Just a shoestring-budget storefront; like a pizza franchise taken over by Mom and Pop. Very friendly.

House specialties: Red snapper in a tomato-onion Veracruz sauce; shrimp and crab enchilada; spicy skillet-browned boneless chicken; sautéed scallops with onions and melted cheese; boneless chicken breast stuffed with pork and cheese. Those familiar with sopa de mondongo, beef tripe soup, will find Acajutla's extremely good.

Other recommendations: Fried seafood chimichanga; fajitas, particularly the shrimp; a sort of sautéed Philly beef stew topped with melted cheese.

Summary & comments: This little suburban strip-mall surprise serves up a lot of food for the money, especially when you consider that most entrees come with rice and beans and, in some cases, a salad. Don't skip the appetizers, though, particularly the fried plantain; impeccable fried yucca; and the "chalupas Acajutla," corn tortillas with shredded beef, pickled cabbage, Parmesan, salsa, and hard-boiled eggs.

Aditi

Zone 5   Georgetown
3299 M Street, NW
(202) 625-6825

Indian	
★★★	
Inexpensive	
Quality 84	Value B

Reservations:	Suggested
When to go:	Any time
Entree range:	$5.95−13.95
Payment:	VISA, MC, AMEX, DC, D
Service rating:	★★½
Friendliness rating:	★★★
Parking:	Street
Bar:	Full service
Wine selection:	Fair
Dress:	Casual
Disabled access:	No
Customers:	Local, tourist, ethnic
Lunch:	Monday−Saturday, 11:30 A.M.−2:30 P.M.; Sunday, noon−2:30 P.M.
Dinner:	Sunday−Thursday, 5:30−10 P.M.; Friday and Saturday, 5:30−10:30 P.M.

Atmosphere / setting: To frayed nerves, Aditi offers the Arabian Nights hidden-courtyard effect: From the busy street, one enters through a whitewashed brick exterior—sometimes with the flourish of a turbaned doorman—into a soothing, two-story, burgundy-and-celadon den.

House specialties: Twice-cooked chicken Makhanwala, tandoori-roasted and then sautéed with tomatoes; a delicate almond-sauced chicken (or lamb); spicy lamb vindaloo; fried vegetarian "meatballs."

Other recommendations: Malabar fish curry with tamarind; stir-fried lamb Kadai with ginger sauce; okra curry; the $4.95 bread sampler.

Summary & comments: Because Aditi substitutes olive oil for the usual clarified butter and knows about keeping the oil hot, it can be said to serve the healthiest, least greasy, and best-tasting samosas. The tandoori oven does fine service here as well. The "Aditi dinner," a thali platter combining tandoori and curry dishes, is a bargain at $13.95; a vegetarian platter is $11.95. Incidentally, "Aditi" is Sanskrit for "abundance," a nice promise.

Andalucia

Spanish
★★
Moderate

Quality 74   Value B

Zone 10A   Maryland suburbs
4931 Elm Street, Bethesda
(301) 907-0052
Zone 10B   Maryland suburbs
12300 Wilkins Avenue, Rockville
(301) 770-1880

Reservations:	Recommended; required on weekends (Bethesda)
When to go:	Any time
Entree range:	$13.95−18.95
Payment:	VISA, MC, AMEX, DC, D
Service rating:	★★★
Friendliness rating:	★★★½
Parking:	Lot, street
Bar:	Full service
Wine selection:	Fair
Dress:	Informal, casual
Disabled access:	Good
Customers:	Local, ethnic
Lunch:	Monday, 11:30 A.M.−2:30 P.M. (Bethesda only); Tuesday−Friday, 11:30 A.M.−2:30 P.M.
Dinner:	Monday−Friday, 5:30−10 P.M.; Saturday, 5:30−10:30 P.M.; Sunday, 4:30−9:30 P.M.; Monday, closed (Rockville).

Atmosphere/setting: From the original restaurant, an unassuming family-style storefront in a semi-industrial warehouse/office park, Andalucia has expanded into a much prettier, white-lace-curtained Bethesda restaurant with painted tiles and stucco.

House specialties: Paella and zarzuella, a Spanish bouillabaisse; roast duck; whole red snapper on rock salt; grilled squid and steamed clam appetizers.

Other recommendations: Daily specials, often as many as eight or ten, often featuring veal sirloin with dry sherry and fresh seafood such as grouper with lobster sauce or smoky grilled squid on roasted sweet peppers.

Entertainment & amenities: Classical/flamenco guitar weeknights.

Summary & comments: These southern Spanish restaurants are, happily, more Mediterranean than "Latin," are more tomato and onion sauce than salsa, and have a modern penchant for lightly cooked seafood. This is family-style cooking, but Sunday-dinner quality; the many bilingual family groups prove it.

Angkor Wat GONE

Zone 11A   Virginia suburbs
6703 Lowell Avenue, McLean
(703) 893-6077

Cambodian
★★½
Inexpensive
Quality 79   Value B

Reservations:	Helpful for 4 or more
When to go:	Any time
Entree range:	$5.25 − 18.99
Payment:	VISA, MC, AMEX, D, DC
Service rating:	★★½
Friendliness rating:	★★★
Parking:	Free lot
Bar:	Beer and wine
Wine selection:	House
Dress:	Casual
Disabled access:	No
Customers:	Ethnic, local
Lunch:	Monday − Friday, 11 A.M. − 2:30 P.M.
Dinner:	Monday − Thursday, 5 − 9:30 P.M.;
	Friday and Saturday, 5 − 10 P.M.;
	Sunday, 5 − 9:30 P.M.
	(Closed on Sundays in the summer.)

Atmosphere / setting: This very small room is painted a soothing mauve and a waterfall seems to pour water down the staircase. A few fairly standard paintings of Cambodia decorate the walls, and background music wafts through the air.

House specialties: The most astonishing stuffed chicken wings ever seen, with the two larger joints entirely deboned and stuffed with a mixture of ground pork, malty roasted rice powder, onions, and spices; it's scored, then broiled and served with lettuce leaves for wrapping, and then dipped in a peanut-vinegar sauce. Also, the Cambodian hot pot of beef, seafood, and vegetables called yao hawn (much like Japanese shabu shabu or Mongolian fondue); kuong, the Cambodian version of summer rolls with pork and shrimp; big pots of soup with or without noodles.

Other recommendations: Char-grilled beef; shrimp in hot sauce.

Summary & comments: Cambodian food is, not surprisingly, closely related to Thai and Malay: It tends to Thai-style coconut-milk curries, lime juice, chiles, lemongrass, and a fish sauce similar (though unfermented) to those found in Thai and Vietnamese restaurants, plus the tamarind and peanuts popular in Malaysian recipes. Since this is a no-frills operation in most respects, the food has to be pretty good to keep so many non-Cambodian diners coming in; it is, and they do.

AQUARELLE

Zone 4   Foggy Bottom
2650 Virginia Avenue, NW
    (Watergate Hotel)
(202) 298-4455

Modern American
★★★
Expensive

Quality 80   Value B

Reservations:	Recommended
When to go:	Lunch; pretheater
Entree range:	$17−27
Payment:	VISA, MC, AMEX, CB, D, DC
Service rating:	★★½
Friendliness rating:	★★★
Parking:	Valet validated at restaurant
Bar:	Full service
Wine selection:	Good
Dress:	Business (jacket required at dinner)
Disabled access:	Good
Customers:	Locals, tourists, expense accounters, food trendies
Lunch:	Every day, 11:30 A.M.−2:30 P.M.
Dinner:	Every day, 5:30−10:30 P.M.

Atmosphere/setting: If it weren't for the Potomac River beyond the windows (and visibly clunky iron fence), it would have almost no visual attraction at all; floral plates and pastel-colored carafes aren't enough to warm this cool room.

House specialties: Game and fowl—stuffed quail, braised pheasant, roast squab, buffalo, and roulade of rabbit—have enough big flavor to survive the sometimes over-vigorous seasoning. Flavors for seafood are more carefully considered: A miniature bouillabaisse of coin-sliced scallops and lobster morsels is a fine first course; and roasted striped bass lay prostrate on a perfect risotto.

Other recommendations: The chef's primary fun is dishing up the daily menu du gustacione: five courses for about $65. You can have the staff provide glasses of wine; however, the selection is uneven, and few will want the sauternes as well as dessert. The three-course pretheater menu for $35 is the real steal.

Summary & comments: Running the Watergate's restaurant, so long the personal domain of star-chef Jean-Louis Palladin, may have made successor Robert Wiedmaier a little careless. While most of the dishes are beautifully conceived and presented, a few star-and-sauce mismatches leave a strange taste. A spice-crusted beef with a classically strong reduction was layered over a ham-studded vegetable pilaf and topped with a caramelized garlic-carrot puree also heavily salted—too much salt altogether. And, as if the cooking were too casual, or hurried, too much of the veal, seafood, and even poultry comes out tough even when still pink in the middle.

ARGENTINE GRILL

Zone 6   Dupont Circle/
          Adams-Morgan
2433 18th Street, NW
(202) 234-1818

Argentine	
★★½	
Moderate	
Quality 75	Value B

Reservations:	Accepted
When to go:	Any time
Entree range:	$7.95 – 18.95
Payment:	VISA, MC
Service rating:	★★★
Friendliness rating:	★★½
Parking:	Street, lot
Bar:	Full service
Wine selection:	Fair
Dress:	Business, informal
Disabled access:	Fair
Customers:	Local, international
Dinner:	Monday – Thursday, 5 – 10:30 P.M.;
	Friday and Saturday, 5 – 11 P.M.;
	Sunday, 5 – 10 P.M.

Atmosphere/setting: Aside from its tourism-special mural, which turns the map of Argentina into the Wide World of Sports, this is a classically clean, two-level Adams-Morgan bistro with exposed brick walls, time-scarred hardwood floors, and white linen tablecloths.

House specialties: Char-grilled sweetbreads, offered as an appetizer but so rich they actually make a meal; grilled kidneys; grilled fish; marinated eggplant (appetizer); lamb chops; shrimp over linguini (surprised?); grilled short ribs.

Other recommendations: Chorizo; filet mignon with green chimichurri sauce; empanadas.

Summary & comments: If the touch of Italian on the menu surprises you, perhaps they ought to touch up the mural: Argentina is truly a melting-pot nation. Even if you opt to jump off the meat bandwagon, the grilling here is the best bet. For sweetbread fans, this is worth the parking bother.

Asia Nora

Zone 6   Dupont Circle/
Adams-Morgan
2213 M Street, NW
(202) 797-4860

Pan Asian
★★★½
Moderate

Quality 86   Value B

Reservations:	Recommended
When to go:	Any time
Entree range:	$18 – 23.50
Payment:	VISA, MC
Service rating:	★★★
Friendliness rating:	★★★½
Parking:	Pay lots, meters
Bar:	Full service
Wine selection:	Limited
Dress:	Business, informal
Disabled access:	No
Customers:	Local, tourist, business
Dinner:	Monday – Thursday, 6 – 10 P.M.;
	Friday and Saturday, 6 – 10:30 P.M.;
	Sunday, closed.

Atmosphere / setting: A small but very romantic two-story Indonesian jewel box (or fantasy boudoir) of a room, with carved wood, mirrors, and intriguing booths and balcony niches.

House specialties: Rockfish with lemongrass and chiles; lacquered spit-roasted duck with a crêpe-light mushroom pancake and chile-hoisin sauce; salmon glazed with Japanese miso and served with ginger-flavored soba noodles.

Other recommendations: Grilled "satays" of shiitake mushrooms and tofu; Asian veal-rice sausage; vegetable or seafood tempura; Vietnamese-style garden rolls with crabmeat, cilantro, mint, and peanut sauce; hot-and-sour coconut soup. At lunch, the "grill of the day" or Japanese-style bento box lunches. A selection of quality sakés and green teas.

Summary & comments: This is a restaurant designed for dawdling. The menu, which is seasonally adjusted, is divided into "small dishes" of three or four bites each and larger dishes of six to eight bites, so that a series of different tastes can be shared. (Of course, this means that you can spend rather more money here if you want.) The dishes are more traditional in attitude than in strict recipes: Japanese udon noodles are topped with portobello mushrooms; salmon "tartare" is lightly pickled, like seviche; and the tuna "sashimi" is seared, just as the flounder "sashimi" is dressed with sizzling-hot oil—a trick made famous by bicoastal star Nobu.

ATAMI

Zone 11B   Virginia suburbs
3155 Wilson Boulevard, Arlington
(703) 522-4787

Japanese
★★
Moderate
Quality 74   Value A

Reservations:	Helpful
When to go:	Any time
Entree range:	$6.50–13
Payment:	VISA, MC, DC, AMEX
Service rating:	★★★
Friendliness rating:	★★★★
Parking:	Street, free lot
Bar:	Beer and wine
Wine selection:	House
Dress:	Casual
Disabled access:	Fair
Customers:	Local, ethnic
Open:	Monday–Thursday, 11 A.M.–10 P.M.;
	Friday, 11 A.M.–10:30 P.M.;
	Saturday, noon–10:30 P.M.; Sunday, 4–9:30 P.M.

Atmosphere/setting: Very simple, dark, and relaxed, with fresh flowers and only a few nods to traditional decor. The staff is attentive, but almost shy.

House specialties: The best-known "entree" on the menu is the all-you-can-eat sushi special for $24.95 (even less if you clip one of their frequent coupons out of the local newspapers). Actually, it's more of a house special, available every night—and if it turns out your eyes are bigger than your stomach, as they used to say, and you don't eat $25 worth, you only pay the per-piece price. Other good choices include the broiled jaw of fresh yellowtail and roast quail.

Other recommendations: Eel roll, here called "Virginia roll"; shishamo, the small fish—the menu says "herring-like," but they're usually smelts—grilled with salt; toro in season (the owner will be glad you asked); giant clam in nuta sauce or thinly sliced rare beef in vinegary ponzu sauce (both appetizers).

Summary & comments: There are so many hyphenated sushi bars these days—Korean-Japanese, Chinese-Japanese, and so on—that this one, owned by Vietnamese-Japanese Taro Koizumi, comes as no surprise. There are many Vietnamese dishes on the menu, and even a somewhat lighter, Vietnamized flavoring to some of the Japanese food, but the Japanese food is better (not first-rate, but good). Atami makes a special attempt to please vegetarian diners, with veggie tempura, vegetarian versions of sukiyaki and noodle soups, and many types of veggie sushi.

ATHENIAN PLAKA

Zone 10A Maryland suburbs	Greek
7833 Woodmont Avenue, Bethesda	★★½
(301) 986-1337	Moderate
	Quality 75 Value B

Reservations:	Accepted
When to go:	Any time
Entree range:	$8.95–14.95
Payment:	VISA, MC, AMEX, CB, DC, D
Service rating:	★★★
Friendliness rating:	★★★
Parking:	Validated, free valet (weekends)
Bar:	Full service
Wine selection:	Limited
Dress:	Informal, casual
Disabled access:	Good
Customers:	Locals
Open:	Monday–Thursday, 11 A.M.–10 P.M.;
	Friday and Saturday, noon–11 P.M.;
	Sunday, noon–10 P.M.

Atmosphere/setting: A quietly proud little dining room, with fresh linen and greenery, plaster arches, and vivid travel-mag murals of the home country. (In fact, it shares ownership with the nearby La Panetteria Italian restaurant.) In good weather, tables are set up on the sidewalk.

House specialties: Among entrees, veal baked with eggplant, wine, and two cheeses; exohikon, lamb sautéed with artichokes, calamata olives, and cheese and then baked in phyllo; pan-fried baby squid. Among appetizers, a combination platter of calf's liver, sweetbreads, meatballs, sausage, and lamb (for two); eggplant stuffed with pine nuts, raisins, and tomato; pan-fried smelt.

Other recommendations: Broiled red snapper; shrimp baked with tomatoes and feta; swordfish.

Summary & comments: Don't let the suburban storefront location fool you; this is not your father's greasy Greek joint. The kitchen says it takes time to prepare dishes to order, and they mean it—it's a little slow, but it's right. A surprising number of these dishes are also available at lunch for a couple of dollars less.

Austin Grill

	Tex-Mex
	★★★
	Inexpensive
	Quality 83　Value A

Zone 5　Georgetown
2404 Wisconsin Avenue, NW
(202) 337-8080

Zone 11C　Virginia suburbs
801 King Street, Alexandria
(703) 684-8969

Zone 11B　Virginia suburbs
8430-A Old Keene Mill Road (Old Keene Mill Center), West
　Springfield
(703) 644-3111

Zone 10A　Maryland suburbs
7278 Woodmont Avenue, Bethesda
(301) 656-1366

Reservations:	Not accepted
When to go:	Late afternoon, late night
Entree range:	$5.75−13.95
Payment:	VISA, MC, AMEX, D, DC
Service rating:	★★★
Friendliness rating:	★★★
Parking:	Street
Bar:	Full service
Wine selection:	Fair
Dress:	Casual
Disabled access:	Good, except for Georgetown
Customers:	Local, student
Breakfast:	*West Springfield:* Saturday and Sunday, 9 A.M.−3 P.M.
Brunch:	Saturday and Sunday, 11 A.M.−3 P.M.
Lunch/Dinner:	Tuesday−Thursday, 11:30 A.M.−11 P.M.;
	Friday and Saturday, 11 A.M.−midnight;
	Sunday, 11 A.M.−10 P.M.;
	Monday, 11:30 A.M.−10 P.M.

Atmosphere/setting:　Hot adobe pastels, Crayola-colored tile, buffalo and lizard stenciling, angular art-joke graphics, and Tex-Mex pun art and T-shirts in a funky vinyl-booth roadhouse setting. Great Texas music on the PA. If not a mom-and-pop joint, it's more like a *Friends* franchise: One of the original prep cooks who started at age 19 in Georgetown became the head chef in Bethesda.

(continued)

House specialties: Potent quesadillas with chorizo or delicate ones with crabmeat; grilled fish of the day; real all-beef chunky chili; "Austin special enchilada" with three sauces; green chicken chili; grilled chili-rubbed shrimp and scallops; grilled fish; pork loin enchilada with mole sauce.

Other recommendations: Margaritas; chili-flavored rib eye; pork chops adobado; eggs Benedict with jalapeño hollandaise (brunch); barbecued brisket.

Summary & comments: The perfect antidote for designer chili cuisine (not that these are plain-Jane spots; in fact, they're corporate cousins of the slick-chic Jaleo). The original Georgetown branch made its first friends just from the smell of the smoker out back. The hot-hot sauces—a choice of four—were the local endorphin addict's drugs before chiles were cool, so to speak. Incidentally, the Springfield location has been experimenting with serving breakfast, but a fairly straight version.

Bacchus

Zone 6   Dupont Circle/
          Adams–Morgan
1827 Jefferson Place, NW
(202) 785-0734

Zone 10A   Maryland suburbs
7945 Norfolk Avenue, Bethesda
(301) 657-1722

Lebanese	
★★★	
Moderate	
Quality 73	Value B

Reservations:	Suggested
When to go:	Any time
Entree range:	$14.25–16.25
Payment:	VISA, MC, AMEX
Service rating:	★★½
Friendliness rating:	★★
Parking:	Street; valet (dinner only)
Bar:	Full service
Wine selection:	Brief
Dress:	Informal, casual
Disabled access:	Jefferson Street, no; Norfolk Avenue, good
Customers:	Local, business
Lunch:	Monday–Friday, noon-2:30 P.M.
Dinner:	Monday–Thursday, 6–10 P.M.;
	Friday and Saturday, 6–10:30 P.M.;
	Sunday, 6–10 P.M. (Bethesda only;
	downtown closed)

Atmosphere/setting: The D.C. location is a simple, pleasantly crowded English basement downtown; in Bethesda, it's a villa with carved screens, white-washed walls, a balcony, and a more leisurely atmosphere.

House specialties: Meze (or "maza" here), a platter of two-bite appetizers served simultaneously, including stuffed phyllo turnovers of spinach or cheese; kibbeh, a steak tartare with cracked wheat; zucchini pancakes; grilled sausages; stuffed baby eggplant; spicy sausages; stuffed grape leaves.

Other recommendations: Lamb almost any fashion, including layered over a fried pita and yogurt or with eggplant; fried smelts; fatayer bel sbanegh, a spinach and coriander pastry; stuffed cabbage with pomegranate sauce; kebabs.

Summary & comments: For whatever reason, the Bethesda location is more consistent, the specials are more interesting, and the food is just a little sprightlier (perhaps because the pace is less frantic), but appetizers in particular are always good at both sites. The Washington location has no separate nonsmoking section.

86

Bangkok Garden

Zone 10A   Maryland suburbs
4906 St. Elmo Avenue, Bethesda
(301) 951-0670

Thai
★★½
Inexpensive

Quality 79   Value B

Reservations:	Accepted on weekends
When to go:	Any time
Entree range:	$6.25–17.25
Payment:	VISA, MC, AMEX
Service rating:	★★★½
Friendliness rating:	★★★★
Parking:	Street, free lot after 6 P.M.
Bar:	Full service
Wine selection:	House
Dress:	Casual
Disabled access:	Fair
Customers:	Local, ethnic
Open:	Monday – Thursday, 11 A.M. – 10:30 P.M.;
	Friday and Saturday, 11 A.M. – 11 P.M.;
	Sunday – Thursday, 4 – 10 P.M.

Atmosphere/setting: Small, cheery, and so crowded with brass and plaster animals—giraffes, elephants, temple foo dogs, peafowl, deer—that the young Buddha enshrined resembles a Thai Francis of Assisi. Enlarged and framed colorful Thai currency and portraits of the ruling family are also prominent.

House specialties: A rich, skin-and-fat duck in five-flavor sauce; fat "drunken" noodles with beef; hoy jawh, a crispy pork and crab appetizer cake; squid with basil and chili (unusually, almost purely squid and scarce vegetable filler); the tangy rather than searing seafood combination.

Other recommendations: Soft-shell crabs in a choice of five sauces, four spicy and one very light version with asparagus and oyster sauce; steamed crab dumplings; shrimp in chili oil.

Summary & comments: Though relatively low profile amidst the Thai boom, this family-run restaurant rewards regular attendance and obvious interest because some of the best dishes aren't on the English menu, but are available to anyone who knows to ask. A particularly delicious example is the "Thai steak tartare," a beef version of a Thai pork classic that is rich with garlic, cilantro, and basil and served with a steaming basket of "sticky rice" intended to be used as the utensil: Take a pinch of rice—about a tablespoon—slightly flatten it and grasp a bite of meat with it and pop the whole morsel into your mouth. At $7.95, it's a steal of a meal.

87

BaNqkok St. Grill aNd NoodlES

	Thai
	★★½

Inexpensive

Quality 79	Value B

Zone 11B   Virginia suburbs
5872 Leesburg Pike, Falls Church
(703) 379-6707

Reservations: Helpful
When to go: Any time
Entree range: $6.75−8.75
Payment: VISA, MC, AMEX, DC
Service rating: ★★★
Friendliness rating: ★★★½
Parking: Free lot
Bar: Full service
Wine selection: House
Dress: Casual
Disabled access: No
Customers: Local, ethnic
Open: Sunday−Thursday, 11:30 A.M.−10 P.M.;
                           Friday and Saturday, 11:30 A.M.−11 P.M.

Atmosphere/setting: Very funny and intentionally "mod," this restaurant looks more like a village grocery with an open-air dining room than the offshoot of the very dignified Duangrat (see profile) that it is. Stunted trees and gracious palms, a brick "sidewalk" in the tile flooring, verandah-ish furniture and road signs pointing to Phuket and Pattaya reinforce the theme of a market strip like those that are the food courts of Asia.

House specialties: Despite the even-handed name, this is more successful as a noodle shop. Try the coconut-curry soup with meatballs and vegetables or shrimp dumplings; clay pot chicken with sausage and mushrooms; the classic "drunken noodles" (thick rice noodles with chicken, hot green chiles, and basil— aptly named because most people drink so much beer to cool the flames).

Other recommendations: Duck marinated in miso and hoisin sauce; grilled leg of pork with chiles and basil (offered as-is or "Bangkok style" with an over-easy fried egg); "yentafo," vermicelli stopped with poached fish, fried fish balls, fried tofu, squid, watercress, crab, and sliced pork in a tomato broth.

Summary & comments: As part of the sidewalk vendor style, the customers are encouraged to spice dishes as they please with a half-dozen bottles and dishes of seasonings and sauces. Do, however, be polite and smart enough to taste first: this is no cowardly kitchen. As evidence, try the fajita-like "strips of Bangkok" in garlic and chili sauce. Texans, defend your honor.

Bangkok-Vientiane

Zone 11B   Virginia suburbs
926-A West Broad Street, Falls Church
(703) 534-0095

Thai-Laotian
★★½
Inexpensive

Quality 75   Value B

Reservations:	Helpful
When to go:	Any time
Entree range:	$5.95−15.95
Payment:	VISA, MC, AMEX, D, DC
Service rating:	★★
Friendliness rating:	★★★
Parking:	Free lot
Bar:	Wine and beer
Wine selection:	House
Dress:	Casual
Disabled access:	Good
Customers:	Local, ethnic
Lunch:	Every day, 11 A.M.−2 P.M.
Dinner:	Sunday−Thursday, 5−10 P.M.; Friday and Saturday, 5−11 P.M.

Atmosphere/setting: The word "atmosphere" barely pertains to a shoebox like this, but the staff is extremely nice and a few nostalgic pictures, particularly of Laos, add interest. And the nearly constant crowd of Laotian, Vietnamese, Thai, and even Cambodian diners makes for a gentle hubbub that testifies to its hospitality.

House specialties: Larb, minced-meat chicken or beef dishes (not raw, as in Thailand) served with sticky rice; papaya salad with dried beef and hot chiles; fried spring rolls that are longer and narrower than the ones common in Vietnamese restaurants.

Other recommendations: A seafood hot pot related to the Mongolian hot pot and Japanese shabu shabu.

Summary & comments: Laotians might protest that their food is not exactly a synthesis of their neighbors on either side, Thailand and Vietnam, but it's pretty close; and this sweet little cafe is apt to be populated by immigrants of any Southeast Asian country. Expect chiles, citrus fruits, and lemongrass to flavor most of the dishes. Among the dishes not widely available is Lao sean dard, beef marinated in a sweetish combination and then dipped into the typical anchovy-based sauce.

Benjarong

Thai
★★★½
Inexpensive

Quality 85   Value B

Zone 10B   Maryland suburbs
855-C Rockville Pike (Wintergreen
    Plaza), Rockville
(301) 424-5533

Reservations:	Suggested
When to go:	Any time
Entree range:	$7.95 – 11.95
Payment:	VISA, MC, AMEX, DC, D
Service rating:	★★★
Friendliness rating:	★★★★
Parking:	Free lot
Bar:	Full service
Wine selection:	House
Dress:	Informal
Disabled access:	Good
Customers:	Local, ethnic
Open:	Monday – Thursday, 11:30 A.M. – 9:30 P.M.;
	Friday and Saturday, 11:30 A.M. – 10:30 P.M.;
	Sunday, 5 – 9:30 P.M.

Atmosphere/setting: A simple but soothing room decorated with off-white grass wallpaper, pink linens, black lacquer chairs, and a few Thai carvings and figurines.

House specialties: Duck with asparagus (in season); spicy duck and coriander salad; mussels steamed in lemongrass and spices; sliced beef filet in red wine sauce; fresh squid sautéed with chiles and basil; and the best pra pla mug—a sort of squid seviche with lime juice and chiles—even in this Thai-smart town.

Other recommendations: Steamed whole snapper with delicate scallions and ginger sauce or crispy fried flounder; spicy shrimp in red curry sauce; red curry duck; seafood combination chow foon noodles; a rattle-shaped chicken drummette appetizer stuffed with ground chicken and pork; soft-shell crabs in a choice of sauces; and a sort of barbecue beef in chili paste with scallions.

Summary & comments: Benjarong (the name refers to a type of multicolored Thai porcelain) used to be part of a local chain called Thai Taste, but like its next-door neighbor, the Kashmir Palace, it seems to have become much stronger since going independent. Many of the dishes here are Southern Thai, meaning the curries are creamier and there's a good pork satay on the menu. There are also several good vegetarian choices, including a delicately peppery sautéed watercress.

BICE

Zone 3   Downtown
601 Pennsylvania Avenue, NW
  (entrance on Indiana Avenue)
(202) 638-2423

Italian
★★½
Moderate

Quality 79   Value C

Reservations:	Recommended
When to go:	Any time
Entree range:	$15−25
Payment:	VISA, MC, AMEX, DC
Service rating:	★★½
Friendliness rating:	★★
Parking:	Street, valet (dinner only)
Bar:	Full service
Wine selection:	Good
Dress:	Dressy, business
Disabled access:	Good
Customers:	Local, business
Lunch:	Monday−Friday, 11:30 A.M.−2:30 P.M.
Dinner:	Every day, 5:30−9 P.M.

Atmosphere/setting: Pleasantly restrained, with a woody, clubby bar and a bright, airy dining room hung with what looks like cleverly framed wallpaper samples.

House specialties: Marinated and sautéed pork loin with olives, tomato, balsamic vinegar, and cannellini beans, or beef tenderloin with cannellini and green peppercorn sauce; a paillard of veal with grilled vegetables; grilled rabbit in rosemary; seafood or porcini risotto. Among appetizers (enough for grazing): warm eggplant timbale; air-dried bresaola with a rustic salad; ravioli stuffed with veal and mushrooms.

Other recommendations: Grilled red snapper with lentil salad; a rich lamb/ pork/rabbit sausage; grilled veal or lamb chops; pastas with substantial rabbit or duck sauce.

Summary & comments: Although this Italian restaurant can be one of the town's best, it can occasionally be sloppy and condescending. Risottos are creamy and heavenly three times, but cobby the fourth. And this is one of the places that instituted the habit of bringing a $5 bottle in response to a request for water. But with the advent of executive chef Francesco Ricchi, it is beginning to get its act back together, and might well have regained its third star by the time you get in.

The Bistro at the ANA

	Mediterranean
	★★½
	Moderate
Zone 5 Georgetown	
2401 M Street, NW	Quality 79 Value B
(202) 457-5020	

Reservations:	Helpful
When to go:	Any time
Entree range:	$17−25
Payment:	VISA, MC, AMEX, D, DC
Service rating:	★★★
Friendliness rating:	★★★
Parking:	Valet, street
Bar:	Full service
Wine selection:	Good
Dress:	Business, casual
Disabled access:	Good
Customers:	Local, business
Breakfast:	Every day, 6:30−11 A.M.
Lunch/Dinner:	Every day, 11 A.M.−10:30 P.M.

Atmosphere/setting: As befits the "bistro" of such an upscale restaurant, this is very sleek but low-gloss: polished wood, dark green paint, white marble, and a great view of the hotel's courtyard, where good-weather dining is available.

House specialties: Pan-roasted scallops with olive ragout; warm roast lamb on flatbread with roasted eggplant salad; pasta with smoked trout and pesto; first or light courses of seafood risotto and oxtail ragout.

Other recommendations: Even the most classical dishes, left on to honor the hotel trade, have something new to offer: The beef tenderloin is sweetened by an onion gratinée and a marrow and mushroom ragout; the grilled duck gets not a cloyingly sweet glaze, but a barely bitter bed of Swiss chard and a juniper sauce; and if you must have mashed potatoes, try these, flavored with olive instead of the now-ubiquitous garlic.

Summary & comments: You can take Mediterranean chef Peter Moutsos out of the West End, but you can't take the Mediterranean out of . . . well, you get it. (And this still is, after all, the West End.) Moutsos' signature is all over dishes like the scallops and cod, but even with all those rich flavorings—olives, capers, eggplant, cheeses, and pesto—it doesn't get heavy. Even feta cheese is worth another chance when used to pump up grilled flank steak and snap peas.

BISTRO BISTRO

French	
★★½	
Inexpensive	
Quality 79	Value B

Zone 11B   Virginia suburbs
4021 South 28th Street, Arlington
   (Shirlington Village)
(703) 379-0300

Zone 11B   Virginia suburbs
1811 Library Street, Reston (Reston Town Center)
(703) 834-6300

Zone 11B   Virginia suburbs
4301 North Fairfax Drive, Arlington
(703) 522-1800

Reservations:	Recommended
When to go:	Any time
Entree range:	$4.95 – 16.95
Payment:	VISA, MC, AMEX
Service rating:	★★★
Friendliness rating:	★★★
Parking:	Free lot
Bar:	Full service
Wine selection:	House
Dress:	Casual
Disabled access:	Good
Customers:	Local, ethnic
Open:	Monday – Thursday, 11 A.M. – 10 P.M.;
	Friday and Saturday, 11 A.M. – 11 P.M.;
	Sunday, 3 – 10 P.M.

Atmosphere/setting: These are all family-comfy combo kitchens, perhaps a little decor-for-everybody; the newest branch on Fairfax Drive, previously D'Angelo's family-style Italian restaurant, is a microcosm of what's-hot-today: outdoor seating, brick oven pizza, etc.

House specialties: Classic bistro fare such as oyster stew with chard; roast chicken, rack of lamb, fried calamari, burgers, and pastas, but with more modern touches such as Southwestern spice rubs on the lamb.

Summary & comments: Although generally referred to as a French bistro, this is at least half modern-suburban cuisine. The meat loaf is made of veal, for example; the burgers are available in beef, turkey, or tuna; and one of the signature dishes, a white bean – turkey chili, could only have been invented in the *eastern* United States. These are great hangouts and the staffs are extremely friendly; the food is rarely a surprise, though. (Menus vary slightly from site to site.)

BISTRO FRANÇAIS

Zone 5   Georgetown
3128 M Street, NW
(202) 338-3830

French	
★★½	
Inexpensive	
Quality 79	Value B

Reservations:	Recommended
When to go:	Any time
Entree range:	$12.95−19.95
Payment:	VISA, MC, AMEX, DC
Service rating:	★★★
Friendliness rating:	★★★
Parking:	Street (valet on weekends)
Bar:	Full service
Wine selection:	House
Dress:	Casual
Disabled access:	Good
Customers:	Local, ethnic
Open:	Sunday−Thursday, 11 A.M.−3 A.M.;
	Friday and Saturday, 11 A.M.−4 A.M.

Atmosphere/setting: This hasn't changed much since the word *bistro* was new to Washington—hanging pots, rotisserie spits, and clanking trays. In other words, just right.

House specialties: This is the sort of place where as nice as the menu is—especially Dover sole, coq au vin, quennelles of pike, its signature spit-roasted chicken—the daily specials are even better: for instance, duck confits and roast game birds or lamb with artichokes.

Other recommendations: The steak-and-fries here is probably the standard against which all others should be measured. And there are fixed-price lunch and pre-theater menus for $18, including wine.

Summary & comments: For all its many pleasures—its famous late-night service and the especially telling fact that many local chefs eat here after-hours—it sometimes seems as if this old favorite gets the Rodney Dangerfield treatment from the fashionable crowds.

Bistro Twenty-Fifteen

Zone 6   Dupont Circle/
             Adams-Morgan
2015 Massachusetts Avenue, NW
    (Embassy Row Hotel)
(202) 939-4250

Modern American
★★½
Inexpensive

Quality 79   Value B

Reservations:	Recommended
When to go:	Any time
Entree range:	$12−29
Payment:	VISA, MC, AMEX, DC
Service rating:	★★★
Friendliness rating:	★★★
Parking:	Free lot, valet
Bar:	Full service
Wine selection:	House
Dress:	Casual
Disabled access:	Good
Customers:	Local, ethnic
Lunch:	Every day, 11:30 A.M.−2:30 P.M.
Dinner:	Sunday−Thursday, 6−10 P.M.;
	Friday and Saturday, 6−10:30 P.M.

Atmosphere/setting: Reasonably simple for a hotel dining room, with pastel linen, comfy banquettes, and simple flowers.

House specialties: Seafood is the chef's strong suit and his personal interest as well, as suggested by the house-smoked salmon topped with caviar; pan-seared salmon and lobster over caramelized cabbage; and a daily assortment of grilled marinated vegetables for even lighter eaters. Check the chef's fixed-price dinner offerings, four courses for $30.

Other recommendations: Seafood pastas; catches of the day and other choices of fish available grilled, poached, or roasted.

Summary & comments: Oddly enough, the more chef Jim Papovich tries to create a straightforward cuisine, and the fewer frills he tosses on (particularly in terms of menu descriptions), the less attention even his former admirers tend to pay. And, of course, being in a hotel is somewhat limiting—a certain amount of steak and potatoes is unavoidable. Nevertheless, the food is carefully prepared, nicely balanced, and a terrific bargain; and whenever possible, Papovich goes on a binge of "specials"—either cooking with a particular winery's product, going up on the roof, or spotlighting fresh seafood. Those times are the best.

Bistrot Lepic

	French
Zone 5 Georgetown	★★½
1736 Wisconsin Avenue, NW	Moderate
(202) 333-0111	
	Quality 79 Value B

Reservations:	Recommended
When to go:	Any time
Entree range:	$13.95–18.95
Payment:	VISA, MC, AMEX
Service rating:	★★★
Friendliness rating:	★★★
Parking:	Street
Bar:	Full service
Wine selection:	Good
Dress:	Casual
Disabled access:	Good
Customers:	Locals
Lunch:	Tuesday–Sunday, 11:30 A.M.–2:30 P.M.
Dinner:	Tuesday–Thursday, 5:30–10 P.M.;
	Friday and Saturday, 5:30–10:30 P.M.;
	Sunday, 5:30–9:30 P.M.

Atmosphere/setting: This is a true bistro, one plain little room that seats about 40, with huge art reproduction murals on the wall and a view of the upper Georgetown street life.

House specialties: Satisfying and for the most part traditional dishes such as cassoulet, the French casserole of white beans, sausage, and duck confit; calf's liver with olives and capers; chicken in the pot; and also more authentic and flavorful bistro fare, including braised veal cheeks and rich chicken stew.

Other recommendations: Kidneys in mustard sauce; grilled fish; potato-crusted salmon.

Summary & comments: This cheery room burst out in a blaze of publicity and got the usual Georgetown trend victims' rush; the good news is, it's getting even better, and the fad audience has settled into real fans.

BLUE POINT GRILL

Zone 11C   Virginia suburbs
600 Franklin Street, Alexandria
(703) 739-0404

Seafood
★★½
Expensive

Quality 77   Value B

Reservations:	Helpful
When to go:	Any time
Entree range:	$12.95−20.95
Payment:	VISA, MC, AMEX, D
Service rating:	★★★
Friendliness rating:	★★★
Parking:	Free lot
Bar:	Full service
Wine selection:	House
Dress:	Casual
Disabled access:	Good
Customers:	Local, ethnic
Lunch:	Monday−Saturday, 11:30 A.M.−3 P.M.; Sunday, 11 A.M.−2:30 P.M.
Dinner:	Sunday−Friday, 5:30−10 P.M.; Saturday, 5−11 P.M.

Atmosphere/setting: Intended to recall the straightforward fish houses of half-a-century ago, this has intentionally unpolished wood floors and a minimum of color—a few gold and purple swags—so that the raw bar really shines.

House specialties: Cold lobster and shellfish platters; tuna tartare drizzled not with Asian flavorings, as at most places, but with a more tartare-like mustard sauce; fish selections of the day, roasted or grilled; seasonal Alaskan halibut.

Other recommendations: A variety of fish roasted in the wood-burning oven; seafood pastas; blue corn meal−crusted grouper with a smoky, hot, tomato sauce.

Summary & comments: This is something like a seafood market with tables: raw bar platters and roasted or grilled fish, big bowls of seafood stews, and a few trendy items such as the tuna tartare (although, to tell the truth, that's so common it's not even a trend anymore).

Bombay Bistro

<table>
<tr><td></td><td>Indian</td></tr>
<tr><td></td><td>★★★</td></tr>
<tr><td></td><td>Inexpensive</td></tr>
<tr><td></td><td>Quality 83   Value A</td></tr>
</table>

Zone 10B   Maryland suburbs
98 West Montgomery Avenue,
   Rockville
(301) 762-8798

Zone 11B   Virginia suburbs
3570 Chain Bridge Road, Fairfax
(703) 359-5810

Reservations:	Not accepted
When to go:	Early evening; lunch buffet
Entree range:	$6.95 – 15.95
Payment:	VISA, MC, AMEX, DC, D
Service rating:	★★★
Friendliness rating:	★★★
Parking:	Free lot
Bar:	Beer and wine
Wine selection:	House
Dress:	Casual
Disabled access:	Yes
Customers:	Local, ethnic, business
Lunch:	*Rockville:* Monday – Friday, 11 A.M. – 2:30 P.M.;
	Saturday and Sunday, noon – 3 P.M.;
	Fairfax: Monday – Friday, 11:30 A.M. – 2:30 P.M.
Dinner:	*Rockville:* Sunday – Thursday, 5 – 9:30 P.M.;
	Friday and Saturday, 5 – 10 P.M.;
	Fairfax: Sunday – Thursday, 5 – 10 P.M.;
	Friday and Saturday, 5 – 10:30 P.M.

Atmosphere/setting: This storefront family-style diner is made cheery in an almost Christmasy way, with red and green native costumes and gilded slippers hung on the wall along with strings of stuffed birds above wooden booths. Its new offshoot is equally simple and comfy.

House specialties: Tandoori chicken or, even better, tandoori salmon; lamb vindaloo, the hottest item on the menu; el maru, a bowlful of rice and crispy noodles with a texture between granola and trail mix; Goan fish curry with a golden sauce; many fine vegetarian choices, notably an aromatic clove-and-cinnamon-flavored okra curry and baingan bhartha (tandoori eggplant); roasted vegetables; mild chicken tikka or spicy chicken madras; oothapam, a South India "crêpe" of lentil and rice dough, stuffed with onions, tomatoes, and green peppers.

(continued)

Other recommendations: Lamb rogan josh or shish kebab; chicken or vegetable biryani; beef badam pasandra, an almond-spiked stew; a sampler platter with chicken tikka, rogan josh, cucumber raita, puri, lentils, and spinach or eggplant.

Summary & comments: Located among the lawyers' warrens of historic Rockville, this squeeze-'em-in eatery started out as an Indians' Indian lunch spot, but the word leaked out. Now, even with three or four cooks working, you may have to wait at dinner for a table at the original location, which is the second good reason to go for the all-you-can-eat lunchtime buffet (at both branches). The first good reason is the price: $6.95 on weekdays and $8.95 on weekends. Meanwhile, the cooking keeps getting better.

Bombay Club

	Indian
	★★★½
	Expensive
	Quality 89 Value C

Zone 3   Downtown
815 Connecticut Avenue, NW
(202) 659-3727

Reservations:	Recommended
When to go:	Any time
Entree range:	$7.95−18
Payment:	VISA, MC, AMEX, DC
Service rating:	★★★½
Friendliness rating:	★★★★
Parking:	Street, garage, valet (dinner)
Bar:	Full service
Wine selection:	Very good
Dress:	Jacket and tie suggested
Disabled access:	Good
Customers:	Local, business, ethnic
Brunch:	Sunday, 11:30 A.M.−2:30 P.M.
Lunch:	Monday−Friday, 11:30 A.M.−2:30 P.M.
Dinner:	Monday−Thursday, 6−10:30 P.M.;
	Friday and Saturday, 6−11 P.M.;
	Sunday, 5:30−9 P.M.

Atmosphere/setting: British officers' club decor, with pale salmon and aquamarine walls, giant palms, ceiling fans, and shutters; a dark wood lounge to one side; and a conservatory-style piano bar in the front.

House specialties: Tandoori-marinated and roasted trout; green chile chicken; a Bengali seafood curry with shrimp, scallops, fish, and lobster; a vegetarian appetizer of crisp puri crackers topped with pureed mango and potato.

Other recommendations: Lamb curry with green chiles or the vinegar-marinated vindaloo; okra curry; curried fish with coconut milk; grilled eggplant. Vegetarian dishes are available in full or appetizer portions. A sampler of dishes called a "thali" is a good introduction: $16.95 for meat and seafood, $15.50 for the veggie version.

Entertainment & amenities: Piano-bar entertainment at happy hour.

Summary & comments: This kitchen brings a nice distinction to its myriad breads, its vegetable dishes, and particularly its seafood, which sets it apart from typical curry houses: The flavors are unusually clean and engrossing. The chile-fired chicken is as hot as advertised but not salty, for a pleasant change.

BUKOM

Zone 6	Dupont Circle/
	Adams-Morgan
2442 18th Street, NW	
(202) 265-4600	

West African
★★
Inexpensive
Quality 72   Value B

Reservations:	Accepted
When to go:	Sunday dinner
Entree range:	$8.25 – 9.25
Payment:	VISA, MC, AMEX
Service rating:	★★
Friendliness rating:	★★★
Parking:	Street
Bar:	Full service
Wine selection:	House
Dress:	Casual
Disabled access:	Fair
Customers:	Ethnic, local
Dinner:	Tuesday, 4 P.M.– 1 A.M.;
	Wednesday and Thursday, 4 P.M.– 2 A.M.;
	Friday and Saturday, 4 P.M.– 3 A.M.;
	Sunday, 4 P.M.– 2 A.M.

Atmosphere/setting: Considering that Bukom is named for a prominent social/political area in Accra, Ghana, filled with speakers and rallies by day and lit by the flames of food vendors at night, Bukom is perfect—small, gossipy, and heavily scented by simmering pots of stew.

House specialties: Oxtail stewed with peanut butter and tomatoes or with smoked fish; goat and spinach stew with melon seeds; fried plantains; a veggie plate of sautéed eggplant and zucchini over black-eyed peas.

Other recommendations: Smoked fish and okra, cooked in flavorful "cholesterol-free" but high-fat palm oil; mustard-coated chicken; pan-fried trout ("croakers") in tomato sauce or with spicy black-eyed pea stew. And if you think you've had hot wings before, try their three-day marinated "devil wings."

Entertainment & amenities: Live music (a mix of reggae, highlife, soukous, etc.) Tuesday through Sunday nights.

Summary & comments: West African cuisine shows clearly its parental relationship to Caribbean and Jamaican dishes, although the heavier use of greens and smoked rather than vinegar-preserved fish is distinctive. Both fresh fish and chicken are somewhat overcooked.

BURMA

Zone 3   Downtown
740 6th Street NW (upstairs)
(202) 638-1280

	Burmese
	★★½
	Inexpensive
Quality 79	Value B

Reservations:	Accepted
When to go:	Any time
Entree range:	$5.95−7.95
Payment:	VISA, MC, AMEX, D, DC
Service rating:	★★★★
Friendliness rating:	★★★★
Parking:	Street
Bar:	Beer and wine
Wine selection:	House
Dress:	Casual, informal
Disabled access:	Yes
Customers:	Ethnic, local, tourist
Lunch:	Monday−Friday, 11 A.M.−3 P.M.
Dinner:	Every day, 6−10 P.M.

Atmosphere/setting: This is a modest and unobtrusive second-floor warren with only a handful of small native arts on the walls to advertise its ethnicity, but owner and ex-diplomat Henry Tin Pe, whose Oxfordian accent is almost cinematic in its exactitude, makes this restaurant not only intriguingly ethnic but exotic.

House specialties: Kaukswe thoke, a tangy noodle dish with ground shrimp, cilantro and red pepper, and peanuts; pickled green tea leaf salad, a slightly sour, spicy slaw with caramelized onions and peanuts dressed in a green tea pesto; squid with ham and scallions; a chile-spiked tofu-and-shrimp stir-fry; and an almost soul-food version of mustard greens with shrimp, pork, or chicken.

Other recommendations: Gold fingers, strips of squash-like calabash in a peppery dipping sauce; chile- and mango-flavored pork; a macrobiotic delight of substantial dried tofu with cruciferous veggies; roast duck (requires 24 hours' notice).

Summary & comments: Using familiar ingredients from any Asian grocery, this Burmese holdout manages to turn out flavors surprisingly distinct from its near relatives: not so "fishy" (no fermented fish sauce or soy) or seafood-conscious as Vietnamese, less purely peppery and more sour-tangy than Thai, and with the concentrated tea and smoke background of classic Chinese and Japanese cuisine. Disabled patrons should call ahead to make sure the elevator is unlocked.

BUSARA

Zone 5   Georgetown
2340 Wisconsin Avenue, NW
(202) 337-2340

Zone 11A   Virginia suburbs
8142 Watson Street, McLean
(703) 356-2288

Thai	
★★★½	
Moderate	
Quality 87	Value B

Reservations:	Recommended
When to go:	Before 7:30 or after 9:30
Entree range:	$7.50−22.95
Payment:	VISA, MC, AMEX, DC, D
Service rating:	★★★½
Friendliness rating:	★★★
Parking:	Street, lot, valet after 6 P.M.
Bar:	Full service
Wine selection:	Fair
Dress:	Informal
Disabled access:	No
Customers:	Local, ethnic
Lunch:	Monday−Friday, 11:30 A.M.−3 P.M.;
	Saturday and Sunday, 11:30 A.M.−4 P.M.
Dinner:	Sunday−Thursday, 5−11 P.M.;
	Friday and Saturday, 5 P.M.−midnight

Atmosphere/setting: These Thai siblings are aggressively and cheekily modern. The decor of molded hard black rubber, brushed steel, slate, and heavily lacquered flame-streaked tabletops looks as if it were created by a former hot rod customizer—not to mention the ice-blue neon overhead ("busara" means "blue topaz") and post-Pop art. Outside, a partially covered patio curves around a miniature, but elegant, Japanese garden with a fountain. The Tysons Corner branch is even brighter, and although it doesn't yet have a garden, it may in the future.

House specialties: Rice-fattened eesan sausage with pork and cabbage; roasted quail with asparagus and oyster sauce; cellophane noodles with three kinds of mushrooms; fillet of sea trout with salmon mousse served on a banana leaf; marinated pork satay with both a tomato-peanut sauce and a chile-spiked vinegar dip; duck in red curry; Thai bouillabaisse in coconut milk; country-style lamb curry.

Other recommendations: Tiger shrimp grilled over watercress; vegetarian pad thai; soft-shell crabs and whole flounder; lobster tail in white pepper. The

(continued)

Tysons branch has a grill that turns out chicken, lean pork, and assorted fresh fish and shellfish as well.

Entertainment & amenities: Live jazz in the upstairs bar suite in town, Wednesday through Saturday.

Summary & comments: These are Siamese grins with the emphasis on presentation as much as preparation and a lightened-up attitude toward greens and veggies that makes them crisp and filling. A wide variety of spicing is represented (the chile-pod symbols next to menu items are fairly reliable for gauging heat; the Tysons branch sticks to the more familiar stars), and extra sauces or peppers are easy to obtain. Even nicer, there is no MSG in anything.

Cafe Asia

Zone 6 Dupont Circle/ Adams-Morgan 1134 19th Street, NW (202) 659-2696	Pan Asian ★½ Inexpensive Quality 69 Value A

Reservations:	Accepted
When to go:	Any time
Entree range:	$6.95−13.95
Payment:	VISA, MC, AMEX, DC
Service rating:	★★★
Friendliness rating:	★★★
Parking:	Street
Bar:	Full service
Wine selection:	House
Dress:	Casual
Disabled access:	No
Customers:	Local, business, ethnic
Open:	Monday−Friday, 11:30 A.M.−10 P.M.; Saturday, noon−10 P.M.; Sunday, 5−10 P.M.

Atmosphere/setting: A simple but cheerful and extremely aromatic version of the typical town house turned downtown-business-district-quick-stop.

House specialties: Marinated spicy bluefish grilled in a banana leaf; charcoal-broiled salmon with teriyaki glaze; grilled Indonesian tofu; gado gado, a salad of sautéed veggies, tofu, and shrimp chips in peanut sauce.

Other recommendations: Grilled shrimp in peanut, lime, and lemongrass dressing; pad thai; a Thai-style chicken curry with coconut milk; pan-fried steak with lemongrass.

Summary & comments: This melting pot we-know-what-we-like eatery—offering Chinese, Indonesian, Japanese, Singaporean, Thai, and Vietnamese favorites—is the sort of place that becomes a pet, with an eager-to-please staff, simple but tangy and satisfying food, and incredibly affordable prices: All but a half-dozen dishes come in at $6.95 or less. And even if most of the dishes can be had elsewhere, the bluefish in banana leaf is worth a stop.

Cafe Atlantico

Zone 3   Downtown
405 8th Street, NW
(202) 393-0812

Nuevo Latino	
★★★½	
Inexpensive	
Quality 85	Value B

Reservations: Recommended
When to go: Any time
Entree range: $12.95 – 16.95
Payment: VISA, MC, AMEX, DC
Service rating: ★★★
Friendliness rating: ★★★
Parking: Street, valet (dinner only)
Bar: Full service
Wine selection: Good
Dress: Casual
Disabled access: Good
Customers: Local, ethnic
Open: Monday, 11:30 A.M. – 10 P.M.;
                      Tuesday – Thursday, 11:30 A.M. – 11 P.M.;
                      Friday, 11:30 A.M. – midnight;
                      Saturday, 5:30 P.M. – midnight;
                      Sunday, 5:30 – 10 P.M.

Atmosphere / setting: A very stylish salon, like the living room of an art collector: brilliant fabrics, large and vibrant paintings, loft-like balconies and windows, mosaics, and richly oiled wood. The clientele tends to match the decor — very vibrant, very "on," and frequently very loud.

House specialties: Baby fowl with Mexican mole (cocoa-cinnamon) sauce; a miniature (traditionally speaking) Argentine mixed grill with steak, two kinds of sausage, and the teaspoon-sized sweetbread; mushroom-stuffed boned quail; and a nueva feijoada, the Brazilian national stew that vaguely resembles cassoulet.

Other recommendations: Guacamole prepared tableside; chicken pieces skewered on sugar cane; the Portuguese-imported brandade of salt cod appetizer; fresh fish Veracruzano.

Summary & comments: Cafe Atlantico is riding two waves at once: location and cuisine. It has moved into the heart of the new arts-intelligentsia neighborhood around the Shakespeare Theatre and Landsburg Building, and it's the first major restaurant in this area to specialize in *cocina nueva*, the Latin version of New Continental. That means that although dishes salute various Central and South American traditions, they are apt to be lighter, more fashionably presented and, depending on your perspective, less homey and more expensive than the originals.

Cafe Berlin

Zone 2   Capitol Hill
322 Massachusetts Avenue, NE
(202) 543-7656

German
★★½
Inexpensive

Quality 79   Value C

Reservations:	Helpful
When to go:	Any time
Entree range:	$5.95−16.95
Payment:	VISA, MC, AMEX, DC
Service rating:	★★★
Friendliness rating:	★★½
Parking:	Street
Bar:	Full service
Wine selection:	Limited
Dress:	Business, casual
Disabled access:	To sidewalk tables only
Customers:	Business, local
Open:	Monday−Thursday, 11:30 A.M.−10 P.M.;
	Friday and Saturday, 11:30 A.M.−11 P.M.;
	Sunday, 4−10 P.M.

Atmosphere/setting: Pretty in a light-hearted way that (fortunately) goes against both the stereotype and the area standards for German restaurants. The sidewalk seating is, like several of those in its east−Union Station nook, full of young Hillies and interns.

House specialties: Game in season, including venison and fowl; sauerbraten; duck breast with gooseberries; poached grouper with root vegetables and sour cream; snapper en papillote.

Other recommendations: Pork stuffed with apples, roasted and sauced with Calvados; the classic goulash and sausage plates; chicken ragout.

Summary & comments: It's difficult to be evocative in a town house that looks so much like the town houses (and restaurants) all around, but Cafe Berlin is not only hospitable, it's convincing in an easygoing way. And its constant experimentation with chicken and fish dishes takes some of the dietary *oomph* out of the image. A 15% gratuity is added for tables of six or more.

Café Bethesda/ Café Bethesda North

	Modern American
	★★★
Zone 10A Maryland suburbs	Expensive
5027 Wilson Lane, Bethesda	Quality 80 Value B
(301) 657-3383	

Zone 10A   Maryland suburbs
5027 Wilson Lane, Bethesda
(301) 657-3383

Zone 10B   Maryland suburbs
121 Congressional Lane, Rockville
(301) 770-3185

Reservations:	Recommended
When to go:	Any time
Entree range:	$14−25
Payment:	VISA, MC, AMEX
Service rating:	★★★
Friendliness rating:	★★★
Parking:	Street, pay lots (Bethesda); street, free lot (Rockville)
Bar:	Full service (Rockville); wine and beer (Bethesda)
Wine selection:	Good
Dress:	Business, informal
Disabled access:	Rockville only
Customers:	Business, local
Lunch:	*Bethesda:* Monday−Friday, 11:30 A.M.−2 P.M.; *Rockville:* Monday−Friday, 11:30 A.M.−2:30 P.M.
Dinner:	*Bethesda:* Monday−Thursday, 5:30−9 P.M.; Friday and Saturday, 5:30−10 P.M.; Sunday, 5−9:30 P.M.; *Rockville:* every day, 5:30−10 P.M.

Atmosphere/setting: The Bethesda location is an elegant but smallish cottage, all dove grey and Wedgewood blue, on one of the less traveled side streets. The newer Rockville branch, taken over from a series of unsuccessful Italian spots, is larger and more traditional, with a mahogany bar, white linen, and still-life prints.

House specialties: Spinach-pasta ravioli stuffed with rabbit and wild mushrooms over sautéed spinach; a surprisingly successful veal sausage with sun-dried blueberries; eggplant rolls stuffed with goat cheese; and a very light lemon angelhair pasta with scallops and asparagus (all appetizers, but substantial); sautéed or sometimes poached red snapper with lobster, artichokes, and tomato; seared rare tuna.

(continued)

Other recommendations: Grilled veal chops; duck breast with cassis; sautéed veal and portobellos over spinach pasta.

Summary & comments: The original branch was already gathering steam and, paradoxically, having two kitchens seems to have given the staff more confidence: The food continues to improve. The menu is not enormous, but there is something for everyone. They set high standards for themselves, too: When a rack of lamb, ordered rare, arrived too done, it was returned; and when it took (much) too long to replace, the waiter produced a second bottle of wine on the house. Both branches have a pleasantly old-suburb atmosphere, with lots of 30- and 40-something couples out for a pleasant meal.

Cafe Dalat

Vietnamese	
★★½	
Inexpensive	
Quality 79	Value B

Zone 11B   Virginia suburbs
3143 Wilson Boulevard, Arlington
(703) 276-0935

Reservations:	Helpful
When to go:	Any time; lunch for buffet
Entree range:	$6.95−8.95
Payment:	VISA, MC
Service rating:	★★★
Friendliness rating:	★★★
Parking:	Free lot
Bar:	Full service
Wine selection:	House
Dress:	Casual
Disabled access:	Good
Customers:	Local, ethnic
Open:	Monday−Thursday, 11 A.M.−9:30 P.M.;
	Friday and Saturday, 11 A.M.−10:30 P.M.;
	Sunday, 11 A.M.−9:30 P.M.

Atmosphere / setting: Like most Clarendon eateries, pretty simple: Plywood panelling of the old rec room sort, fading pink linoleum, and textured plaster walls. The music can only be said to tinkle.

House specialties: A sort of soft seafood kebab of shrimp, scallops, and a ground shellfish that will erase those painful memories of cafeteria salmon croquettes; seafood curry; fried whole fish with ginger; braised, chronella-scented tofu with mushrooms; grilled five-spice pork.

Other recommendations: Stir-fried vegetables, available plain or with shrimp, chicken, or beef, but promised—and delivered—al dente.

Summary & comments: Cafe Dalat, like its neighbor Atami, is particularly solicitous of vegetarian diners; it offers a long list of tofu dishes and even veggie versions of such traditional dishes as banh xeo, the crispy omelet called "happy pancake."

Cafe Milano

Zone 5   Georgetown
3251 Prospect Street, NW
(202) 333-6183

Italian	
★★★	
Moderate	
Quality 82	Value C

Reservations:	Helpful
When to go:	Late lunch, late dinner
Entree range:	$10−20
Payment:	VISA, MC, AMEX, DC
Service rating:	★★★½
Friendliness rating:	★★★½
Parking:	Street, pay lots
Bar:	Full service
Wine selection:	Good
Dress:	Business, hip informal
Disabled access:	Through rear entrance
Customers:	Local, embassy
Lunch:	Monday−Friday, 11:30 A.M.−2:30 P.M.
Dinner:	Monday−Wednesday, 5:30 P.M.−1 A.M.;
	Thursday and Friday, 5:30 P.M.−2 A.M.
Lunch/Dinner:	Saturday, 11:30−2 A.M.; Sunday, noon−11 P.M.

Atmosphere/setting: A cross between an haute couturier's salon and a Milan disco, with a subway map painted on the ceiling (which makes for interesting philosophical speculation on the direction Italian interests have taken since the days of the Sistine Chapel). At Bice, where owner Franco Nuschese was manager, the shadowboxes held wallpaper samples; here they frame the even hip-jokier designer ties—presumably from his closet, as he never seems to be wearing one—and limited-edition scarves. And the pastas are named after designers.

House specialties: Pastas, from the deceptively simple and often bland angel-hair with basil and tomatoes and a similar "summer version" with chopped raw tomato, to a lavish but light lobster linguini or pappardelle with broccoli rabe and anchovies. There are heartier dishes as well (there's a pair o' chefs) including stuffed eggplant, quail with artichokes, and a non-cacciatore rabbit stew, almost a blanquette.

Entertainment & amenities: A Euro-techno singles scene after about 10:30.

Summary & comments: This is not the capo's Oldsmobile. It's loud, lively, brash, almost deconstructionist: The staff urges you to throw together meals in an almost naughtily nontraditional manner—for instance, pizza, then veal, or pasta before antipasto—the way the younger designers mix and match clothing. And it helps to dress with a little flash yourself, as if you're in on the joke—the joke, presumably, being not only designer cuisine but those willing to follow any trend.

111

Cafe Oggi

Zone 11A   Virginia suburbs
6671 Old Dominion Drive, McLean
(703) 442-7360

Italian
★★½
Moderate
Quality 75   Value B

Reservations:	Recommended
When to go:	Any time
Entree range:	$9.95−19.95
Payment:	VISA, MC, AMEX, D, DC
Service rating:	★★★
Friendliness rating:	★★★
Parking:	Free lot
Bar:	Full service
Wine selection:	Limited
Dress:	Informal
Disabled access:	Good
Customers:	Local, ethnic
Lunch:	Monday−Friday, 11:30 A.M.−2:30 P.M.
Dinner:	Sunday−Thursday, 5:30−10 P.M.;
	Friday and Saturday, 5:30−10:30 P.M.

Atmosphere/setting: Simple suburban Italian trattoria style, with pink linen, long rows of tables and simple art, and "windows" of glass bricks to shut out the traffic.

House specialties: Seafood, simple but freshly considered, such as broiled black pearl salmon with capers or shrimp; calf's liver prepared to your taste; risotto with your favorite ingredients; veal in fresh artichoke sauce; and a rich lamb shank.

Other recommendations: Pasta, of course: with mixed seafood, with smoked salmon, with lobster, with eggplant, or for lite-fare trendies, with sun-dried tomatoes, shiitake mushrooms, and shallots.

Summary & comments: The nicest thing about this place is its poise, which is somehow symbolized by the absence of any trendy wood-burning pizza oven. And the service is respectful and attentive without being familiar, another increasingly rare pleasure.

CAFE SAIGON

	Vietnamese
Zone 11B Virginia suburbs	★★★
1135 North Highland Street, Arlington	Inexpensive
(703) 243-6522; (703) 276-7110	Quality 84 Value A

Reservations:	Helpful
When to go:	Any time
Entree range:	$5.95 – 22.95
Payment:	VISA, MC, AMEX
Service rating:	★★★
Friendliness rating:	★★½
Parking:	Street, lot after 6 P.M.
Bar:	Beer and wine
Wine selection:	House
Dress:	Informal, casual
Disabled access:	Good
Customers:	Local, ethnic
Open:	Sunday – Thursday, 10 A.M. – 10 P.M.; Friday and Saturday, 10 A.M. – 11 P.M.

Atmosphere/setting: Nothing much to look at; it's almost a lunchroom (there's even a soft-serve ice cream dispenser in the back), but tellingly fragrant and busy. It's on a corner, so two walls are mostly window; most of the wall space is covered with tacked-up, highly colorized lists of daily specials.

House specialties: Incredibly large and crisp soft-shell crabs, in a much thinner and crunchier coating than anywhere else, but not tempura-fried; roast quail appetizer in an unusually sweet glaze on a bed of watercress and coriander; wine- and honey-marinated beef, charbroiled and served over rice noodles; combination seafood over soft yellow noodles; orange beef (mild or spicy) with fresh orange slices; whole fried flounder with ginger sauce.

Other recommendations: Grilled beef in grape leaves; roasted quail; boneless chicken breast in lemongrass; Saigon "muffin" (like a shrimp-paste potato pancake) with ground pork and sprouts.

Summary & comments: This is another of those brash, bright, adventuresome Vietnamese establishments that inexplicably remains in the shadow, let us say, of publicity, while older and more self-satisfied kitchens continue to hog the customers (the better for us, said the wolf). Cafe Saigon makes a point of inviting customers to specify whether they like food spicy or mild, which is a smart concession in a city gone wild for Thai. It also knows a lot about sauces—the glazes are extra rich—and the simple but apparently arcane fact that the hotter the oil, the crispier the fry. It's worth the hike across town for the soft-shells in season.

Cafe Taj

Zone 11A   Virginia suburbs
1379 Beverly Road, McLean
(703) 827-0444

Indian	
★★½	
Inexpensive	
Quality 77	Value B

Reservations:	Accepted
When to go:	Lunch
Entree range:	$7.95 – 15.95
Payment:	VISA, MC, AMEX, DC
Service rating:	★★★
Friendliness rating:	★★★½
Parking:	Free lot
Bar:	Full service
Wine selection:	House
Dress:	Business, casual
Disabled access:	No
Customers:	Locals
Lunch:	Every day, 11:30 A.M.–2:30 P.M.
Dinner:	Sunday–Thursday, 5:30–10 P.M.;
	Friday and Saturday, 5:30–10:30 P.M.

Atmosphere/setting: Extremely pretty and elegant, a swath of black stone-top tables and hot neon on the second floor of a very suburban office building. Actually, it looks as though the owners bought an upscale Italian restaurant and didn't change the decor, not even the trickling birdbath of a fountain in the middle of the dining room. (Maybe that explains the "Cafe" in the name—it's a leftover, too.) At least they bought a new music tape.

House specialties: Tandoori-rubbed shrimp or salmon; a better-than-average lamb vindaloo for spice lovers; skewered chicken tidbits.

Other recommendations: A mixed vegetarian curry with nuts for protein and interest; breads that are more side order than condiment, including versions stuffed with chicken or lamb; grilled, marinated eggplant.

Summary & comments: The lunch buffet here, which includes the signature tandoori chicken, is $8 per person, weekends as well as workdays, and makes braving the crowd well worthwhile. All tandoori dishes, incidentally, come with a side dish of lentils that alone are worth the trip.

Cajun Bangkok

	Cajun/Thai
Zone 11C Virginia suburbs	★★½
907 King Street, Alexandria	Inexpensive
(703) 836-0038	
	Quality 77 Value B

Reservations:	Accepted
When to go:	Any time
Entree range:	$10.95 – 14.95
Payment:	VISA, MC, AMEX
Service rating:	★★★
Friendliness rating:	★★★
Parking:	Street
Bar:	Full service
Wine selection:	House
Dress:	Informal
Disabled access:	Good
Customers:	Local, tourist, ethnic
Dinner:	Sunday – Thursday, 5 – 10 P.M.;
	Friday and Saturday, 5 – 11 P.M.

Atmosphere/setting: A long, rather plain, pale-grey and lavender room with the bar along one wall and kibbitzing green plants here and there.

House specialties: Tiger steak, a muscular little rib eye in chili pepper sauce; chicken breast with green coconut curry; shrimp in bourbon sauce; crawfish meat sautéed with scallions and Cajun spices (special).

Entertainment & amenities: The chef won't do carry-out because he doesn't think the food will be as appetizing if the presentation gets all squashed around—which is sort of an entertaining concept.

Summary & comments: Okay, the name gives you pause, but consider— how different is blackened seafood from Thai dishes in black pepper dips? Or red chili-garlic sauces? And after all, Southeast Asian cuisines are as strong on collards and mustard greens as any Southerner's. In fact, for those who find most "pot greens" dull and greasy, the appetizer version here—almost a miniature rijsttafel called meang khan with lime, ginger, peanuts, coconut, and dried shrimp—is a revelation. The tiger steak rib eye may be a little chewy, but at $7.95, it's pretty good—as long as you like it cooked at least medium.

The Capital Grille

Zone 3   Downtown
601 Pennsylvania Avenue, NW
(202) 737-6200

Steak	
★★½	
Expensive	
Quality 78	Value C

Reservations:	Recommended
When to go:	Any time
Entree range:	$15.95 – 27.95
Payment:	VISA, MC, AMEX, DC, D
Service rating:	★★★
Friendliness rating:	★★★
Parking:	Valet after 5 P.M.; paid lots
Bar:	Full service
Wine selection:	Good
Dress:	Business, informal
Disabled access:	Good
Customers:	Politicos, lawyers, lobbyists, and tourists looking for them
Lunch:	Monday – Friday, 11:30 A.M.–2:30 P.M.
Dinner:	Sunday – Thursday, 5 – 10 P.M.; Friday and Saturday, 5 – 11 P.M.

Atmosphere / setting: Very gentlemen's clubbish, with dark wood, white linen, and polished brass. The streetside bar is quite atmospheric, combining as it does the old-boys' look and the Fed City vista. (The gas lanterns at the doorway, à la carriage house chic, are almost always lit: Bring me your prosperous, your power-tied, your huddled lobbyists yearning to eat free.) However, some may find the display of darkening and apparently somewhat dessicated dry-aged slabs of meat stacked like firewood in the vestibule window a little stark.

House specialties: Pan-fried, chile-spiked calamari; cold baby lobster; and lobster-crab cakes (appetizers); porterhouse; the house special Delmonico, a classic but nowadays less popular cut; and a signature veal steak.

Other recommendations: Fresh grilled swordfish or salmon; double-cut lamb chops; a near-pound of filet mignon; lobsters by the pound.

Summary & comments: Capital Grille steaks come in merely greedy portions (10 or 14 ounces) or true pig-out sizes (20 to 24 ounces). "Dry-aging" means that instead of being kept in vacuum bags, which keeps the blood in and the weight higher, the meat is drained, making for a heartier texture that either does or doesn't attract you. Otherwise, its menu and its side orders of asparagus hollandaise, creamed spinach, and potatoes don't differ much from the other red-blooded steakhouses in town, except perhaps that its propinquity to Congress makes it a political hot spot.

116

Carlyle Grand Café

	Modern American
Zone 11B Virginia suburbs	★★★
4000 South 28th Street, Arlington	Moderate
(703) 931-0777	Quality 81 Value C

Reservations:	Recommended for 6 or more
When to go:	Late night, afternoon
Entree range:	$10.95−15.95
Payment:	VISA, MC, AMEX
Service rating:	★★½
Friendliness rating:	★★★
Parking:	Free lot, street
Bar:	Full service
Wine selection:	Good
Dress:	Casual
Disabled access:	Good
Customers:	Locals
Open:	Monday−Wednesday, 11:30 A.M.−11 P.M.;
	Thursday, 11:30 A.M.−midnight;
	Friday and Saturday, 11:30 A.M.−1 A.M.;
	Sunday, 10:30 A.M.−11 P.M.

Atmosphere/setting: Simple and attractive, though often over-bustly, a mix of black-and-white and pink paint upstairs, but bistro style rather than Deco.

House specialties: Lobster pot stickers with a spicy ginger sauce; porterhouse-cut lamb chops with minted papaya chutney; roast duck with mango sauce and curried greens; barbecue-spiced oysters; sautéed scallops on lemon fettuccine with a hint of bacon and ginger.

Other recommendations: A smoked chicken and wild mushroom tamale with roasted chili sauce; rock shrimp and sea scallop risotto (an appetizer); a big salad with seared rare tuna or grilled tuna steak with mango relish.

Summary & comments: Chef Bill Jackson, who's popular with his peers as well as his patrons, is interested in providing varied and unobtrusively healthful food and air: It's a smoke-free zone, and there are plenty of heart-healthy options as well as hearty ones. He likes to mix and match styles, although it isn't fusion food, just fun. He believes in light spirits as well as light food: consider his own description, "chef and fearless sailboarder," on the menu, and the name of his adjoining bread bakery, Best Buns. Note that while the downstairs area is open all afternoon and into the late hours, the more formal upstairs dining room closes between lunch and dinner and also shuts down earlier in the evening.

Cashion's Eat Place

	Modern American
Zone 6 Dupont Circle/	★ ★ ★
Adams-Morgan	Moderate
1819 Columbia Road, NW	
(202) 797-1819	Quality 82 Value B

Reservations:	Recommended
When to go:	Any time
Entree range:	$12.95 − 17.95
Payment:	VISA, MC
Service rating:	★ ★ ★
Friendliness rating:	★ ★ ★ ★
Parking:	Street, valet (evenings)
Bar:	Full service
Wine selection:	Good
Dress:	Business/casual
Disabled access:	Fair
Customers:	Locals
Brunch:	Sunday, 11:30 A.M.−2:30 P.M.
Dinner:	Tuesday, 5:30−10 P.M.;
	Wednesday−Saturday, 5:30−11 P.M.;
	Sunday, 5:30−10 P.M.

Atmosphere/setting: Crammed into the hodgepodge wedge of Columbia Road, this tongue-in-cheekily modest bistro ("Eat Place," indeed) manages to seem bustling, lively, streetwise, and sleek all at the same time, thanks to a smart mix of old photos, exposed wine bins, and architectural detailing.

House specialties: "Old-fashioned rabbit and dumplings"; sautéed scallops with a gingery "bordelaise" over tender savoy cabbage; osso bucco; hearty but moist pork chops; big-flavor-for-the-bite buffalo hanger steak.

Other recommendations: Roast chicken or Cornish hen is a frequent theme, and any version of it is welcome. Ditto with grilled seafood or mussels.

Summary & comments: Ann Cashion's Southwest-flavored cooking helped launch the Austin Grills and Jaleo; however, her style here is what you might think of as boomer comfort food. It's a little bit mid-America, a little bit Euro-peasant, a bit o' bistro, a fillip of fusion . . . and all with a solid comprehension of the pleasures of texture. You can have light or filling, rich or delicate, and side dishes are sauced as complementary, not "creative." It may be the kind of stuff some people would make at home, but they'd have to have subscriptions to gourmet mags and time to cruise the markets for inspiration. And with "homestyle" places like this, who needs a kitchen, anyway?

CHINA INN

Zone 3   Downtown
631 H Street, NW
(202) 842-0909

Chinese	
★★★	
Inexpensive	
Quality 83	Value B

Reservations:	Helpful
When to go:	Lunch for dim sum, late night
Entree range:	$9.95 – 24.95
Payment:	VISA, MC, AMEX, DC
Service rating:	★★½
Friendliness rating:	★★½
Parking:	Street
Bar:	Full service
Wine selection:	House
Dress:	Casual, informal
Disabled access:	No
Customers:	Ethnic, local, tourist
Open:	Sunday – Thursday, 11 A.M. – 1 A.M.;
	Friday and Saturday, 11 A.M. – 2 A.M.

Atmosphere / setting: This isn't a place that feels the need to look "authentic" (meaning touristy) or dangle roasted ducks in the window. It's just a hodge-podge of small dining rooms on various levels, simply painted teal and pink, but what you do see—the large number of Chinese diners—is more telling.

House specialties: Crabs "smoked" in ginger and scallions; boneless duck in watercress (not on the menu, but ask); "fish dipping in boiling water with spices" (a fantastic poached sea bass); hearty chow foon noodle dishes; seafood dumplings.

Other recommendations: One of the most fun lunches in any Chinatown is dim sum, the little wheelabout trays of hot dumplings, stuffed bean curd, spare ribs, and so on that you order by the dish (usually three pieces or servings). It goes like this: The cook sends out something hot; the waiter wheels it by; you point; they put a check on your bill and the plate on your table. Most restaurants make dim sum only on the weekends, but China Inn offers this traditional tea house fair every day between 11 A.M. and 3 P.M.

Summary & comments: China Inn has a very strong and loyal following in the Chinese community, and like many such places, it has more than one menu— the "authentic" version and the tourist guide (although here, even some of the more revisionist dishes are very good). Peruse the "chef's specials," and if you see something on someone else's table that attracts you, be brave and order it. And since it's only a block from the subway and near the great Chinese arch, it's a great place for tourists.

119

Citronelle

Zone 5   Georgetown
3000 M Street, NW (Latham Hotel)
(202) 625-2150

	Modern American
	★★★
	Expensive
	Quality 81 Value C

Reservations:	Recommended
When to go:	Lunch; before 9
Entree range:	$24−28
Payment:	VISA, MC, AMEX, DC, D
Service rating:	★★½
Friendliness rating:	★★★
Parking:	Valet
Bar:	Full service
Wine selection:	Good
Dress:	Business, dressy
Disabled access:	Excellent
Customers:	Local, tourist, business
Brunch:	Sunday, 10:30 A.M.−3:30 P.M.
Lunch:	Every day, 11:30 A.M.−2 P.M.
Dinner:	Sunday−Thursday, 6−10 P.M.;
	Friday and Saturday, 5:30−10 P.M.

Atmosphere/setting: Using a series of small level shifts and cutaway ceilings, the designers of this pretty but not showy establishment have made the space seem both intimate and expansive. The upstairs lounge is classic flannel grey and green; the downstairs rooms have a conservatory touch, with dark green wicker armchairs, glass accent doors, and blessedly simple greenery. The star attractions are the exposed kitchen and its six chefs, two preppers, and salad chef.

House specialties: Appetizers: white tuna carpaccio (actually yellowtail) with ginger vinaigrette; luxuriant sautéed foie gras with chanterelles; creamy crab coleslaw wrapped in savoy cabbage; crab cannelloni; wild mushroom napoleon. Entrees: roasted lobster; veal chop with mini−goat cheese ravioli; penne with shiitakes and veal glacé; grilled swordfish; rib eye; rare tuna Châteaubriand; rack of lamb.

Summary & comments: It's tempting to pass up the entrees and load up on appetizers which, at between $8 and $14, make more of a meal for the money and are more reliably handled. This is food art: Simple grilled swordfish is made memorable by a wreath of angelhair-fine potato crisps and a bed of lentils; the peony of transparently sliced yellowtail lies on a painted bed of sauce and under a garnish of seaweed and baby endive. Monkfish is bacon-wrapped à la tournedo and accompanied by a standing pastry "vase" filled with wild mushrooms; a crabmeat "cannelloni" is actually a seafood terrine rolled in a broad noodle canopy and striped with saffron and squid ink.

120

City Lights of China

	Chinese
Zone 6 Dupont Circle/	★★★
Adams-Morgan	Moderate
1731 Connecticut Avenue, NW	
(202) 265-6688	Quality 81 Value B

Reservations:	Helpful
When to go:	Any time
Entree range:	$6.95 − 21.95
Payment:	VISA, MC, AMEX, DC, D
Service rating:	★★½
Friendliness rating:	★★★½
Parking:	Validated after 6 P.M.
Bar:	Full service
Wine selection:	House
Dress:	Informal or casual
Disabled access:	Yes
Customers:	Local
Open:	Monday – Thursday, 11:30 A.M. – 10:30 P.M.;
	Friday, 11:30 A.M. – 11 P.M.;
	Saturday, noon – 11 P.M.;
	Sunday, 11:30 A.M. – 11 P.M.

Atmosphere / setting: A surprisingly cheery underground warren with a reasonable volume setting. It has expanded a couple of times, which may explain the minimal decor of celadon paint; it's sort of like those portable walls in office buildings that are made to be reconfigured at any time.

House specialties: Tinkling bells pork, named for the spitting noises produced when the fried wontons and pork tidbits hit the hot metal platter; a peppery version of caramelized shredded beef; a strongly-flavored Szechuan lamb; twice-cooked duck; pan-fried dumplings; lobster so fresh you're introduced to it first.

Other recommendations: Shredded pork with chiles; Peking duck; sea cucumber with scallions; bean curd with crabmeat.

Summary & comments: One of the attractions of this young-professional-neighborhood restaurant is the breadth of its menu, from the authentic entree soups (combination chicken, pork, and shrimp; pork and pickle mustard with noodles; etc.), through a middle-class range of seafood and meat dishes, up to perfectly executed steamed whole sea bass and shrimp on coarse salt. One of its drawbacks is the lack of "serious" dishes — no organ meats or exotic sea creatures — but then the really ethnic eaters aren't the target audience here. The nouvelle attitude toward traditional sauces is something of a toss-up; when they're good, they're very good, but when they're bland, they're boring.

121

Clyde's

	American
	★★½
	Moderate

Zone 5   Georgetown
3236 M Street, NW
(202) 333-9180

Quality 77   Value B

Zone 10A   Maryland suburbs
70 Wisconsin Circle (Chevy Chase
   Center), Chevy Chase
(301) 951-9600

Zone 11A   Virginia suburbs
8332 Leesburg Pike, Tysons
   Corner
(703) 734-1901

Zone 11B   Virginia suburbs
Market Street, Reston Town
   Center, Reston
(703) 787-6601

Reservations:	Recommended
When to go:	Any time
Entree range:	$6.95 – 14.95
Payment:	VISA, MC, AMEX, DC, D
Service rating:	★★★½
Friendliness rating:	★★★½
Parking:	Free lots; pay lots in Georgetown
Bar:	Full service
Wine selection:	Limited
Dress:	Business, casual
Disabled access:	Good
Customers:	Local, business
Brunch:	*Georgetown:* Saturday and Sunday, 9 A.M.–4 P.M.; *Reston:* Sunday, 10 A.M.–4 P.M.
Lunch/Dinner:	*Georgetown:* Monday – Thursday, noon – 10 P.M.; Friday, noon – 11 P.M.; Saturday, 4:30 – 11 P.M.; Sunday, 4:30 – 10 P.M.; *Reston:* Monday – Saturday, 11 A.M.– midnight; Sunday, 4 – 10 P.M.; *Chevy Chase and Tysons:* Monday – Saturday, 11 A.M.– 2 A.M.; Sunday, 10 A.M.– 2 A.M.

Atmosphere/setting: Although all the Clyde's branches resemble the origi-nal M Street gaslight-era chophouse in atmosphere, they each have a theme: Re-ston's is a sporting club, with paraphernalia from sculls to sailboat models; Tyson's Corner has a pseudo-European style, with murals of nude bathers and lots

(continued)

of neo-nouveau glass and sculpture; and the branch in Columbia Mall is that sort of helter-skelter fake Tiffany and patent medicine sort of saloon. The Clyde's of Chevy Chase is a showplace of etched "Orient Express" glass, model cars—we mean production models—and real race cars, plus a huge downstairs bar larger than many nightclubs.

House specialties: The foods vary somewhat, too, with some similarities (and slight variations in price range). In general, look for smoked salmon, one of the company's signatures; lamb stew; beer-batter shrimp with an orange marmalade/mustard sauce; crab cakes; real old-fashioned burgers. (Which is to say, these kitchens are still American at heart.) However, a new, more serious attitude toward cooking is beginning to manifest itself; watch these spaces.

Other recommendations: Steaks; scallop and shrimp sautées; a chili that many people swear by (it's the company's other signature dish, canned and sold by neo-prep catalogs); seafood specials (including the annual halibut feasts, lobster specials, and in Reston, huge clambakes and Oktoberfest feeds). The menus and prices vary a bit from site to site, but have obvious family relationships.

Entertainment & amenities: Bar nibbles at happy hour, most notably an old-fashioned club cheese or smoked salmon tray at M Street and hot, fresh, butter-dipped soft pretzels in Reston—worth the trip alone. So are the sweet rolls served at Sunday brunch in Tysons.

Summary & comments: Clyde's was Georgetown's first "scene" bar, a sort of party and political hangout for post-grads who couldn't let go. Now it's almost an institution, but always dependable and welcoming. The Tysons Corner branch is a major singles center; Reston and Columbia are more family-oriented. Chevy Chase is a more serious restaurant, with sweetbreads, smoked duck, and other slightly more Bethesda-neighborhood entrees. All are heavy on the ice cream and spiked coffee drinks, and on cholesterol-spiking desserts.

Coco Loco

Zone 3   Downtown
810 Seventh Street, NW
(202) 289-2626

Reservations:	Strongly recommended on weekends
When to go:	Early or late; lunch for lower prices
Entree range:	$29.95 fixed price
Payment:	VISA, MC, AMEX
Service rating:	★★★
Friendliness rating:	★★★½
Parking:	Street, garage, valet (dinner only)
Bar:	Full service
Wine selection:	Good
Dress:	Business, informal
Disabled access:	Fair
Customers:	Local, international
Lunch:	Monday – Friday, 11:30 A.M. – 2:30 P.M.
Dinner:	Monday – Thursday, 6 – 10:30 P.M.;
	Friday and Saturday, 6 – 11 P.M.

Atmosphere/setting: Splashily modern tropical decor includes tile floors, bright primary colors and parrot-print uniforms, suspended canoes, and geometrically shaped columns. The cafe in front and big horseshoe bar serve tapas; the main dining room features an all-you-can-eat Brazilian-style mixed grill.

House specialties: The all-you-can-eat churrascaria grill includes skewered meats — lamb, beef flank and tenderloin, pork spareribs, chicken, and chorizo — carved directly onto your plate, plus a huge salad bar with fruit, asparagus, marinated mushrooms, couscous, etc. From the tapas menu: beef brochette with chili sauce; crab cakes; mini-paella; duck enchiladas with mole sauce.

Other recommendations: Bacon-wrapped shrimp; chicken-stuffed ravioli with poblanos; steamed salmon; side dishes of coconut rice.

Entertainment & amenities: Good-weather dining in a walled courtyard; hot Latin dancing after 11 P.M. Wednesday through Saturday, with Rio-style "pros" atop the bar on Saturdays.

Summary & comments: This is a very high-energy joint, a crowd- and trend-watcher's paradise; even with reservations you may have to wait a while. The mixed grill is more food than anyone but a pro football player could eat. The wine list includes several lesser-known but good and bargain-priced Chilean and Argentine wines. If you can afford to go straight to bed at 4 in the afternoon, go for the all-you-can-eat churrascaria at lunch, when it's only $20.95.

Cottonwood Cafe

New Southwestern
★★★
Moderate

Quality 80   Value B

Zone 10A   Maryland suburbs
4844 Cordell Avenue, Bethesda
(301) 656-4844

Reservations:	Recommended
When to go:	Any time
Entree range:	$9.95−20.95
Payment:	VISA, MC, AMEX
Service rating:	★★★
Friendliness rating:	★★★
Parking:	Lot, valet (dinner only)
Bar:	Full service
Wine selection:	Fair
Dress:	Informal, business, casual
Disabled access:	Good
Customers:	Local, business
Open:	Monday−Thursday, 11:30 A.M.−10 P.M.;
	Friday and Saturday, 11:30 A.M.−11 P.M.;
	Sunday, 5:30−10 P.M.

Atmosphere/setting: A very pretty, jewel-toned bow to the American Southwest, with terra cotta walls, murals of pueblos, wall sconces like mood rings, a few artifacts, and wrought-iron salamander door pulls—and a staff uniformed in turquoise and amethyst shirts with bolos and boots.

House specialties: Real "rattlesnake bites" (jalapeños stuffed with rattlesnake meat and cheese); blue cornmeal-crusted calamari with tomato chili glaze; a Southwest-style paella with sun-dried Indian corn and black beans amongst the shellfish; roast duck glazed with habanero-flavored molasses.

Other recommendations: Chile sausage and smoked shrimp tossed with black pepper pasta, sun-dried tomatoes, and shiitakes; Navajo fry bread topped with smoked salmon.

Summary & comments: Cottonwood continues to experiment with chili peppers, varying its flavors as well as heat levels. Sauces are cleaner and lighter than before, the quality is consistent, and the experimentation informed, not frantic. Lunch is a real bargain. The wine list is all-American, and the beer list is fair.

Dar es Salaam

Zone 5   Georgetown
3056 M Street, NW
(202) 337-6680

Moroccan	
★★½	
Moderate	
Quality 79	Value B

Reservations:	Helpful
When to go:	Any time
Entree range:	$11.95−14.95
Payment:	VISA, MC, AMEX
Service rating:	★★★
Friendliness rating:	★★★
Parking:	Street
Bar:	Full service
Wine selection:	House
Dress:	Casual
Disabled access:	Limited
Customers:	Local, ethnic
Dinner:	Daily, 5−11 P.M.

Atmosphere/setting: Even after being closed for several years, the authentic tilework and plaster of this escapist fantasy is in beautiful condition; add the flowery pillowcases, brass jugs, and background music and you have a romantic date to reckon with.

House specialties: Mechoui, roast whole lamb (requires 24 hours' notice); an unusual tajine of red snapper and more common lamb and chicken versions of this classic preserved-citrus and olive stew.

Other recommendations: Bisteeya, the sugar-dusted pastry filled with chicken and used not as dessert but as first course; harrira, a pepper-potent stew-thick soup with lamb and lentils.

Summary & comments: It's a little sad that, while so many other ethnic restaurants in Washington feel increasingly emboldened to ask diners to eat traditional style, Dar es Salaam has gone the other way: The handwashing ceremony which formerly preceded eating with fingers has given way to forks and knives and the low banquette seating has been topped with another layer of cushions. But the food is as good as ever. (Some people complain that the couscous seems skimpy, compared to the typically exaggerated versions served around town, but it's plenty filling and more traditional.)

Delhi Dhaba

Zone 11A   Virginia suburbs
2424 Wilson Boulevard, Arlington
(703) 524-0008

Zone 10B   Maryland suburbs
7236 Woodmont Avenue, Bethesda
(301) 718-0008

Indian
★★½
Inexpensive

Quality 78   Value A

Reservations:	Accepted
When to go:	Any time
Entree range:	$3.95−5.75
Payment:	VISA, MC
Service rating:	★★
Friendliness rating:	★★★
Parking:	Street
Bar:	Beer and wine
Wine selection:	House
Dress:	Casual, business
Disabled access:	No
Customers:	Local, ethnic
Open:	Sunday−Thursday, 11 A.M.−10 P.M.;
	Friday and Saturday, 11 A.M.−11 P.M.

Atmosphere/setting: A carryout with a touch of class—steam tables, coolers of beer and soda, and tables set off from the kitchen by carved wooden screens. And while some may be distracted by the Indian MTV-style videos (you should see the third-hand translation of the "Macarena"), they're kind of cheerful.

House specialties: Stewed goat chopped on the bone; okra curry; a creamy vegetable stew with nuts; tandoori lamb.

Other recommendations: Eggplant; shrimp specials.

Summary & comments: Another of those seemingly casual Indian fast-food steam table joints, but one where the hot buffet turns out to be a lot better than you expect—and covers more territory than most. They usually set out six or eight curries and stews a day, along with the tikka and tandoori, which explains the mountains of chickens visible in the kitchen. A carryout dish is a surprise, since each includes salad and either rice or a big slab of bread. The $7.95 all-you-can-eat Sunday buffet (11 A.M.−3:30 P.M.) is a staggering version of that local staple. Note that some of these family-style dishes seem oily to American tastes but are authentic to Indian palates.

DUANGRAT

Zone 11B Virginia suburbs	Thai
5878 Leesburg Pike, Falls Church	★★½
(703) 820-5775	Moderate
	Quality 79 Value C

Reservations:	Helpful
When to go:	Any time
Entree range:	$6.95−19.95
Payment:	VISA, MC, AMEX, CB, DC
Service rating:	★★★½
Friendliness rating:	★★★
Parking:	Free lot
Bar:	Full service
Wine selection:	Limited
Dress:	Informal, casual
Disabled access:	Fair
Customers:	Locals
Lunch:	Monday−Friday, 11:30 A.M.−2:30 P.M.
Lunch/Dinner:	Saturday and Sunday, 11:30 A.M.−11 P.M.
Dinner:	Monday−Thursday, 5−10:30 P.M.;
	Friday, 5−11 P.M.

Atmosphere/setting: A delicate, almost Art Deco−style restaurant, especially the upstairs dining room: pink linens, curio cabinets, and black-and-gray sconces. Waitresses in bright silk seem to match the floral arrangements.

House specialties: Whole fish with basil and chiles; charbroiled fish wrapped in banana leaves; chili-marinated squid and shrimp salads; ground peanut curries with coconut milk.

Other recommendations: Seafood dishes, particularly the mixed seafood over rice noodles, which includes soft-shell crabs in season; pork dishes; fried chicken wings stuffed with pork and crabmeat; quail in white rather than the usual black pepper.

Entertainment & amenities: On weekend evenings traditional dancers perform in full costume; it's free, but make reservations specifically for upstairs.

Summary & comments: This kitchen's spicy dishes lack some of the bite and variety some of the newer Thai establishments offer, and it isn't as generous with portions as some, but it has a consistently reliable quality and often exquisite presentation. This is becoming a mini-empire, in fact; the owners also have the flip-flop, country-style Thai Rabieng star nearby (see profile), and although its assertively French-Thai offshoot, Le Chef d'Oeuvre, failed, its trendy Bangkok Street Grill & Noodles shop is hauling them in (see profile).

128

Dusit

	Thai
Zone 10C Maryland suburbs	★★
2404 University Boulevard West, Wheaton	Inexpensive
(301) 949-4140	Quality 70 Value A

Reservations:	Accepted
When to go:	Any time
Entree range:	$5.95 – 10.95
Payment:	VISA, MC, AMEX, DC
Service rating:	★★★
Friendliness rating:	★★½
Parking:	Small lot, street
Bar:	Full service
Wine selection:	House
Dress:	Casual
Disabled access:	No
Customers:	Local, ethnic
Open:	Sunday – Thursday, 11:30 A.M. – 10 P.M.; Friday and Saturday, 11:30 A.M. – 11 P.M.

Atmosphere/setting: This otherwise plain mauve-and-lilac room is enlivened by a few splashes of neon; a small shrine hoisted on the rear wall gazes benignly out over the customers.

House specialties: Marinated shrimp, butterflied raw and topped with peppers and garlic; crab and potato "puffs" (more like empanadas); squid with white pepper; twice-cooked duck; crispy whole flounder with pork and black bean sauce.

Other recommendations: Squid with basil; red (sweet) curried pork; diced duck roll; stir-fried crabs in black bean sauce.

Summary & comments: This is a deceptively modest restaurant, with 20 appetizers and more than 80 entrees that run from mild to spanky, although none is blistering. Dishes are simple, too, almost purist, without so much of the onion and vegetable stretchers common to many Asian kitchens. There are four types of curries here, all good: green, red, Panang-style, and country-style, without coconut milk.

Elysium

Zone 11C   Virginia suburbs
116 South Alfred Street, Old
  Town Alexandria
(703) 838-8000

Reservations:	Recommended
When to go:	Any time
Entree range:	Fixed price: $35, $45, and $55
Payment:	VISA, MC, AMEX, DC
Service rating:	★★★★
Friendliness rating:	★★★½
Parking:	Valet, street
Bar:	Full service
Wine selection:	Very good ·
Dress:	Jacket and tie (dining room); informal (grill)
Disabled access:	No
Customers:	Local, tourist
Dinner:	*Dining room:* Tuesday – Saturday, 6 – 10 P.M.;
	Grill: Every day, 6 – 10 P.M.

Atmosphere / setting: A lovely newer but Old Town–style inn, with a curving white marble stairway and various small, pretty dining rooms; some more formal with classic white linen, oil paintings, and definitely modern but stylish china; some more like libraries and old smoking rooms.

House specialties: For such a shifting menu, it's hard to specify, but game dishes, including ostrich in a rich wine reduction and wild boar with a mole sauce and Cervena venison, are beautifully handled; a mini-bouillabaisse, though not the richest, was light and succulent; and a cannelloni of pheasant and duck was rich without being cloying. Grilled marinated quail with red cabbage choucroute is a good example of traditional recipes made fresh.

Summary & comments: Under different chefs, different names, and different cuisines, this restaurant has wandered from fine to frustrating, but it's been riding high lately as a showcase for chef Jim Garrison's fancies. The menu changes almost nightly, which is good for those intrigued by market-fresh ingredients, but not all Washingtonians are so off-the-cuff, and some may find this a little overwhelming. In addition, some dishes seem more carefully considered and original than others. But there is no doubt that if you're at all food-savvy, his chef's menus—$35 for three courses, $45 for four, and $55 for five, each including dessert and quite likely a little lagniappe from the kitchen—are as intriguing as any. And you can opt for a glass of wine or even a tasting flight for each course.

Faccia Luna

	Pizza
	★★
	Inexpensive
	Quality 73 Value B

Zone 5   Georgetown
2400 Wisconsin Avenue
(202) 337-3132

Zone 11A   Virginia suburbs
2909 Wilson Boulevard, Arlington
(703) 276-3099

Zone 11C   Virginia suburbs
823 South Washington Boulevard, Alexandria
(703) 838-5998

Reservations:	Not accepted
When to go:	Any time
Entree range:	$4.95 – 10.95
Payment:	Cash only
Service rating:	★★½
Friendliness rating:	★★★
Parking:	Street
Bar:	Full service
Wine selection:	House
Dress:	Casual
Disabled access:	Fair
Customers:	Local, student
Lunch/Dinner:	Monday – Thursday, 11:30 A.M. – 11 P.M.; Friday and Saturday, 11:30 A.M. – midnight
Dinner:	Sunday, 4 – 11 P.M.

Atmosphere/setting: A modern, straightforward office building of exposed brick cuts away in a wedge to allow outdoor dining and a simultaneous view of the bar at one side and the spinning dough at the far end. Inside, the otherwise plain booths are nicely labyrinth'd with glass-brick walls.

House specialties: Slow-rising yeast dough pizzas or calzones, which are pizzas folded in on themselves and stuffed with ricotta as well as mozzarella and tomato sauce; a prosciutto, mortadella, and salami grinder.

Other recommendations: Charbroiled chicken breast sandwich with home-made Dijon and walnut dressing; chocolate pistachio shortcake.

Entertainment & amenities: In D.C., the night-lit George Mason ball field across the street, which hosts fast-pitch softball and hardball games all summer.

Summary & comments: Faccia Luna is not only a good pizza stop (it offers about 20 toppings), it's a pretty good beer bar, offering a mix of imports and microbrews. Its "Luna Mary" cocktail is a Bloody Mary with Parmesan cheese.

Fasika's

Zone 6   Dupont Circle/
          Adams-Morgan
2447 18th Street, NW
(202) 797-7673

Ethiopian	
★★★	
Inexpensive	
Quality 82	Value A

Reservations:	Accepted
When to go:	Any time
Entree range:	$9−23
Payment:	VISA, MC, AMEX, DC
Service rating:	★★★
Friendliness rating:	★★★
Parking:	Street, lot
Bar:	Full service
Wine selection:	House; tej (honey wine)
Dress:	Informal, casual
Disabled access:	Fair
Customers:	Local, ethnic
Open:	Every day, noon−midnight

Atmosphere/setting: What might be called generic Ethiopian—whitewashed walls, a bit of travel poster color, and greenery. The most interesting tables are those where the local discussion groups spend hours nibbling and debating the latest political shift. The music and talk continue until 3 A.M.

House specialties: A combination platter with honey-chili dressed fish, jalapeño shrimp alecha and house special shrimp; lamb braised in a mild green chili sauce, marinated in white wine, or strip-marinated in honey-chili sauce and fried; a liver-tripe stew; double-cooked hand-chopped beef with ginger and cardamom.

Other recommendations: Cold lentil salad with chiles; carrots, potatoes, and green beans in tomatoes.

Summary & comments: Although often lost in the horde (close to a dozen) of Ethiopian establishments in the Adams-Morgan neighborhood, Fasika's is easily one of the best. It also offers several particularly interesting vegetarian dishes.

Filomena

Zone 5 Georgetown	**Italian**
1063 Wisconsin Avenue, NW	★★½
(202) 337-2782	Moderate
	Quality 79 Value B

Reservations:	Recommended
When to go:	Any time
Entree range:	$11.95−29.95
Payment:	VISA, MC, AMEX, DC, D
Service rating:	★★★½
Friendliness rating:	★★★★
Parking:	Pay lots, street
Bar:	Full service
Wine selection:	Good
Dress:	Business, informal
Disabled access:	No
Customers:	Local, business
Open:	Every day, 11:30 A.M.−11 P.M.

Atmosphere/setting: Think of this as a fairy-tale witch's cottage of a kitchen, packed to the very nooks with ribbons, pictures, dolls, pie safes, vintage bottles and cans and crates, copper utensils, and above all, the sidewalk pastry room, where Italian ladies (so picturesque you'd think they were character actors) mix, roll, cut, and hang the fresh pasta served downstairs.

House specialties: A multiseafood pasta with or without a lobster tail; jumbo shrimp stuffed with crabmeat; a hearty version of saltimbocca, scaloppine with prosciutto, fresh sage, and mozzarella; a rich-but-twist-my-arm linguini cardinale dressed in a sauce of lobster meat and rose wine.

Other recommendations: Real lasagna; oysters Rockefeller over the top with shrimp and crabmeat; specials such as crab ravioli.

Entertainment & amenities: After dinner, two carafes—one of sambuca, one of amaretto—are placed on the table.

Summary & comments: Okay, so Filomena's isn't the trendiest Italian around. Or the nouvellest, or the most famous, or the fastest (or the slowest). It's far and away the friendliest, the funniest, the warmest, and the most mamma's kitchen reassuring—comfort food for the head as well as the stomach. And what's wrong with a little traditional mangia, mangia anyway? Its adherents are legion, with reason (just look around at the crowd); the luckiest of them are invited to dine in the sanctum sanctorum—a dining room within the dining room, with a big oak table, wreaths and pots, and memorabilia galore. This is the kind of place where you can actually enjoy having the staff sing "Happy Birthday."

FOUR RIVERS

	Chinese
Zone 10B Maryland suburbs	★★★
184 Rollins Avenue, Rockville	Moderate
(301) 230-2900	
	Quality 83 Value B

Reservations:	Recommended for 4 or more on weekends
When to go:	Weekends for dim sum
Entree range:	$5.95−12.95
Payment:	VISA, MC, AMEX, D
Service rating:	★★★
Friendliness rating:	★★★½
Parking:	Free lot
Bar:	Full service
Wine selection:	House
Dress:	Casual or informal
Disabled access:	Good
Customers:	Ethnic, local
Open:	Sunday−Thursday, 11:30 A.M.−10 P.M.;
	Friday and Saturday, 11:30 A.M.−11 P.M.

Atmosphere/setting: Simple but comfortable, with red vinyl booths, plain wood wainscotting, and easy Oriental paintings and posters around the walls.

House specialties: Fresh seafood, particularly lobster (sweetly cooked, even in the black bean sauce version); shredded stomach (tripe) in chile oil; fried baby eggplant; squid in ginger; fresh scallops with black ear mushrooms in spicy ginger and garlic-tomato sauce, and a similar version including shrimp.

Other recommendations: Lobster with scallions and ginger; a hot version of orange beef; double-cooked crispy shredded beef; whole fish steamed or fried in a variety of sauces.

Summary & comments: This is the former home of the Seven Seas restaurant, which moved into larger quarters a block away and resembles it in its stocking of live seafood tanks; but this is a fine restaurant in its own right. The staff is not merely tolerant of novices, it's positively protective, and proud of both you and the food when you like something odd (in truth, shredded stomach is great, and tastes, as they say, like chicken). Don't be afraid to attack things in shells, like lobster, with your hands; they do. And if you're not sure what's polite, just ask. There is an all-Chinese menu, too; if you ask for it, even if you can't read it, it will alert the managers to come over and ask, and then you can get really good advice.

Full Key

Zone 10C   Maryland suburbs
2227 University Boulevard West,
    Wheaton
(301) 933-8388

Chinese
★½
Inexpensive
Quality 69   Value A

Reservations:	Not accepted
When to go:	Any time
Entree range:	$5.25−9.50
Payment:	VISA, MC, AMEX
Service rating:	★★★
Friendliness rating:	★★★
Parking:	Street
Bar:	No
Wine selection:	None
Dress:	Casual
Disabled access:	Fair
Customers:	Ethnic, local
Open:	Every day, 11 A.M.−2 A.M.

Atmosphere / setting: Rather plain except for the traditional green and red round-tiled pagoda roof hung overhead, but the immaculately white tiling and stainless steel stove, in plain view behind the hanging fowl, is an advertisement for swift and demanding efficiency. The staff's bright blue bowties (pre-tied) and cummerbunds go sweetly with the down-home menu.

House specialties: One-bowl soup "meals" with dumplings or noodles (or both), the Chinese equivalent of Vietnamese pho dinner; the rice equivalent, that seagoers' favorite gruel called congee, also with a dozen topping choices.

Other recommendations: Sour cabbage and tripe; pig skin and duck blood; for the pedestrian, chicken and scallops with mixed veggies; scallops in garlic sauce.

Summary & comments: Everything you really need to know about Full Key, especially in Wheaton, is in the plastic "specials" holder on the table: a list of noodle dishes, rice congees (including those with kidneys and livers and one with pork, squid, and peanuts), and Hong Kong−style noodle soups, of which the shrimp dumpling rendition is the town darling. While the version with roasted duck means slices of duck on the bone and with skin and fat (which gives the anise broth texture and flavor) intact, it's worth the indulgence. And at $4.75, it's a steal. The menu and the style bear a resemblance to Paul Kee around the corner: Compare duck blood dishes if you dare.

Gabriel

Zone 6   Dupont Circle/
           Adams-Morgan
2121 P Street, NW (Radisson
   Barcelo Hotel)
(202) 956-6690

Nuevo Latino
★★★
Moderate
Quality 84   Value A

Reservations:	Recommended
When to go:	Lunch, brunch, happy hour
Entree range:	$15.50−22
Payment:	AMEX, VISA, MC, DC, D
Service rating:	★★½
Friendliness rating:	★★★
Parking:	Street, hotel valet
Bar:	Full service
Wine selection:	Good and affordable
Dress:	Business, casual
Disabled access:	Good
Customers:	Business, local
Breakfast:	Monday−Friday, 6:30−11 A.M.;
	Saturday and Sunday, 7−10:30 A.M.
Brunch:	Sunday, 11 A.M.−3 P.M.
Lunch:	Monday−Friday, 11:30 A.M.−2:30 P.M.
Dinner:	Monday−Thursday, 6−10 P.M.;
	Friday and Saturday, 6−10:30 P.M.;
	Sunday, 6−9:30 P.M.

Atmosphere/setting: Sunny yellow paint, ocre and red art, and lots of wood and windows makes this English basement seem like an enclosed courtyard.

House specialties: Tapas: grilled quail stuffed with sausage; neo-Salvadoran pupusas with a crunchy cornmeal batter; scallops and spicy chorizo with cilantro and lime; figs stuffed with chorizo. Entrees: vegetable stew with rice croquettes; roast monkfish with caramelized oranges and corn fungus sauce; seared salmon with serrano ham and saffron-tomato broth.

Summary & comments: At $9.50, the lunch buffet seems to be the best bargain, including paella, quesadillas, rice and vegetable salads, and cured meats and cheeses. The $7.95 happy-hour spread, 5−8:30 P.M. Wednesday−Friday, could easily pass for dinner. The real pig-out, so to speak, is Sunday brunch, complete with suckling pigs; paella; cassoulet; rolls, danishes, and pastries; cheese and fruit; vegetable and couscous salads; sardines and cold cuts; omelets; polenta and potatoes; roast beef, lamb, and ham; plus unlimited champagne and a dessert bar, all for $16.75. Holy mole!

Galileo

	Italian
Zone 6 Dupont Circle/	★ ★ ★ ★ ★
Adams–Morgan	Expensive
1110 21st Street, NW	
(202) 293-7191	Quality 98 Value C

Reservations:	A must
When to go:	Any time
Entree range:	$19.95−29.95
Payment:	VISA, MC, AMEX, CB, DC, D
Service rating:	★ ★ ★ ★
Friendliness rating:	★ ★ ★ ½
Parking:	Lot, valet (dinner, except Sunday)
Bar:	Full service
Wine selection:	Excellent
Dress:	Dressy, business
Disabled access:	Good
Customers:	Local, tourist, business, gourmet mag groupies
Breakfast:	Monday – Friday, 7:30 – 9 A.M.
Lunch:	Monday – Friday, 11:30 A.M.– 2 P.M.
Dinner:	Monday – Thursday, 5:30 – 10 P.M.;
	Friday and Saturday, 5:30 – 10:30 P.M.;
	Sunday, 5 – 10 P.M.

Atmosphere/setting: A gracious stone and plaster palazzo with vaulted recessed booths and a trompe l'oeil mural leading into a Renaissance eternity.

House specialties: Five-course menus du gustacione for about $50. Among the frequent offerings are game birds—squab, woodcock, guinea hen—and red game such as venison and wild hare. Sea urchin appears fairly often, usually caressing a delicate pasta, as do wild mushrooms or truffles.

Other recommendations: Ravioli stuffed with scallops and served with black truffles, or stuffed with veal and topped with roasted foie gras; grilled rack of veal or venison; sweetbreads; grilled or roasted seafood; gnocchi.

Summary & comments: Among the city's finest restaurants by any account. Chef Roberto Donna's creations quickly appear on menus elsewhere in town. He also offers the longest, best, and probably priciest Italian wine list in Washington, but with style: Even the bread sticks and loaves, which come in a half-dozen flavors, are to be savored. Sauces and presentations are rarely showy and purees often stand in for cream. Regular customers get white-glove treatment; tourists (and obvious food-trend victims) may find the staff showily condescending, but spit-and-polish precise nonetheless.

George

	Mediterranean
Zone 3 Downtown	★★★½
2020 K Street, NW	Moderate
(202) 452-9898	
	Quality 85 Value B

Reservations:	Recommended
When to go:	Any time; lunch
Entree range:	$13.50−20.50
Payment:	VISA, MC, AMEX, DC
Service rating:	★★★
Friendliness rating:	★★★★
Parking:	Valet at night; street or lot
Bar:	Full service
Wine selection:	Good
Dress:	Business, informal
Disabled access:	Good
Customers:	Local
Lunch:	Monday−Friday, 11:30 A.M.−2 P.M.
Dinner:	Monday−Thursday, 5:30−10 P.M.;
	Friday and Saturday, 5:30−10:30 P.M.

Atmosphere/setting: A stately, but not stiff, room with a hint of Riviera-style stucco paint, Italian marble floor, and polished wood.

House specialties: Scallop-stuffed lasagna with eels and white wine sauce; chunky lobster ravioli with lime, ginger, shiitakes, and roasted fennel; a novel seafood soup with kohlrabi, tomatoes, and crab fritters.

Other recommendations: A sort of pared-down couscous with honey-ginger-marinated lamb chops, eggplant mousse, and fennel; a rich-spirited ag-nolotti stuffed with wild mushrooms and topped with a ham-asparagus cream; lemony chicken over caponata; pork chops marinated in buttermilk and honey with horseradish; roasted shiitake and lamb kidney salad.

Summary & comments: It may seem as odd a name for a restaurant as for a magazine, but it has a better excuse: It's the eponymous kitchen of chef George Vetsch, who not only was one of the first chefs to offer a combination of North African/Middle Eastern/Riviera cooking at the Mediterraneo restaurant in Arlington, but who pushed the envelope even more by making the real stuff, like sautéed rabbit giblets and brandied lamb liver. The menu here is only a little more subdued, but the rich flavors—fennel, chicken livers, calamata olives, goat cheese, eggplant, and spicy harissa—are the same. And the majority of these dishes are available at lunch for a few dollars less. Even the supposedly jaded sophisticates of K Street ought to find real pleasure in some of these combinations.

Georgetown Seafood Grill

Seafood	
★★½	
Inexpensive	
Quality 79	Value B

Zone 5   Georgetown
3063 M Street, NW
(202) 333-7038

Zone 6   Dupont Circle/Adams-Morgan
1200 19th Street, NW
(202) 530-4430

Reservations:	Helpful
When to go:	Any time
Entree range:	$10−21.95
Payment:	VISA, MC, AMEX, D, DC, CB
Service rating:	★★★
Friendliness rating:	★★★
Parking:	Pay lot
Bar:	Full service
Wine selection:	House
Dress:	Casual
Disabled access:	Good
Customers:	Local, ethnic
Open:	Sunday–Thursday, 11:30 A.M.–10:30 P.M.;
	Friday and Saturday, 11:30 A.M.–11:30 P.M.

Atmosphere/setting: The M Street original is pretty straightforward, though chummy, with the raw bar itself the main decoration; but the new 19th Street site is a real surprise, an upscale Carolina coastal decor in the middle of the silk stocking Steak Alley. Ceiling fans, stuffed trophy fish, the usual boat shell or two in the rafters, and even table umbrellas.

House specialties: Raw oysters and clams; crab cakes; seafood gumbo; a not-too-rich oyster stew; fresh fish selection simply grilled.

Other recommendations: Have it your way: Any fish of the day can be ordered grilled, blackened, broiled, poached, or pan-fried and with a variety of dipping sauces.

Summary & comments: The original branch on M Street never got much attention, although it plugged along nicely anyhow; but with the seafood grill boom of recent years, its good nature is finally being rewarded.

GEORGIA BROWN'S

Zone 3 Downtown	Southern
950 15th Street, NW	★★★
(202) 393-4499	Moderate
	Quality 80 Value B

Reservations:	Suggested
When to go:	Any time
Entree range:	$10.95 – 19.95
Payment:	VISA, MC, AMEX, DC, CB, D
Service rating:	★★★½
Friendliness rating:	★★★½
Parking:	Street, valet (after 6 P.M.), $5
Bar:	Full service
Wine selection:	Very good
Dress:	Business, informal
Disabled access:	Good
Customers:	Business, local, tourist
Brunch:	Sunday, 11:30 A.M.–3 P.M.
Lunch/Dinner:	Monday – Thursday, 11:30 A.M.–11 P.M.;
	Friday, 11:30 A.M.–midnight;
	Saturday, 5:30 P.M.–midnight;
	Sunday, 5:30–11 P.M.

Atmosphere/setting: An almost too-sophisticated take on Southern garden district graciousness, with vinelike wrought iron overhead, sleek wood curves and conversation nooks; window tables are prime.

House specialties: A very in-joke take on osso buco made with ham hock (possibly the smartest pun in Washington cuisine); beautiful white shrimp, heads still on, with spicy sausage over grits; the same extravagant shrimp in an untypical coconut milk – rum – green onion gravy; grilled black grouper with peach chutney; spicy duck sausage gumbo; pan-crisped sweetbreads with Madeira.

Other recommendations: Braised rabbit with wild mushrooms; crab cakes; medallions of beef with bourbon-pecan sauce; a Caribbean-spiced catfish fried in cornmeal; an appetizer of eggplant rolls stuffed with bleu cheese and fried.

Entertainment & amenities: Live jazz at Sunday brunch.

Summary & comments: This is not low-country cuisine. It's haute country, updated versions of dishes you might have found in Charleston or Savannah. Presentation is distinctive without being showy, and portions are generous. Homesick Southerners can indulge in the fried chicken livers and the farm-biscuit-like scones and still look uptown. The wine list is all-American and fairly priced; barrel-aged bourbons and single-malt Scotches available as well.

Gerard's Place

Zone 3   Downtown
915 15th Street, NW
(202) 737-4445

Reservations:	Recommended
When to go:	Monday
Entree range:	$16.50−29.50
Payment:	VISA, MC, AMEX, CB, DC
Service rating:	★★★
Friendliness rating:	★★½
Parking:	Street, valet (evenings)
Bar:	Full service
Wine selection:	Good
Dress:	Business, casual
Disabled access:	Very good
Customers:	Business, local, tourist
Lunch:	Monday−Friday, 11:30 A.M.−2:30 P.M.
Dinner:	Monday−Thursday, 5:30−10 P.M.;
	Friday and Saturday, 5:30−10:30 P.M.;
	Sunday, closed.

Atmosphere/setting: A quietly powerful room, painted simply in charcoal and terra cotta and studded with a series of stark pencil lithographs.

House specialties: The menu changes weekly, but look for any sweetbread or venison dish; perfectly poached lobster topped with a tricolor confetti of mango, avocado, and red bell pepper in lime-sauterne sauce; "foie gras of the sea" (known to sushi connoisseurs as ankimo or monkfish liver), lightly crusted and grilled rare, as rich as real foie gras but with a fraction of the calories and guilt; terrine of quail bound by quail liver; boned rabbit rolled and wrapped in Japanese seaweed; soft-shell crabs not with almonds but sweeter, unexpected hazelnuts.

Other recommendations: Hearty bistro-max dishes such as pot-au-feu of cured duck and savoy cabbage; cod cheeks; braised oxtail; breast of duck with shepherd's pie of the leg. Or you can try the tasting menu, five courses for $58 or with wine for $85. A vegetarian tasting menu is also offered.

Entertainment & amenities: On Monday, Gerard's Place waives not only the corkage fee on wines but the markup as well.

Summary & comments: Gerard Pangaud prepares classic food, often long-cooked and incredibly tender, but unobtrusively lightened to modern nutritional standards and keyed to seasonal specialties. Presentation is discreet but stunning.

Honors & awards: Pangaud's restaurant in Paris earned two Michelin stars.

GERMAINE'S

Zone 5   Georgetown
2400 Wisconsin Avenue, NW
(202) 965-1185

Pan Asian	
★★½	
Moderate	
Quality 79	Value B

Reservations: Recommended
When to go: Any time
Entree range: $14−22
Payment: VISA, MC, AMEX, DC
Service rating: ★★★
Friendliness rating: ★★★
Parking: Valet (dinner), meters
Bar: Full service
Wine selection: Fair
Dress: Business, informal
Disabled access: No
Customers: Local, media, tourist
Lunch: Monday−Friday, 11:30 A.M.−2:30 P.M.
Dinner: Sunday−Thursday, 5:30−10 P.M.;
                       Friday and Saturday, 5:30−11 P.M.

Atmosphere/setting: Oriental only in its discretion and elegance, with airy skylights, semiformal banquettes, and large and striking plants for dividers.

House specialties: Cha gio, the traditional spring rolls (better than most); chicken or pork satay; Thai chicken with basil; tea-leaf seafood in a coconut milk sauce; sautéed calamari with tomato and leeks; grilled fresh fish.

Other recommendations: Rockfish steamed in foil with shrimp and chopped seafood; shrimp or mixed seafood in fried-noodle baskets; Peking duck.

Summary & comments: Despite the owner's Vietnamese heritage, Germaine's has turned into what is even more pan-hemispheric than pan-Asian. Elements of Korean, Japanese, Filipino, Indonesian, Thai, Chinese, Burmese, and French cuisines are mixed together in what is really the chef's best interest. She cooks what she likes, which is, after all, the definition of any art. After 15 years, it may not be quite the prime people-watching spot it used to be (image is everything) but it's still intelligently populated, particularly by professionals who haven't rotated with the administrations.

Goldoni

Zone 6   Dupont Circle/
          Adams-Morgan
1113 23rd Street, NW
(202) 293-1511

Italian
★★★½
Inexpensive

Quality 85   Value C

Reservations:	Recommended
When to go:	Any time
Entree range:	$9.95 – 24.95
Payment:	VISA, MC, AMEX, D, DC
Service rating:	★★★½
Friendliness rating:	★★★
Parking:	Free lot
Bar:	Full service
Wine selection:	Good
Dress:	Business/informal
Disabled access:	No
Customers:	Local, ethnic
Lunch:	Every day, 11:30 A.M.– 2 P.M.
Dinner:	Monday – Thursday, 5:30 – 10 P.M.;
	Friday and Saturday, 5 – 10:30 P.M.;
	Sunday 5 – 9:30 P.M.

Atmosphere/setting: This has always been a beautiful restaurant, no matter under which regime: The skylights and white marble bar contrast with deep green tones and old-fashioned candelabra.

House specialties: Pappardelle with duck ragout or fettuccine with lamb ragout and mushrooms; portobello-stuffed tortellini; veal that goes cordon bleu one better, on a roll with asparagus, prosciutto, spinach, and egg frittata; veal-stuffed ravioli; appetizers such as a terrine of rabbit and sweetbreads with black olive sauce or a salad composed of smoked salmon, goat cheese, and asparagus.

Other recommendations: Dishes wrapped for delicacy, including a scallop wrapped in spinach and a snapper en papillote; break-your-resolution risottos with mascarpone or even sausage; rack of lamb pan-sautéed rather than roasted (and more tender for it) but served, with a wink to Tuscany, with cannellini beans and Swiss chard; and surprisingly light but flavorful mixed grilled seafoods.

Summary & comments: Chef Fabrizio Aielli is one of Roberto Donna's former sous-chefs, and it shows: The dishes here (and their menu descriptions) are every bit as elaborate as those at Galileo—and, as at Galileo, you're always surprised at just how satisfying such imagination can be. These are richly flavored dishes, particularly the pastas: Notice the number of gamey ragout sauces.

Good FORTUNE

Chinese

★★★

Inexpensive

Quality 80   Value B

Zone 10B   Maryland suburbs
2646 University Boulevard West,
    Wheaton
(301) 929-8818

Reservations:	Suggested
When to go:	Lunch
Entree range:	$8.95 – 12.95
Payment:	VISA, MC
Service rating:	★★★
Friendliness rating:	★★★
Parking:	Street
Bar:	Full service
Wine selection:	House
Dress:	Informal, casual
Disabled access:	Good
Customers:	Local, ethnic
Open:	Monday – Friday, 11:30 A.M. – 1 A.M.;
	Saturday, 11:30 A.M. – 2 A.M.;
	Sunday, 11 A.M. – 1 A.M.

Atmosphere/setting: An odd cinderblock sort of pagoda outside; a large, pink banquet room inside, with carved lions and an ancestor altar at one end.

House specialties: Unusual dishes featuring conch, sea anemone, squid, and frog legs; sautéed squid with tangy sweet-and-sour cabbage; shrimp and scallops in black bean sauce; oyster stew with ginger and scallions; dim sum at lunch every day.

Other recommendations: Whole fried fish or, more healthfully, steamed with julienned ginger; appetizers of bouncy shrimp mousse mounded and fried around snow-crab claws like seafood lollipops; scallop and shrimp mousse with black bean sauce.

Summary & comments: Cantonese cooking is the Rodney Dangerfield of Chinese cuisine, but this wide-ranging kitchen deserves plenty of respect. Larger groups may want to order the eight- or ten-course banquets ($17 – 20 a person). Good Fortune is especially popular at lunch, and rightfully, for its Hong Kong–style dim sum served traditionally from carts (and served seven days a week). The seafood is more consistent than the beef and pork dishes, which are sometimes chewy.

Greenwood

Zone 7   Upper Northwest
3311 Connecticut Avenue, NW
(202) 833-6572

Modern American	
★ ★ ★	
Moderate	
Quality 84	Value B

Reservations:	Accepted
When to go:	Any time
Entree range:	$11.50 – 16.95
Payment:	VISA, MC, AMEX
Service rating:	★ ★ ★
Friendliness rating:	★ ★ ★ ★
Parking:	Street
Bar:	Full service
Wine selection:	Limited
Dress:	Business, casual
Disabled access:	Yes
Customers:	Youngish, nutrition-conscious locals
Lunch:	Monday – Friday, noon – 3 P.M.
Dinner:	Every day, 6 – 10 P.M.

Atmosphere/setting: A simple but inviting cafe, pretty in pink but smartly modernized by antique tablecloths, faux marbling, and iron sconces.

House specialties: "New-wave salmon," served over a red lentil dhal with cucumber salad, is a signature dish; "mile-high" lobster or shrimp pad thai; open-faced buckwheat ravioli with mushrooms, potato, and smoked mozzarella filling; lobster-scallop cakes; open-faced spinach ravioli filled with potatoes, chanterelles, spinach, and smoked mozzarella; a signature appetizer of three dips, Mediterranean carrot-cashew, spicy lentil, and beet with caraway.

Other recommendations: A vegetable pho (Vietnamese noodle soup); seared rare tuna; artichoke and mushroom risotto; baklava stuffed with eggplant, potato, roasted onion, and walnuts; a bastila (North African pastry) filled with red snapper, caramelized onions, and spices, served with almond couscous and preserved lemons.

Entertainment & amenities: Live music on Sunday evenings only; but several of the staff are musicians, so even the recorded music tends to be interesting.

Summary & comments: Greenwood, named for owner/chef Carole Wagner Greenwood, is billed as providing "seasonal California cooking," and that pretty much sums it up: light, market-savvy, and not recipe-bound. Meals can be either light or heavy (in fact, the menu is divided into small and large dishes, so you can nibble in the neo-Asian fashion). Her cooking is still world-view, however, working in Asian and Middle Eastern flavors in ways that don't overwhelm the palate. This is home-style fusion, if you can understand that.

Grill from Ipanema

Zone 6   Dupont Circle/
         Adams-Morgan
1858 Columbia Road, NW
(202) 986-0757

Brazilian	
★★½	
Moderate	
Quality 78	Value C

Reservations:	Recommended for weekends
When to go:	Early, especially Wednesday and Saturday; or after 10.
Entree range:	$12.95−19.95
Payment:	VISA, MC, AMEX, DC, D
Service rating:	★★½
Friendliness rating:	★★★½
Parking:	Street
Bar:	Full service
Wine selection:	Limited
Dress:	Informal, casual
Disabled access:	Good
Customers:	Local, ethnic, embassy
Brunch:	Saturday and Sunday, noon−4 P.M.
Dinner:	Monday−Thursday, 5−11 P.M.; Friday, 5 P.M.−midnight; Saturday, noon−midnight; Sunday, 4−11 P.M.

Atmosphere/setting: Spare and nouveau; its Brazilian rosewood, slate mountainscape mirrors, and darkly tinted windows suggest a huge celebrity limo on cruise control, and the black artist palm trees look like the back drop for a fashion shoot.

House specialties: Feijoada, a black bean/smoked pork/collard greens stew served only on Wednesday and Saturday for dinner and Sunday all day (hence the crush); shellfish stews in either cilantro and pepper or palm oil and coconut sauces; carne de sol, a salt-cured, milk-resuscitated beef roast grilled and thinly sliced.

Other recommendations: Grouper and leeks in phyllo dough; marinated grilled shrimp; a mug of smooth black bean soup spiked with cachaca (Brazilian rum).

Summary & comments: A young and lively atmosphere, especially after 10 P.M. when the bar gets busy and the music turns up. The caipirinha, a mix of fresh lime and cachaca (somewhere between rum and moonshine), is particularly popular and potent. Because of the no reservations policy, and a certain tendency of the Portuguese-speaking staff to prefer regular customers, the wait can be annoying—which also adds to the caipirinhas' popularity.

Guapo's

	Tex-Mex
	★★½
	Inexpensive

Zone 7   Upper Northwest
4515 Wisconsin Avenue, NW
(202) 686-3588

Zone 10B   Maryland suburbs
9811 Washingtonian Boulevard
    (Rio Center), Gaithersburg
(301) 977-5655

Quality 76   Value B

Reservations:	Helpful
When to go:	Off-peak hours (if possible)
Entree range:	$8.95 – 13.95
Payment:	VISA, MC, AMEX, D, DC
Service rating:	★★★
Friendliness rating:	★★★
Parking:	Free lot
Bar:	Full service
Wine selection:	House
Dress:	Casual
Disabled access:	Good
Customers:	Local, ethnic
Open:	Every day, 11:30 A.M.–11 P.M.

Atmosphere/setting: The Tenleytown original is an O.K. Corral, especially during soccer matches on the satellite; the Rio Center location has to overcome murals of cowpokes, overly florid decoration, and karaoke.

House specialties: Fajitas, particularly the quail version, which offers two semi-boned birds that taste as if they had been marinated in bacon; the "Acapulco steak," something like a jalapeño-flavored Palm steak grilled over mesquite; tequila-sautéed shrimp (of course); and a dangerously fragrant half-dozen shrimp stuffed with jalapeños and cheese, wrapped in bacon, and served with thick garlicky butter. Feel your arteries closing yet?

Other recommendations: If you really want to get your money's worth, try the two-appetite-sized "plato grande" with beef and chicken fajitas, ribs, spicy shrimp, and all the sides for $30. Or hit the all-you-can-eat buffet for a weekday lunch or Sunday brunch.

Summary & comments: This is almost more bar than restaurant, which is not surprising, since the menu pushes margaritas right on the front. Tenley gets a more authentically Central American crowd, along with AU students and young locals; the Rio branch feeds the nearby town house developments and the multiplex crowd. There's a carryout location in the Farragut North Metro food court.

Haandi

Indian
★★½
Inexpensive

Quality 77   Value B

Zone 11B   Virginia suburbs
1222 West Broad Street (Falls Plaza
   Shopping Center), Falls Church
(703) 533-3501

Zone 10A   Maryland suburbs
4904 Fairmont Avenue, Bethesda
(301) 718-0121

Reservations:	Accepted (except Friday and Saturday)
When to go:	Any time
Entree range:	$6.95 – 14.95
Payment:	VISA, MC, AMEX, DC
Service rating:	★★★
Friendliness rating:	★★½
Parking:	Lots
Bar:	Full service
Wine selection:	Fair
Dress:	Informal, casual, business
Disabled access:	Good
Customers:	Local, business, ethnic
Lunch:	Every day, 11:30 A.M. – 2:30 P.M.
Dinner:	Sunday – Thursday, 5 – 10 P.M.;
	Friday and Saturday, 5 – 10:30 P.M.

Atmosphere/setting: Both are discreet, Empire-influenced dining rooms with pastel paint and white tablecloths.

House specialties: Tandoori-marinated or char-grilled salmon; chicken or lamb karahi, boneless cubed meat half-cooked in the clay oven then wok-fried with a tomato-onion sauce; murg, a popular tandoori-roasted half-chicken.

Other recommendations: Roasted eggplant; marinated skewered lamb chops; shrimp and saffron biryani.

Summary & comments: At Haandi, you get formal care in presentation with informal welcome and moderate prices. Recipes are sometimes a surprise, though not unwelcome: The rogan josh here is made with sour cream rather than yogurt, rather like stroganoff, and the barbecued salmon is served in a dark ragout. Cardamom-studded rice is excellent. The condiments are particularly good here as well.

Hard Times Cafe

Zone 10B   Maryland suburbs
1117 Nelson Street (Woodley Gardens
    Shopping Center), Rockville
(301) 294-9720

Zone 11B   Virginia suburbs
3028 Wilson Boulevard, Clarendon
(703) 528-2233

Zone 11C   Virginia suburbs
1404 King Street, Alexandria
(703) 683-5340

Zone 11A   Virginia suburbs
394 Elden Street (K-Mart Shopping Center), Herndon
(703) 318-8941

Chili
★★½
Inexpensive
Quality 75   Value A

Reservations:	Accepted for 10 or more at Rockville and Alexandria; for 15 or more at Clarendon
When to go:	Non−rush hour
Entree range:	$4.50−6.10
Payment:	VISA, MC, AMEX
Service rating:	★★★
Friendliness rating:	★★★½
Parking:	Free lot (Rockville); street
Bar:	Beer and wine
Wine selection:	House
Dress:	Casual
Disabled access:	Good
Customers:	Local, business
Open:	Monday−Thursday, 11:30 A.M.−10 P.M.; Friday and Saturday, 11:30 A.M.−11 P.M.; Sunday, noon−9 P.M.

Atmosphere/setting: These are fun and sincerely family-owned joints, with old photos, some farm implements, and old and new western paraphernalia. A collection of Wurlitzer bubblers plays appropriate Tex-a-Co'try and the occasional brief flare-up of grease from the french fry basket adds sizzle.

House specialties: A great microbrew selection, particularly emphasizing the Western and Southwestern labels and seasonal beers; vegetarian chili; for the meek, a grilled chicken sandwich; for the gut of iron, a beef frank covered in Cincinnati chili, cheddar, and fried onions.

(continued)

Other recommendations: A loaf of fried onion rings; Old Dominion root beer.

Summary & comments: A Hard Times menu is sort of like the old real estate joke about location: You can order chili, chili, or chili. Texas is the familiar coarsely ground beef in spicy brown sauce; Cincinnati style is ground more finely and has a sweetish, cinnamony tomato sauce; and the veggie, with textured protein, mushrooms, and peanuts, is a personal favorite. None of the three could be called authentic except in America, and all require heavy remedial dosing with Tabasco. All three may be ordered with onions, cheese, beans, or spaghetti—chili three ways, four ways, or five ways. It's best to go the sixth way, too, with a side of chopped jalapeños.

Hibiscus Cafe

Zone 5   Georgetown
3401 K Street, NW
(202) 965-7170

Jamaican
★★★½
Inexpensive
Quality 85   Value B

Reservations:	Accepted; required for 6 or more
When to go:	Any time
Entree range:	$12.50−18.50
Payment:	AMEX, VISA
Service rating:	★★★
Friendliness rating:	★★★½
Parking:	Street
Bar:	Beer and wine
Wine selection:	Moderate
Dress:	Casual
Disabled access:	Fair
Customers:	Local, international
Dinner:	Tuesday − Thursday, 6 − 11 P.M.; Friday and Saturday, 6 P.M. − midnight; Sunday and Monday, closed.

Atmosphere/setting: A bright and roadhouse-cheery but extremely modern cafe, with oversized art-metal furnishings, multiple seating levels, potted mini-trees (to earn the name), and infectious music.

House specialties: Jerk quail; smoked rack of lamb with plantain mousse; blackened Creole grouper; lobster and shrimp in spicy coconut butter sauce; "shark and bake" (shark-filled fried appetizers); and a searing habanero-marinated "peppa shrimp," head-on and wildly pungent.

Other recommendations: A yuppie but addictive smoked salmon and Brie pizza; salmon, shrimp, and mussels Creole; homemade ginger beer. For the less spicy-minded, chicken breasts stuffed with spinach and crabmeat; grilled salmon or veal chops.

Summary & comments: The menu changes a bit every day, mostly depending on the choices of fish and curry meat available. The newest weekend special is whole-roasted goat, the most aromatic dish on the riverfront. The jerk chicken wings here are legendary (owners Sharon and Jimmie Banks started out at Adams-Morgan's legendary — and never quite replaced — Fish Wings & Tings). There is a mixed-veggie curry as well that is popular among PC neighbors.

Hinodᴇ

Zone 10A   Maryland suburbs
4914 Hampden Lane, Bethesda
(301) 654-0908

Zone 10B   Maryland suburbs
134 Congressional Lane, Rockville
(301) 816-2190

<table>
<tr><td></td><td>Japanese</td></tr>
<tr><td></td><td>★★½</td></tr>
<tr><td></td><td>Inexpensive</td></tr>
<tr><td>Quality 75</td><td>Value B</td></tr>
</table>

Reservations:	Accepted
When to go:	Any time
Entree range:	$8−18
Payment:	VISA, MC, AMEX, D
Service rating:	★★½
Friendliness rating:	★★★
Parking:	Two hours' free lot parking with validation; street
Bar:	Beer and wine
Wine selection:	House
Dress:	Casual, business
Disabled access:	Good
Customers:	Locals
Lunch:	Monday−Friday, 11 A.M.−2:30 P.M.
Lunch/Dinner:	Saturday, noon−10:30 P.M.
Dinner:	Monday−Thursday, 4:30−10 P.M.;
	Friday, 4:30−10:30 P.M.; Sunday, 4−9:30 P.M.

Atmosphere/setting: Small but elegant, with shoji-grid woodwork, stone garden lantern, mini-gardens, and celadon-green touches.

House specialties: Home-style salted and broiled yellowtail or salmon steaks; buckwheat noodles with ponzu sauce; the house roll, a sort of seafood futomaki with broiled salmon, crab, and squid with veggies.

Other recommendations: The "Hinode box" meals, bargain-priced ($7.95) combos of soup, tempura, and California roll with a choice of sashimi, teriyaki, etc.; sushi in general (Hinode is generous in slicing fish, but balances it on an easily swallowed nugget of rice); yellowtail mini-fillets in teriyaki sauce.

Summary & comments: Hinode has a few surprises up its sleeve—the first being that various members of the staff are speaking Korean or Chinese (or even, occasionally, a snatch of Vietnamese). The others are culinary concessions to American food habits: a crab-stick (surimi) tempura that might be considered the Asian alternative to fried mozzarella sticks, and the far more intriguing tataki, thin-sliced rare beef in vinegary ponzu, a tit-for-tat for all those "tuna carpaccio" appetizers in New American restaurants.

Hope Key

Zone 11B   Virginia suburbs
3131 Wilson Boulevard, Arlington
(703) 243-8388

	Chinese
	★★½
	Inexpensive
Quality 79	Value B

Reservations:	Not necessary
When to go:	Any time
Entree range:	$4.95–13.95
Payment:	VISA, MC, AMEX, D, DC
Service rating:	★★★
Friendliness rating:	★★★
Parking:	Free lot (evenings), meters
Bar:	Wine and beer
Wine selection:	House
Dress:	Casual
Disabled access:	Good
Customers:	Local, ethnic
Open:	Sunday–Thursday, 11–1 A.M.;
	Friday and Saturday, 11 A.M.–3 A.M.

Atmosphere/setting: This is just what it is: white walls, red leatherette banquettes and chair cushions, and red ribbons of daily specials like fortunes hanging from the walls.

House specialties: Hong Kong–style chow foon (the thick egg noodles) and chow mein (the thin kind) served with just about any variety of seafood, meat, or vegetables you can imagine (not to mention the variety of dumpling soups and noodle soups); ditto the hot pots, which range from bean curd to pho-like beef tendon and tripe, to squab and mushroom. Be a little adventurous (it's so inexpensive, anyway!): Try conch, snails, steamed fish head with black bean sauce or fish head in a hot pot (the best part of the fish, as habituees of Japanese restaurants can attest), or frog with chives (yes, it does taste kind of like chicken). Vegetable dishes are very good here, too, especially watercress with bean curd paste, sautéed mustard greens, and tofu with salted fish and diced chicken.

Other recommendations: Although this calls itself a Chinese restaurant, it also has a long list of com dia, the Vietnamese rice dishes, which come with the full range of seafood, meat, or poultry; or the offal (not at all awful) congee with pork kidney, liver, and stomach.

Summary & comments: This is the Bistro Francais of Clarendon, in that it's the after-hours hangout for all the other Asian chefs in the neighborhood. The fun part about this place is that if you ask you can pretty much custom-design your meal, because the kitchen offers virtually everything.

HUNAN NO. 1

Zone 11B Virginia suburbs	Chinese
3033 Wilson Boulevard, Clarendon	★★½
(703) 528-1177	Inexpensive
	Quality 78 Value B

Reservations:	Accepted for 10 or more
When to go:	Any time
Entree range:	$7.25−13.50
Payment:	VISA, MC, D
Service rating:	★★½
Friendliness rating:	★★½
Parking:	Street, lot
Bar:	Full service
Wine selection:	House
Dress:	Casual
Disabled access:	Fair
Customers:	Local, ethnic
Open:	Every day, 11 A.M.−2 A.M.

Atmosphere/setting: This could be one of a hundred suburban Chinese kitchens, with tassled decor touches and suspiciously generic photo-displays of menu options; but you have to like the two giant foo dogs guarding the front door.

House specialties: Salt-baked fried squid and scallops with chiles; shrimp in the shell with black bean sauce, steamed in a lotus leaf envelope; clams or oysters steamed with black beans; a low-cal feast of a seafood hot pot mixing shrimp, scallops, squid, lobsters, and crab with Chinese cabbage, rice noodles, and broth.

Other recommendations: A good version of Singapore noodles.

Summary & comments: Despite the name, and the presence of the dependable kung paos and Szechuans on the menu, the chef's specialties are Cantonese, which leads to such oxymorons as the "Hunan #1 combination," a classic stir-fry of shrimp, chicken, beef, broccoli, straw mushrooms, and mini-cobs in brown sauce; and the even more inexplicable "lobster nouvelle" (baked in herbal salt and garlic). Still, when he's right, he's right; the Hong Kong−style dishes, particularly seafood, are very good.

Hunan Palace

	Chinese
Zone 10B Maryland suburbs	★★★
9011 Gaither Road, Gaithersburg	Inexpensive
(301) 977-8600	
	Quality 81 Value B

Reservations:	Helpful at lunch
When to go:	Any time; weekends for dim sum
Entree range:	$5.95 – 19.95
Payment:	VISA, MC, AMEX
Service rating:	★★★
Friendliness rating:	★★½
Parking:	Free lot
Bar:	Full service
Wine selection:	House
Dress:	Casual
Disabled access:	Good
Customers:	Ethnic, local
Open:	Sunday – Thursday, 11:30 A.M. – 10 P.M.;
	Friday and Saturday, 11:30 A.M. – 10:30 P.M.

Atmosphere / setting: Once primarily a Clark Kent restaurant, turning out quarts of beef and broccoli for area office workers in the orange-boothed front room and julienned eel and leeks for large Taiwanese family groups and fundraisers in the back room, the Hunan Palace has acquired both more elegance (ivory wallpaper and lavender upholstery) and a more knowledgeable audience. (The better menu is called the "Chinese menu," but it's in English as well.)

House specialties: Thin-sliced tripe in chile oil; kidneys and sour cabbage; eel with shrimp; combination seafood soup for two, only $5.95; scallops with fresh pepper (all from the special Taiwanese but bilingual menu—ask your waitress); Peking or home-style (salt-rubbed and grilled) duck; moist and unusually meaty pork pan-fried dumplings; scallops and shrimp with garlic and ginger sauce.

Other recommendations: Specials of the day, including fresh lobster with either Szechuan hot or Cantonese ginger/scallion sauce or steamed perch; kung pao chicken; vegetarian yellow birds (stuffed bean curd); crispy sesame beef.

Summary & comments: This makes a great place to bring both beginners and experienced diners, and familiar faces sometimes get little tidbits and surprise recommendations. Also ask for adjustments—plainer dishes such as yellow birds or moo shi pork can be made peppery on request. And remember that sauces are a little thick. A sign of the restaurant's stability is that many of the employees have been working here for ten years.

I Matti

Zone 6   Dupont Circle/
           Adams–Morgan
2436 18th Street, NW
(202) 462-8844

Italian	
★★★	
Moderate	
Quality 84	Value B

Reservations:	Suggested
When to go:	Any time
Entree range:	$8.75−18.95
Payment:	VISA, MC, AMEX, DC
Service rating:	★★★
Friendliness rating:	★★★½
Parking:	Valet, $5
Bar:	Full service
Wine selection:	Very good
Dress:	Casual
Disabled access:	Good
Customers:	Locals, business lunchers
Lunch:	Monday–Saturday, noon–3 P.M.
Dinner:	Monday–Thursday, 5:30–11 P.M.; Friday and Saturday, 5:30 P.M.–midnight; Sunday, 5–11 P.M.

Atmosphere/setting: A bright, welcoming, wood-and-plaster trattoria with a cutaway balcony upstairs, a smaller dining area near the partially exposed kitchen, and a friendly, crowded stone bar.

House specialties: The menu changes seasonally, but among its general successes are slow-cooked dishes such as osso buco and bollito misto; a mixed skewer of chicken, rabbit, sausages, pancetta, and vegetables; a rabbit cutlet topped with prosciutto and fontina; crêpes filled with braised duck and topped with a mustard "jam."

Other recommendations: Game specials such as quail roasted with slivers of garlic tucked under the skin; capellini dressed with fresh crabmeat and bits of fresh tomato; a benevolent rather than salty caponata made tangy by rings of calamari; grape leaves stuffed with cheese, wrapped in pancetta, and grilled.

Summary & comments: At this less formal sibling of Roberto Donna's Galileo restaurant, the food is often as good and only slightly less ornate. The only factor keeping it from a higher rating is lingering inconsistency—infrequent in the food, a little more frequent in the service. The homemade pastas have both heft and delicacy; even the pizzas and polentas here will revive your interest. I Matti hosts monthly wine dinners worth the Adams-Morgan crush.

i Ricchi

Italian
★★★
Expensive

Quality 84   Value B

Reservations:	Suggested
When to go:	Lunch (almost the same menu but a few dollars less) or early dinner
Entree range:	$10.50−29.95
Payment:	VISA, MC, AMEX
Service rating:	★★★★
Friendliness rating:	★★★★
Parking:	Street, garage, valet (dinner only)
Bar:	Full service
Wine selection:	Fine
Dress:	Dressy, business
Disabled access:	Good
Customers:	Business, local, tourist
Lunch:	Monday−Friday, 11:30 A.M.−2 P.M.
Dinner:	Monday−Saturday, 5:30−10 P.M.; Sunday, closed.

Atmosphere/setting: This stone and terra cotta−tile room evokes a villa courtyard with *Better Homes & Gardens* detailing—gilded magnolia branches draped in muslin, floral tiles, and heavy cloth. The wood-burning stove makes the whole restaurant smell like fresh bread.

House specialties: Brick-pressed grilled half-chicken; rolled florentine of pork and rabbit; pasta with hare; a miraculously light fritto misto; a mixed grill of sausage, quail, and veal; scottiaglia, a mixed platter of braised meats.

Other recommendations: The risotto of the day; grilled fresh fish; the warm salad of shrimp, cannellini, and green beans; the punning "ricchi e poveni," roasted goat chops; thick winter soups; Tuscan toast slathered with chicken livers.

Summary & comments: The oak-fired grill is the other fiery attraction, and the fresh breads and grilled meats and seafoods taste, with pure Tuscan assurance, of smoke and rosemary. (Like many of the finer restaurants in town, i Ricchi changes its menu seasonally and has moved beyond strictly regional fare, but the grill is always featured.) Despite its prime law-and-lobby location, i Ricchi is arguably the most affordable fancy Italian restaurant in town, although the competition is quickening. Incidentally, it's a rare tribute to someone's cooking when he can leave and people still take his name with pleasure: Founding chef and former co-owner Francesco Ricchi is now trying to rescue the Bice reputation.

Ichiban

<table>
<tr><td></td><td>Korean/Japanese</td></tr>
<tr><td>Zone 10B   Maryland suburbs</td><td>★★★</td></tr>
<tr><td>637 North Frederick Avenue,</td><td>Moderate</td></tr>
<tr><td>   Gaithersburg</td><td></td></tr>
<tr><td>(301) 670-0560</td><td>Quality 83   Value B</td></tr>
</table>

Reservations:	Recommended
When to go:	Any time
Entree range:	$9.95 − 20.95
Payment:	VISA, MC, AMEX, DC, D
Service rating:	★★★
Friendliness rating:	★★★
Parking:	Free lot
Bar:	Full service
Wine selection:	House
Dress:	Informal
Disabled access:	Good
Customers:	Local, ethnic
Open:	Every day, 11:30 A.M.− 10:30 P.M.

Atmosphere / setting: A pleasant, simple room with screened-off tatami (or banquet) rooms for special parties, a stone garden lantern at the entrance, a sushi bar with a few stools, and hoods and built-in gas grills in the booths.

House specialties: Grilled split squid that you barbecue yourself on a portable grill top; tripe casserole (for two); choice yook hwe bibimbap, the Korean steak tartare; negimayaki, marinated beef sliced thin and pin-rolled around scallions; sushi and sashimi; rice vermicelli with chopped beef and vegetables.

Summary & comments: Although Korean-Japanese restaurants competent at both cuisines aren't so rare anymore, Ichiban was one of the first. It also braved what was then the frontier of mid-county business traffic and managed to make bulgoki a household word in Germantown. Sushi order prices here are a touch higher than some, but the quality is usually very high and the sushi staff more knowledgeable than at some other non-Japanese bars. And as it has become more of a neighborhood fixture, it has become more self-assured: its spices more assertive and the staff more outgoing.

Il Pizzico

Zone 10B   Maryland suburbs
15209 Frederick Road/Route 355,
  Rockville
(301) 309-0610

Italian	
★★½	
Inexpensive	
Quality 77	Value A

Reservations:	Not accepted
When to go:	Before 7 or after 8:30
Entree range:	$8.95−13.95
Payment:	VISA, MC, AMEX
Service rating:	★★★
Friendliness rating:	★★★★
Parking:	Small lot
Bar:	Wine and beer
Wine selection:	Fair
Dress:	Informal, casual
Disabled access:	Good
Customers:	Locals
Lunch:	Monday−Friday, 11 A.M.−2:30 P.M.
Dinner:	Monday−Thursday, 5−9:30 P.M.;
	Friday and Saturday, 5−10 P.M.; Sunday, closed.

Atmosphere/setting: A strip-mall storefront with no pretense and a recently acquired set of linens—not "real" Italian, exactly, but even more hospitable—like a stage set or Italian family kitchen with humor. Check out the food-lovers' murals on the wall.

House specialties: Mushroom-stuffed ravioli with pistachio sauce; veal scaloppine with pine nuts, raisins, and red wine; penne with eggplant and mozzarella; thin spaghetti with strips of tomato and olive oil.

Other recommendations: Penne with sausage in a tomato-tinged ricotta sauce; bowtie pasta with mushrooms.

Summary & comments: "Il Pizzico" means "the pinch," and although this mom-and-pop shop has doubled in size, it's still a squeeze, and waiting customers usually hang out the door. But because service is so swift, you can be in and out in 30 minutes—or a pinch—and the atmosphere so congenial, nobody seems to mind. And even if the prices have crept up a couple of dollars, they are still almost unbelievably low. This really is dinner the way Mamma would have served it—three small slices of veal, lightly steamed zucchini, and a small wedge of polenta for $9.95—lovingly prepared and joyously informal.

Il Radicchio

<table>
<tr><td colspan="2">Italian</td></tr>
<tr><td colspan="2">★★½</td></tr>
<tr><td colspan="2">Inexpensive</td></tr>
<tr><td>Quality 79</td><td>Value A</td></tr>
</table>

Zone 6   Dupont Circle/
               Adams-Morgan
1509 17th Street, NW
(202) 986-2627

Zone 5   Georgetown
1211 Wisconsin Ave, NW
(202) 337-2627

Zone 11B   Virginia suburbs
1801 Clarendon Boulevard, Arlington
(703) 276-2627

Reservations:	Not accepted
When to go:	Early or late
Entree range:	$4.25 – 10
Payment:	VISA, MC, AMEX, DC
Service rating:	★★★
Friendliness rating:	★★★½
Parking:	Street
Bar:	Beer and wine (17th Street); full service (Wisconsin Ave.)
Wine selection:	Good
Dress:	Informal
Disabled access:	No
Customers:	Local, business, tourist
Lunch/Dinner:	Monday – Thursday, 11:30 A.M. – 11 P.M.; Friday and Saturday, 11:30 A.M. – midnight
Dinner:	Sunday, 5 – 10:30 P.M.

Atmosphere/setting: These restaurants are cheeky but relaxed; a town house-turned-cafe or a storefront gone freestyle, with murals of farm animals and whole forests of the eponymous chickory.

House specialties: Wood-fired pizzas; suckling pig on Wednesday and roast lamb on Thursday; a variety of carpaccios.

Other recommendations: Sandwiches on fresh focaccia, rotisserie chicken.

Summary & comments: This is a sort of gimmick spot, but an old dependable one—an all-you-can-eat spaghetti house with your choice of nearly two dozen sauces almost all for under $10, including seasonal favorites such as pesto, rabbit and other game stews, and primavera. Designer chef Roberto Donna of Galileo and I Matti runs these as, well, his off-the-rack line.

Il Ritrovo

Zone 10A   Maryland suburbs
4838 Rugby Avenue, Bethesda
(301) 986-1447

Mediterranean
★★★
Moderate

Quality 80   Value B

Reservations:	Helpful
When to go:	Any time
Entree range:	$7.95–17.95
Payment:	MC, VISA, AMEX, DC, D
Service rating:	★★★★
Friendliness rating:	★★★★
Parking:	Street, lot (free after 5:30 P.M.)
Bar:	Full service
Wine selection:	Limited
Dress:	Business, informal
Disabled access:	Good
Customers:	Locals
Lunch:	Monday–Friday, 11:30 A.M.–2:30 P.M.
Dinner:	Every day, 5:30–11 P.M.

Atmosphere/setting: Simple but attractive, with whitewashed brick, white linen, and a sort of schoolroom-sized mural map of the Mediterranean.

House specialties: Moroccan lamb scaloppine marinated with mint; paella and couscous offered with meat or seafood; potato gnocchi with spinach, fresh tomatoes, feta cheese, and black olives; and specials of grilled fresh fish. Daily specials have included duck-stuffed ravioli; Lebanese-style trout with tahini; bouillabaisse and even the classic escargot Escoffier in puff pastry.

Other recommendations: A heart-stoppingly rich risotto of four cheeses, including Gorgonzola; seafood brochette; vegetarian options including the risottos and pasta and a couscous with seven vegetables.

Summary & comments: "All menu items are just suggestions," the menu says, and you can certainly have it your own way, but you might never want to. The chef and owners between them have worked at a half-dozen well-liked area restaurants, mostly French and Italian, but this restaurant encompasses Greece, Spain, and North Africa as well. It even offers tasting each course with wines from different countries. And although it hasn't been so highly publicized as some places, it's developed a strong enough following that it's branched out into catering and broadened the menu a little more. In fact, the menu has been broadened almost into confusion: There are four fixed-price menus from $17.50 to $32 and a nightly raft of specials.

Inn at Glen Echo

Zone 10A Maryland suburbs	Modern American
6119 Tulane Avenue, Glen Echo	★★½
(301) 229-2280	Moderate
	Quality 75 Value B

Reservations:	Recommended
When to go:	Afternoons for a drink outside; Sunday brunch
Entree range:	$13−20
Payment:	VISA, MC, AMEX, DC
Service rating:	★★★
Friendliness rating:	★★★
Parking:	Free lot
Bar:	Full service
Wine selection:	Limited
Dress:	Informal
Disabled access:	Good
Customers:	Locals
Breakfast:	Saturday, 7:30−11:30 A.M.
Brunch:	Sunday, 11 A.M.−3 P.M.
Lunch:	Monday−Saturday, 11:30 A.M.−2:30 P.M.
Dinner:	Monday−Saturday, 6−10 P.M.;
	Sunday, 5:30−9:30 P.M.

Atmosphere/setting: An old rambler of a country home with comfy, un-fussy dining rooms. The balcony is a popular lunch spot during the summer and the bar area, where oldtimers and joggers off the nearby canal are tolerated, is filled with pictures of the park's heyday.

House specialties: Grilled swordfish with avocado and jalapeños; venison in season; orange-rubbed quail over couscous; chicken marinated in lime and te-quila; lamb chops with roasted jalapeños; new-era pizza in the bar.

Entertainment & amenities: Live jazz Sunday evening.

Summary & comments: The life and times of the Inn is a miniature of the so-cial history of the whole Glen Echo neighborhood. Originally a fine old home in the style of its neighbors, it had declined along with the amusement park next door and spent many years as a boisterous biker bar known for big cockroaches and killer chili. Nevertheless, having lived through a mercifully brief fern-bar adolescence, the Inn has become particularly popular during porch-sitting weather. Sunday brunch is an all-you-can-eat bonanza, mixing hot casseroles, omelets and waffles to order, smoked fish, and sweetbreads with a glass of champagne; $14.95 for adults and $7.95—no champagne—for kids.

162

The Inn at Little Washington

Zone 11B   Virginia suburbs
Middle and Main streets,
    Washington, VA
(540) 675-3800

Modern American
★★★★★
Expensive

Quality 98   Value B

Reservations:	Recommended
When to go:	Any time
Entree range:	Prix fixe: $78 during the week,
	Friday $98 and Saturday $108
Payment:	VISA, MC
Service rating:	★★★½
Friendliness rating:	★★½
Parking:	Free lot
Bar:	Full service
Wine selection:	Very good
Dress:	Dressy, informal
Disabled access:	Fair
Customers:	Local, tourist
Dinner:	Monday, Wednesday – Friday, 6 – 9:30 P.M.;
	Saturday, seatings at 5:30, 6, 9, and 9:30 P.M.;
	Sunday, 4 – 8:30 P.M.; Tuesday, closed.

Atmosphere/setting: An elegantly appointed but unfussy frame building with an enclosed garden (with many romantic seatings on the patio) and rich, hand-painted walls, velvet upholstery, and the clean glint of real crystal and silver in all directions.

House specialties: The menu changes continually, but look for dishes such as seafood and wild mushroom risotto; veal or lamb carpaccio; tenderloin of beef that reminds you why that's such a classic entree; home-smoked trout; sweetbreads with whole baby artichokes; baby lamb morsels with lamb sausage alongside. And although the dinner is purportedly four courses, here, as at several other top-flight restaurants, there are apt to be extras along the way.

Other recommendations: Soft-shell crabs however offered (usually respectfully simple); a signature appetizer of black-eyed peas and Smithfield ham topped with foie gras; that same ham, sliced thin as prosciutto, wrapped around fresh local figs; portobello mushroom pretending to be a filet mignon.

(continued)

Summary & comments: Like Roberto Donna, Yannick Cam, and Jean-Louis Palladin, chef Patrick O'Connell is a name to conjure within gourmet (and gourmand) circles all over the country. O'Connell's strength is a sense of balance: Dishes are never overwhelmed or overfussy; local produce is emphasized (which guarantees freshness); and a lot of fine ingredients are allowed to speak for themselves, which is sadly rare. Everyone remembers his or her first passion here—homemade white chocolate ice cream with bitter chocolate sauce—and for some Washingtonians, driving down to the other Washington becomes an addiction, a compulsion. It's the single biggest reason (besides horses, perhaps) for the boom in yuppie commuting to the hills. Incidentally, for fans of Cam, it was O'Connell who bought up the wine cellar when Le Pavillion went bankrupt; and one can almost not regret it.

Isabella

Mediterranean
★★★
Moderate

Quality 80   Value B

Reservations:	Recommended
When to go:	Any time
Entree range:	$13–21
Payment:	VISA, MC, AMEX
Service rating:	★★★
Friendliness rating:	★★★
Parking:	Valet ($3 after 5:30 P.M.), street
Bar:	Full service
Wine selection:	Good
Dress:	Business, casual
Disabled access:	Good
Customers:	Local, ethnic
Lunch:	Monday–Friday, 11:30 A.M.–3 P.M.
Dinner:	Monday–Saturday, 5:30–10 P.M.

Atmosphere/setting: A smart and fresh take on Spanish Mediterranean decor: leopard-like patina'd copper panels, carved wood, bits of iron, touches of deep marine blue (particularly the taverna-like heavy cobalt glassware); a richly appointed galleon of a room that rides the eye line back to the great curving wave of the chef's table. The mood is light, however; check out the funky videos and the world beat music.

House specialties: Seared lamb carpaccio with roasted eggplant; duck-stuffed rigatoni dressed with calamata olives, artichokes, and oven-dried tomatoes on a pool of broth; lamb tagine, the citrusy North African stew; grilled snapper on wilted Swiss chard.

Other recommendations: For unrepentant foie gras fanatics, a different tack with artichokes, potato, and tomato jam; tabbouleh-crusted lamb chops with mint and pomegranates; black bass with preserved lemons.

Summary & comments: This is the new home of prodigal popular chef Will Greenwood, long of the Jefferson Hotel and back near his old digs after a stint in Nashville. It may surprise some people that he's abandoned his old regional American style for this rich Moorish Mediterranean stew, but Greenwood has lightened his hand with sauces (check his personal profile for evidence) and here takes up the romance of 15th-century Spain—well, mood is mood—with a flourish.

Jaleo

Zone 3 Downtown	Nuevo Latino
480 7th Street, NW	★★★
(202) 628-7949	Moderate
	Quality 77 Value B

Reservations:	Limited
When to go:	Early evening
Entree range:	$9.75 – 14.95
Payment:	VISA, MC, AMEX, DC, D
Service rating:	★★★
Friendliness rating:	★★★
Parking:	Street, valet, $5 (after 5:30 P.M.)
Bar:	Full service
Wine selection:	Good
Dress:	Business, casual
Disabled access:	Good
Customers:	Local, tourist
Brunch:	Sunday, 11:30 A.M.–2:30 P.M.
Lunch/Dinner:	Sunday and Monday, 11:30 A.M.–10 P.M.;
	Tuesday–Thursday, 11:30 A.M.–11:30 P.M.;
	Friday and Saturday, 11:30 A.M.–midnight

Atmosphere/setting: A combination tapas bar, chic competition, and piazza, with bits of wrought iron, a lush suedelike grey decor, and a partial copy of the John Singer Sargent painting from which it takes its name.

House specialties: Tapas—bite-sized appetizers (four to a plate) meant to help wash down glasses of sangria and sherry and pass hours of conversation. Among the best: tuna carpaccio; grilled quail; spinach with apples; pine nuts and raisins; salmon with artichokes; eggplant flan with roasted peppers; serrano ham and tomatoes on focaccia. Daily specials, frequently of shrimp or shellfish, are extremely good bets.

Other recommendations: Sausage with white beans; grilled portobello mushrooms (getting to be a local staple); lightly fried calamari; paella.

Summary & comments: Jaleo has taken tapas, a late-blooming bar fad, and built an entire menu around them—there are five times as many tapas as whole entrees. And if you're with three or four people, you can just about taste everything in sight. (In fact, the first time, you may want to go extra slow: The plates look so small, and the palo cortada goes down so smoothly, that you can overstuff yourself without realizing it.) The bar does a heavy business, too, especially pre- and post-theater. It's already so trendy that if you really want to celeb-spot, go off rush hour; they're already ducking the crowds.

JEAN-MICHEL

Zone 10A   Maryland suburbs
10223 Old Georgetown Road
  (Wildwood Shopping Center),
  Bethesda
(301) 564-4910

French
★★½
Moderate

Quality 78   Value C

Reservations:	Recommended
When to go:	Any time
Entree range:	$12.95−21.75
Payment:	VISA, MC, AMEX, DC
Service rating:	★★★
Friendliness rating:	★★★½
Parking:	Free lot
Bar:	Full service
Wine selection:	Good
Dress:	Informal
Disabled access:	Fair
Customers:	Local, business
Lunch:	Monday−Friday, 11:30 A.M.−2:30 P.M.
Dinner:	Monday−Saturday, 5:30−10 P.M.;
	Sunday, 5:30−9 P.M.

Atmosphere/setting: Though rather small, and limited by its position in a strip shopping mall, this is nevertheless a pretty little room: light, decorated with restraint, and subtly divided by glass to lower the volume and make up for the lack of a foyer.

House specialties: Ravioli with wild mushrooms in a richly flavored but not rich sauce; or ravioli with spinach and duck sauce; classic country-French versions of veal scaloppine, lamb, and venison.

Other recommendations: Grilled rockfish or grilled tuna with black olive sauce; mussels; calf's liver; soft-shell crabs; lobster flamed with whiskey.

Summary & comments: Jean-Michel was the partner and host of what was once considered a good "continental French" restaurant downtown, but somehow this relaxed, comfy version with its simplified dishes seems to suit him—as well as '90s attitudes—better. There is little that's unfamiliar here, but that's part of what makes it easy to enjoy.

JiN-GA

Zone 5   Georgetown
1250 24th Street, NW
(202) 785-0720

Korean	
★★½	
Moderate	
Quality 79	Value B

Reservations:	Helpful
When to go:	Any time
Entree range:	$12 – 20
Payment:	MC, VISA, AMEX, DC, D
Service rating:	★★
Friendliness rating:	★★★
Parking:	Validated
Bar:	Full service
Wine selection:	House
Dress:	Business, informal
Disabled access:	Good
Customers:	Primarily Asian; mixed business crowd at lunch
Open:	Every day, 11:30 A.M. – 10:30 P.M.

Atmosphere / setting: Very sleek—mostly wood-panelled with a small stone garden outside and a few private tatami (straw mat) rooms: You might think of it as the gentlemen's club version of Seoul food.

House specialties: The marinated, cook-it-yourself (if you like) barbecues prepared on grill-top tables are the most visible options, and there are a dozen choices: short ribs, chicken, pork tenderloin, squid. However, the rice or noodle and broth casseroles, topped with a variety of seafood or meats, are what you see the older Koreans enjoying. Also look at the upscale appetizers for grazing on a fine international scale. And if you like the family of dip-into dishes called "hot pots," this is a great place for the Japanese version called shabu shabu in meat, veggie, or seafood versions (all served for two).

Other recommendations: Although Korean restaurants back home tend to specialize in one sort of food—barbecue, casseroles, noodles, sushi, even the rarer (in the United States) vegetarian cuisine—here you can wander happily through the whole countryside. If you really want to wow 'em, or have a business dinner with top Asian or gourmet clients, give the restaurant 24 hours' notice and they'll make up one of three elaborate and fascinating multicourse menus at $30, $40, or $60 a head.

Summary & comments: This is the first downtown Korean restaurant (other than a lunch carryout), and it's a first-class branch of a prosperous Asian chain, but its ambitions haven't been matched by its clientele, so the kitchen has scaled back a little.

Kabob Bazaar

Zone 11B   Virginia suburbs
3133 Wilson Boulevard, Arlington
(703) 522-8999

Persian	
★★½	
Inexpensive	
Quality 79	Value B

Reservations:	Recommended
When to go:	Any time
Entree range:	$5.95 – 11.45
Payment:	VISA, MC
Service rating:	★★½
Friendliness rating:	★★★
Parking:	Street
Bar:	Beer and wine
Wine selection:	House
Dress:	Casual
Disabled access:	Good
Customers:	Local, ethnic
Open:	Monday – Saturday, 11 A.M.–10 P.M.;
	Sunday, 11:30 A.M.–9 P.M.

Atmosphere/setting: Just a carryout with a handful of tables along Clarendon's diner row, but so fragrant from its grilling kebabs that you can practically see people floating down the street on the scent the way they do in cartoons. In fact, even the local food mavens rave about this place.

House specialties: A barg kebab made with New York strip instead of the usual filet, which means it's much more flavorful than the run-of-the-mill kebabery (or the slightly lighter-flavored top sirloin chenjeh); lamb, either by itself or combined, as most Americans expect it, with green peppers, mushrooms, tomato, and onion; a whole skinless Cornish hen; the Persian original of the Green rotisserie chicken (available in whole, half, or quarter); assorted combinations thereof.

Other recommendations: The fried chopped fava bean/sesame seed/herb patties called falafel or a Middle Eastern combination plate with falafel, tabouli salad, and hummus; seafood or fish kebab of the day. If the usual Persian delight, baklava, is too syrupy for you, try the rosewater and pistachio nut ice cream.

Summary & comments: Like the Hautum Kabob in Rockville, Kabob Bazaar knows what it does well and sticks by it. Note that the prices above, bargains as they are, are for the kebabs served with rice; if you prefer them with the equally traditional flatbread, prices are even lower. Check for daily specials, too.

Kashmir Palace

Zone 10B   Maryland suburbs
855-A Rockville Pike (Wintergreen
    Plaza shopping center), Rockville
(301) 251-1152

	Indian
	★★½
	Inexpensive
Quality 79	Value B

Reservations:	Accepted
When to go:	Sunday dinner
Entree range:	$7.25−11.95
Payment:	VISA, MC, AMEX
Service rating:	★★★
Friendliness rating:	★★★½
Parking:	Free lot
Bar:	Full service
Wine selection:	House
Dress:	Informal, casual
Disabled access:	Good
Customers:	Local, ethnic, business lunch
Brunch:	Sunday, noon−3 P.M.
Lunch:	Monday−Friday, 11:30 A.M.−2:30 P.M.
Lunch/Dinner:	Saturday, noon−10:30 P.M.
Dinner:	Monday−Friday, 5:30−10:30 P.M.;
	Sunday, 5:30−9:30 P.M.

Atmosphere/setting: Newly lightened and brightened, with ruby-red brocade linens and a view of the tandoor oven through a glass divider.

House specialties: Lamb kebab to restore your faith, broiled in the tandoor oven rather than grilled; jumbo shrimp in a spicy vindaloo sauce; marinated fish fillets either broiled or lightly fried and tossed with curry; melting roasted eggplant.

Other recommendations: Onion kulcha, a spicy onion-stuffed bread; vegetable biryani; samosas stuffed with eggplant as well as the usual meat or veggie versions; a tandoori sampler of lamb, chicken, shrimp, and ground beef.

Summary & comments: Once part of a local mini-chain of tandoori kitchens, the Wintergreen branch quickly became the best and, with the corporate collapse, kept its chef and staff and acquired, as they say, independent ownership. Little touches mean a lot here; the lemon pickle is among the best in town. The rice is too, so biryani fans will be especially happy here. Like many Indian restaurants, it offers a lunchtime all-you-can-eat buffet weekdays ($5.95) and an especially good one Sunday ($7.95 brunch, $8.45 dinner).

KAZAN

Zone 11A   Virginia suburbs
6813 Redmond Drive, McLean
(703) 734-1960

Turkish	
★★½	
Inexpensive	
Quality 79	Value B

Reservations:	Helpful on weekends
When to go:	Any time
Entree range:	$11.95 − 19.95
Payment:	VISA, MC, AMEX, DC
Service rating:	★★
Friendliness rating:	★★★
Parking:	Free lot
Bar:	Full service
Wine selection:	House
Dress:	Casual
Disabled access:	Good
Customers:	Local, ethnic
Lunch:	Monday − Friday, 11 A.M. − 3 P.M.
Dinner:	Monday − Thursday, 5 − 10 P.M.;
	Friday and Saturday, 5 − 11 P.M.; Sunday, closed.

Atmosphere/setting: Once inside the redwood exterior and away from the supermarket parking lot, you'll find a little Casbah of a restaurant: smoky-patterned blue tiles, tent-shaped cutaway beams, and glints of brass.

House specialties: The layered, rotisserie-grilled, and sliced meat pinwheel called donner kebab, available Wednesday, Friday, and Saturday; paticanli kuzu, sliced lamb grilled and topped with eggplant and yogurt; lamb moussaka and the usual variety of kebabs. Unusually, any dish can be ordered extra spicy.

Other recommendations: Pilic shish kebab, marinated chicken sautéed with a little tomato and butter and served over toasted pita pieces; manti, pasta stuffed with lamb and topped with garlic (much like the Afghani aushak).

Summary & comments: It's a little surprising to see the "continental entrees" list with its tournedos and veal piccata, but in McLean, after all, a certain number of die-hard traditionalists can be expected among the clientele.

Kinkead's

Modern American
★★★★
Moderate

Quality 91   Value C

Zone 4   Foggy Bottom
2000 Pennsylvania Avenue, NW
(202) 296-7700

Reservations:	Recommended; required for upstairs dining
When to go:	Any time
Entree range:	$16−24
Payment:	VISA, MC, AMEX, DC, D
Service rating:	★★★
Friendliness rating:	★★★
Parking:	Valet at dinner; pay lots, meters
Bar:	Full service
Wine selection:	Good
Dress:	Business, informal
Disabled access:	Good
Customers:	Business, local
Brunch:	Sunday, 11:30 A.M.−2:30 P.M.
Lunch:	Monday−Saturday, 11:30 A.M.−2:30 P.M.
Dinner:	Daily, 5:30−10:30 P.M.

Atmosphere/setting: Pleasantly restrained, ranging over two floors and divided into a series of elevated or glass-enclosed areas. The kitchen staff is visible upstairs, as is commonplace these days; it's a little less common to see chef-owner Robert Kinkead, on the consumer side of the glass wall, barking at his cooks via headset like a football coach talking to the booth.

House specialties: A melting char-grilled squid over polenta with tomato confit (appetizer); delicate grilled skate with a veal reduction; rockfish with artichokes; seared tuna with portobellos and flageolets; lobster specials; crispy-fried red snapper with Chinese black bean sauce; hearty seafood chowder.

Other recommendations: Grilled squid, shrimp, and crab pupusa with pickled cabbage; Ipswich-style fried soft-shell clams and crab and lobster cakes (appetizers); lamb shanks with braised leg of lamb and white beans; sautéed cod cheeks; Sicilian swordfish with fennel, olives, currants, and arugula.

Entertainment & amenities: Live jazz weeknights.

Summary & comments: Kinkead's style is simple and straightforward but not shrinking; his sauces are balanced but assured, designed to highlight the food, not the frills. Any available seafood can be ordered broiled or grilled, but "simply grilled" here is almost an oxymoron. And Kinkead, whose first fame came from his Nantucket restaurant, has installed a little home-away-from-home downstairs by way of a raw bar. For those who count Mobil stars, Kinkead's has four.

172

L'Auberge Chez François

Zone 11A   Virginia suburbs
332 Springvale Road, Great Falls
(703) 759-3800

Reservations:	Required 4 weeks in advance
When to go:	Summer evenings in good weather for the terrace
Entree range:	$30—39
Payment:	VISA, MC, AMEX, DC
Service rating:	★★★★
Friendliness rating:	★★★★
Parking:	Free lot
Bar:	Full service
Wine selection:	Very good
Dress:	Dressy, business (jacket required for men at night)
Disabled access:	Very good
Customers:	Locals
Dinner:	Tuesday — Saturday, 5:30 — 9:30 P.M.;
	Sunday, 1:30 — 8 P.M.

Atmosphere/setting: One of the most beloved and romantic dining sites in the area, a real country inn with exposed beams, a mix of views of Alsace (home of pater familias/executive chef Jacques Haeringer), only-a-family-could-love drawings, and a travel-brochure veranda. It's so widely known as an engagement and anniversary mecca that *Regrets Only*, Sally Quinn's semi — roman à clef about journalistic and political circles, included a rather improbable but dramatic tryst in the parking lot (in an MG with a stick shift, no less).

House specialties: Classics such as rack of lamb ($36.50 for one, $72 for two), Châteaubriand for two ($73), and duck foie gras either sautéed with apples or "plain"; the true choucroute royal garni, with Alsatian sauerkraut, sausages, smoked pork, duck, pheasant, and quail; game in season, such as medallions of venison and roast duck; veal kidneys in a rich, mustardy sauce; sweetbreads with wild mushrooms in puff pastry; roasted boneless duck breast paired with the stuffed leg and fruit-dotted rice; seafood fricassee with shrimp, scallops, lobster, rockfish, and salmon in Riesling.

Other recommendations: Various seafood and game pâtés; red snapper braised in beer; boneless rabbit stuffed with leeks and fennel; soft-shell crabs with extra crabmeat stuffed into the body; big scallops in a bright (but not overwhelming) tomato — bell pepper sauce.

(continued)

173

L'Auberge Chez François (continued)

Summary & comments: Although theoretically L'Auberge falls into the "expensive" range, it ought to be called "moderate" to give a fair comparison. What look like entrees on the menu are really whole dinners, and with salads, fancy appetizers, and dessert—not to mention bread and cheese and a bit of sorbet—this is a lot of food. Although the two-to-four weeks' notice rule still applies, competition has increased, along with cancellations: It may be worth a flyer to call in the late afternoon, especially during the week. You can't make reservations for the outdoor terrace, incidentally; just call to make sure it's open (about May through September) and then show up.

L'Auberge Provençal

	French (Provençal)
Zone 11A Virginia suburbs	★★★★★
Route 340, White Post	Expensive
(540) 837-1375	
	Quality 96 Value A

Reservations: Helpful
When to go: Any time
Entree range: Prix fixe dinner, $57
Payment: VISA, MC, AMEX, D, DC
Service rating: ★★★½
Friendliness rating: ★★★★
Parking: Free lot
Bar: Full service
Wine selection: Good
Dress: Jacket and tie required
Disabled access: Good
Customers: Local, Washington food trendies
Dinner: Wednesday – Saturday, 6 – 10:30 P.M.;
                 Sunday, 5 – 9 P.M.; Monday and Tuesday, closed.

Atmosphere / setting: A pretty mid-18th-century fieldstone farmhouse with three smallish and somewhat formal dining rooms furnished in warm "country" antiques (the interior woodwork, incidentally, was crafted by Hessian soldiers during the Revolutionary War), becomingly expanded by wings that resemble small village fronts and surrounded by herb and vegetable gardens and orchards.

House specialties: Dinner is a five-course prix fixe (really four plus a sorbet refresher before the entree) with six or eight choices per course. A fourth-generation chef (his grandfather's place in Avignon had two Michelin stars), Borel's cooking is truly Provençal, but not as heavy as some amateur imitations of that trendy cuisine. Thick roast grouper is stacked atop slices of tomato, zucchini, and eggplant, with a garlic cream poured on the plate, not the fish; and a "salade d'été niçoise" (summer Niçoise salad) was almost a textbook example of Provençal ingredients handled imaginatively: edible flowers, two tiny Brussels sprouts, matchstick-thin green beans, a slice of bulb fennel, tomatoes, fresh goat cheese, a pearl onion, just a morsel of lightly smoked fresh tuna, and a glory of chopped garlic. The menu changes daily, but indicative dishes include pasta with smoked rabbit and morels; sautéed foie gras with fresh mango; sweetbreads in a variety of presentations; Moroccan-spiced salmon; roast pheasant with rosemary and vanilla; lamb medallions with country ham.

(continued)

Other recommendations: Sliced loin of veal stuffed with an olive tapenade; house-smoked rabbit with a mustard cream and whole morel caps, topped with crisped julienned leeks; fresh salmon wrapped in leeks with tomatoes and egg-plant. Breakfast (included in the overnight cost) might be a poached pear, stuffed with currants and pecans and wrapped in homemade puff pastry; followed by muscovy duck breast and shiitakes with demi-glace and a baked slice of tomato topped with a poached egg and African basil; plus scones, croissants, fresh jam, etc.

Entertainment and amenities: The whole complex is decorated with whim-sical carved animals (a three-foot kangaroo [with joey] whose stomach swings open, lots of carousel horses, and rockers), painted straw herons and roosters, and a wealth of imported hand-painted tiles and flatware, all for sale.

Summary & comments: If Patrick O'Connell is the Jean-Louis Palladin of Virginia, then Alain Borel is the Yannick Cam, serving up traditional sun-culture Provençal flavors in the lighter '90s style. The mystery is how so few Washingto-nians—Washingtonians eager to drive an hour or so and spend $98 a head (and $250 a bed) at the Inn at Little Washington—have figured out they could spend $55 (and $150) for a four-star dinner here. And have the breakfast, a superlative version served in the octagonal "peach room," thrown in for free.

La Bergerie

Zone 11C   Virginia suburbs
218 North Lee Street, Alexandria
(703) 683-1007

French
★★★
Moderate

Quality 84   Value C

Reservations:	Recommended
When to go:	Any time
Entree range:	$15.75−24.95
Payment:	VISA, MC, AMEX, DC, D
Service rating:	★★★
Friendliness rating:	★★★
Parking:	Street
Bar:	Full service
Wine selection:	Good
Dress:	Business, informal
Disabled access:	Good (via Thompson Alley)
Customers:	Local, business
Lunch:	Monday−Saturday, 11:30 A.M.−2:30 P.M.
Dinner:	Monday−Thursday, 6−10:30 P.M.;
	Friday and Saturday, 6−11 P.M.; Sunday, closed.

Atmosphere/setting: An "Umbrellas of Cherbourg" dining room with elegant blue and gold wallpaper, some exposed brick, classic chandeliers and banquettes, and booth seating.

House specialties: The nightly specials are always a good bet, but regular dishes include pork tenderloin with lentils "in the Basque style" (a rich confit); salmon braised in Virginia chardonnay; rainbow trout with lobster-crab sauce; roast duck with lingonberries.

Other recommendations: Chicken in a Shenandoah apple glaze (sort of a northern Virginia pun on normande-style); swordfish over pasta with a simple tomato-basil dressing; duck legs and thighs in confit; and pork in confit as well.

Summary & comments: This Basque family kitchen (of the brothers Campagne) has happily adapted the home-grown style of the French plateau to its new region, using local produce (and wine) to ensure freshness and emphasize the soul of a cuisine—honesty. Dishes sound quite rich, incidentally, but are balanced and self-assured rather than showy. La Bergerie is on the second floor, so wheelchair users should turn into the alley alongside and enter the lobby, where there is an elevator.

La Cantinita's Havana Cafe

	Cuban
	★★
Zone 11B Virginia suburbs	Inexpensive
3100 Clarendon Boulevard, Arlington	Quality 73 Value B
(703) 524-3611	

Reservations:	Not accepted
When to go:	Sunday afternoon if you like the scene
Entree range:	$6−12
Payment:	VISA, MC
Service rating:	★★½
Friendliness rating:	★★★★
Parking:	Street, lot
Bar:	Full service
Wine selection:	Limited
Dress:	Informal
Disabled access:	Good
Customers:	Ethnic, local, business after-hours
Lunch/Dinner:	Monday−Friday, 11 A.M.−11 P.M.
Dinner:	Saturday and Sunday, 4−11 P.M.

Atmosphere/setting: A bright two-winged restaurant evocative of both cool adobe and hot tropical nights, far more sophisticated than the old mom-and-pop location down the street (and without the Spanish-language TV in the background), but just as hospitable.

House specialties: Puerco asado, a pork roast slit and stuffed with a garlic/citrus paste, then slow-roasted and served in reduced drippings; ropa vieja, the shredded beef cooked in winey tomato broth (and called, perhaps because of the shredding, "old clothes"); traditional Valencia-style paella (for two only); and bistec empanizado, a cross between chicken-fried steak and veal piccata (breaded and fried but served with lemon instead of flour gravy).

Other recommendations: A chicken "fricassee" that is more au vin than the creamy-gravy version usually passed off under that name; a block-that-artery, no-excuse-but-the-flavor appetizer of sliced chorizo covered with melted cheese; shrimp sautéed with tomatoes and lemon; a tangy mixed seafood stew with vinegar, a very traditional Spanish treatment.

Summary & comments: Just alongside the Clarendon Metro stop, La Cantinitas is a real mom-and-pop establishment (the hostess is their daughter) that has adapted handily to the yuppification of the neighborhood by becoming one of the mainstays of happy hours and of community events, such as the annual chili tastings.

La Chaumière

<table>
<tr><td></td><td>French</td></tr>
<tr><td>Zone 5   Georgetown</td><td>★★★</td></tr>
<tr><td>2813 M Street, NW</td><td>Moderate</td></tr>
<tr><td>(202) 338-1784</td><td>Quality 81   Value C</td></tr>
</table>

Reservations:	Recommended
When to go:	Any time
Entree range:	$13.75 – 23.95
Payment:	VISA, MC, AMEX, CB, DC
Service rating:	★★★
Friendliness rating:	★★★
Parking:	Two-hour parking at Four Seasons Hotel (dinner), street
Bar:	Full service
Wine selection:	Good
Dress:	Business, informal
Disabled access:	Good
Customers:	Local, embassy, business
Lunch:	Monday – Friday, 11:30 A.M. – 2:30 P.M.
Dinner:	Monday – Saturday, 5:30 – 10:30 P.M.; Sunday, closed.

Atmosphere/setting: After 20 years in the often tumultuous Georgetown culinary competition, the cooking in this big-beamed, in-town country inn, with its freestanding fireplace in the center and old iron tools on the wall, remains solid. And what goes around comes around: Bistro fare of owner Gerard Pain's sort is suddenly booming around him.

House specialties: Oysters; seasonal specials of venison (as uptown as medallions with chestnut puree or as down-home as pot pie), rabbit, or choucroute; seafood crêpes; bouillabaisse; traditional tripe à la mode in Calvados. Here, as at the Bistro Français across the street, the daily specials are even more amazing: terrine of duck foie gras or fresh foie gras with cassis; ostrich loin wrapped in bacon; hearty choucroute with Riesling; seared sea bass with portobello-turnip risotto.

Other recommendations: Calf's liver or brains; quenelles of pike in lobster.

Summary & comments: Part of La Chaumière's charm is its weekly treats: Wednesday it's couscous and Thursday, cassoulet. This is family-style food, and most of its regulars are treated like family. Actually, "regulars" is a key word here; La Chaumière hearkens back to the time when Georgetown was more neighborhood than shopping mall, and a lot of its customers feel as if they graduated into adult dinner-dating here. The fireplace is one of the area's hottest (sorry) soulful-gazing areas.

La Colline

	French
Zone 2 Capitol Hill	★★★
400 North Capitol Street, NW	Moderate
(202) 737-0400	Quality 84 Value A

Reservations:	Recommended
When to go:	Any time
Entree range:	$14.50 – 19.75
Payment:	VISA, MC, AMEX, CB, DC
Service rating:	★★★★
Friendliness rating:	★★★★
Parking:	Garage, validation after 5
Bar:	Full service
Wine selection:	Good
Dress:	Casual, elegant
Disabled access:	Good
Customers:	Business, local, tourist
Breakfast:	Monday – Friday, 7 – 10 A.M.
Lunch:	Monday – Friday, 11:30 A.M. – 3 P.M.
Dinner:	Monday – Saturday, 6 – 10 P.M.;
	Sunday and holidays, closed.

Atmosphere/setting: An unfussy, conference-style reception room at one side is the only concession to the office-building shoebox exterior; the main dining room is large, two-tiered, and made less "executive" with nostalgic paintings, a mix of booths and tables, and French country-kitchen cupboards.

House specialties: Foie gras and homemade pâté; lobster and shellfish fricassee; sweetbreads with wild mushrooms; tripe; cool lobster salad; stuffed quail; venison tournedos.

Other recommendations: Roasted monkfish; crab cakes; appetizers of smoked duck breast, wild mushroom ravioli, or spicy lamb-stuffed pastries.

Summary & comments: La Colline manages to serve old-homey French food in such quantity (and with such hospitable style) that you'd expect the quality to fall off, but somehow it never does. The quantity of business of this Senate-side favorite also keeps the prices steady. Presentation is simple and untrendy, but exact: salmon or swordfish steaks on beds of vermouth-flavored sauce, sweetbreads bull's-eyed over concentric circles of bordelaise and herb wine deglaze. Game dishes and rowdy, hearty stews, along with the organ meats most Americans are still only discovering, are always good bets.

La Côte d'Or Cafe

French (Provençal)
★★½
Expensive

Zone 11B   Virginia suburbs
6876 Lee Highway, Arlington
(703) 538-3033

Quality 78   Value C

Reservations:	Suggested
When to go:	Any time
Entree range:	$18.95−24.50
Payment:	VISA, MC, AMEX
Service rating:	★★★
Friendliness rating:	★★½
Parking:	Street, lot
Bar:	Full service
Wine selection:	Good
Dress:	Business, informal
Disabled access:	Good
Customers:	Local, business
Lunch:	Monday−Saturday, 11:30 A.M.−3 P.M.
Dinner:	Monday−Saturday, 5:30−11:30 P.M.; Sunday, 5:30−9 P.M.

Atmosphere/setting: Although seeming rather out of place at first glance —a stone's throw from I-66 and associated with a motel—this is a very pretty, two-room French town house with armchairs, attractive but not overly formal silver and porcelain, and lots of flowers and windows. There's even a small deck for warm-weather dining, although the view is a little . . . urban.

House specialties: Wild mushrooms with delicate duck "ham" (appetizer); grilled tuna with basil and tomato; rabbit stew with mustard sauce over pasta; entrecôte with bleu cheese sauce; loin of lamb; monkfish with mustard sauce.

Other recommendations: Bouillabaisse with lobster and powerful aïoli; steamed mussels; scallop and shrimp soup; calamari with salmon mousse.

Summary & comments: This menu is part traditional country French, part southern French, and occasionally old-fashion "continental," but all hearty and aromatic comfort food. Sometimes the seasoning can seem overpowering (especially if you've been gradually accustomed to "new" Americanized versions of continental food), but many people will find that one of its virtues. The message is sometimes mixed, however: Suburbanizing seems to have increased the staff's desire to seem uptown, so they can be patronizing in the way that used to give continental dining a bad name. A little more consistency from the kitchen, too, would bring in another star.

181

La Ferme

	French
Zone 10A Maryland suburbs	★★½
7101 Brookville Road, Chevy Chase	Moderate
(301) 986-5255	
	Quality 78 Value B

Reservations:	Recommended
When to go:	Weeknights
Entree range:	$15.50−22.50
Payment:	VISA, MC, AMEX, DC, D
Service rating:	★★★½
Friendliness rating:	★★★
Parking:	Free lot
Bar:	Full service
Wine selection:	Good
Dress:	Dressy, casual elegant
Disabled access:	Good
Customers:	Locals
Lunch:	Tuesday−Friday, noon−2 P.M.
Dinner:	Tuesday−Saturday, 6−10 P.M.;
	Sunday, 5−9 P.M.; Monday, closed.

Atmosphere/setting: An almost perfect stage set of a country inn, with great arts-and-crafts lighting fixtures, a sufficiency of flowery wallpaper, and nicely varied groupings of tables, plus an outdoor dining terrace. (An "inn" joke: There are two "balcony tables" overlooking the village.)

House specialties: Sweetbreads en croûte (and sometimes scallops); braised duck with hard cider and caramelized turnips; medallions of venison; a seafood "fricassee" that is really an array of perfectly prepared scallops, shrimp, and half a lobster in a lobster reduction sauce; a tuna tartare appetizer with a mound of hand-chopped tuna, topped with flower-petal slices; filet of lamb.

Other recommendations: Grilled swordfish over lentils with red wine and peppercorns; pepper-crusted tuna; seafood sausage and lobster ravioli appetizers.

Entertainment & amenities: Live piano music on weekends.

Summary & comments: La Ferme has long been a sort of French country inn for those just inside the (prosperous part) of the Beltway. It's also extremely popular among older couples and lunching ladies. But its recent renovation reflects a spruced-up attitude toward sauces, and perhaps, its somewhat younger, more health-conscious customers. Not that the menu changes much—the kitchen knows exactly on which side that bread is buttered—but it has been polished. Almost everyone offers a thick veal chop these days, but this one has a wake-up dose of Calvados and mushrooms that gives it almost as much character as venison.

La Fourchette

	French
Zone 6 Dupont Circle/	★★
Adams-Morgan	Inexpensive
2429 18th Street, NW	
(202) 332-3077	Quality 74 Value B

Reservations:	Helpful
When to go:	Early dinner
Entree range:	$9.50−21.95
Payment:	VISA, MC, AMEX, CB, DC
Service rating:	★★½
Friendliness rating:	★★★
Parking:	Street, lot
Bar:	Full service
Wine selection:	Good
Dress:	Informal, business
Disabled access:	No
Customers:	Locals, students
Lunch/Dinner:	Monday−Thursday, 11:30 A.M.−10:30 P.M.;
	Friday, 11:30 A.M.−11 P.M.
Dinner:	Saturday, 4−11 P.M.; Sunday, 4−10 P.M.

Atmosphere/setting: This is a cookie-cutter 18th Street rowhouse, only on La Fourchette, it's a perfect fit: worn wood floors, exposed brick, elbow-to-elbow dining, florid murals on the walls, smoky hints of the kitchen, and a terrific din of satisfied chatter.

House specialties: One almost thinks La Fourchette's owners are secret romantics; between the murals and the menu, it almost begs for comparison with a gay-Paree magazine photo from the '30s. Sweetbreads, wine-stewed shanks, stuffed and rolled veal breast, mussels, and smoked salmon are old dependables here; on a good night, the bouillabaisse is the best in town, and not completely overwhelmed by garlic.

Other recommendations: Fresh fish, grilled or sometimes baked; shrimp salads tossed with vinaigrette; sometimes even the no-longer PC (and consequently, rarely accomplished) pan-sautéed steak.

Entertainment & amenities: A three-course "early-bird" dinner (4−7 P.M.) for $12.95.

Summary & comments: Most of Washington's better traditional bistros, like La Chaumiere and Le Gaulois, have regulars who are either late-thirty-something or natives; the number of twenty-somethings and students who are becoming regulars at La Fourchette is a nice bit of testimony to its care as well as classic outlook.

La Miche

	French
Zone 10A Maryland suburbs	★★★
7905 Norfolk Avenue, Bethesda	Inexpensive
(301) 986-0707	Quality 83 Value B

Reservations:	Recommended
When to go:	Any time
Entree range:	$14.95 – 23.95
Payment:	VISA, MC, AMEX, DC
Service rating:	★★★
Friendliness rating:	★★★
Parking:	Valet, street meters
Bar:	Full service
Wine selection:	Good
Dress:	Business, informal
Disabled access:	Good
Customers:	Local, business
Lunch:	Tuesday – Friday, 11:30 A.M. – 2 P.M.
Dinner:	Monday – Saturday, 6 – 9:45 P.M.;
	Sunday, 5:30 – 8:30 P.M.

Atmosphere/setting: The tone is somewhere between an old French inn and an upscale bistro, with white lace curtains, gleaming wood, flowers, and soft, well-laundered linens.

House specialties: Sweetbreads; braised rabbit with wild mushrooms; duck confit with mushroom fricassee or grilled duck or almost any duck presentation here; rack of lamb; tournedos rubbed in cracked black pepper and deglazed with brandy.

Other recommendations: Baked fish stuffed with crabmeat; scallop and shrimp dishes.

Summary & comments: La Miche was a magnet in Bethesda long before the restaurant boom of the '90s, and it's one of those places where food fashions count less than dependable, comfortable (though still fairly rich) fare. The dishes are classically "provincial" in the best, as-you-like-it fashion: duck liver and foie gras, cassoulet, snails, medallions of venison, etc., in a variety of presentations. If you're looking for light-minded treatments, you can find them here, but frankly, that's not the kitchen's forte.

LA PROVENCE

Zone 11A   Virginia suburbs
144 West Maple Avenue, Vienna
(703) 242-3777

French (Provençal)
★★★½
Inexpensive

Quality 85   Value B

Reservations:	Recommended
When to go:	Any time
Entree range:	$15.95 – 21.95
Payment:	VISA, MC, AMEX, D, DC
Service rating:	★★★
Friendliness rating:	★★★
Parking:	Free lot
Bar:	Full service
Wine selection:	Good
Dress:	Informal
Disabled access:	Good
Customers:	Local, ethnic
Lunch:	Monday – Saturday, 11:30 A.M. – 2:30 P.M.
Dinner:	Monday – Saturday, 5:30 – 10 P.M.

Atmosphere / setting: A surprisingly evocative little place, done up in sea-side blues and sunny yellows representing the "sun cuisine" of its Provençal fare. The intriguingly offsetting touches, such as the minimal and vaguely Asian flower arrangements (which are also practical, as they don't interfere with your vision) are a subtle reminder of the chef's Franco-Lao mindset.

House specialties: Grilled tuna (or other fish of the day) with fresh tomatoes, anchovies, and garlic; breast of duck on a mint-flavored mousse; monkfish in a caramelized apple cider sauce with fennel; saddle of rabbit in anise; bourride, a close cousin to bouillabaisse, as well as the Pernod-flavored real thing; or a homey pot-roasted Cornish hen.

Other recommendations: A variety of appetizers intriguing enough to make a grazing meal: calamari stuffed with herbs, duck pâté studded with pistachios, codfish mousse; roasted vegetables on semolina (like a mini-couscous) and the roasted eggplant "cake" with Roquefort cheese, pine nuts, capers, and sweet pepper.

Summary & comments: Keo Koumtakoun, former chef at Lavandou and, until recently, chef-owner of Le Paradis, is entirely at home with the flavors of Provence (as is his French wife): basil, olives, garlic, anchovies, saffron, and fennel. But his Asian background serves even this rich style well by keeping things from being over-rich; the mint mousse, for instance, will make you blink with simple pleasure and surprise. The recipes here seem even more assured, more personalized, than at Le Paradis. This is one of the area's greatest (as yet) undiscovered pleasures.

Lafayette

	Modern American
Zone 3 Downtown	★ ★ ★
16th and H streets, NW	Moderate
(Hay-Adams Hotel)	
(202) 638-2570	Quality 84 Value B

Reservations:	Recommended
When to go:	Pretheater, lunch
Entree range:	$14.50 – 29.75
Payment:	VISA, MC, AMEX, DC, CB, D
Service rating:	★ ★ ★
Friendliness rating:	★ ★ ½
Parking:	Valet
Bar:	Full service
Wine selection:	Good
Dress:	Business, informal
Disabled access:	No
Customers:	Business, local, tourist
Breakfast:	Monday – Friday, 6:30 – 11:30 A.M.
Brunch:	Saturday and Sunday, 11:30 A.M.– 2 P.M.
Lunch:	Monday – Friday, 11:30 A.M.– 2 P.M.
Dinner:	Every day, 6 – 10 P.M.

Atmosphere/setting: A pretty room, almost formal but given a lighter, "parlor-ish" warmth by a mix of armchairs and highbacks, florals, abundant flowers, and light, sunny, yellow walls. The arched windows look across Lafayette Park to the White House (the view Lincoln's secretary John Hay and his good friend Henry Adams had when their houses occupied this spot).

House specialties: Moroccan-barbecued salmon or grilled lacquered swordfish; sautéed veal medallions with a Parmesan soufflé and artichoke puree; roasted lobster over polenta; duck terrine paired with smoked duck. There are hearthealthy options to satisfy the most reluctant, such as sesame-and-ginger-crusted tuna; steamed lobster over couscous; or tomato linguine with grilled chicken.

Entertainment & amenities: Piano music, mostly pops, during dinner.

Summary & comments: Although chef Martin Saylor had big shoes to fill when Patrick Clark moved to New York's Tavern on the Green, his lightened-up classic cuisine fills the bill: One night's pretheater prix fixe (three courses for $30 or with two glasses of wine for $40) began with a seafood risotto that included four huge shrimp, four scallops, and four mussels, moved on to a hearty strip of salmon over couscous, and ended with a frieze of three sherbets and fresh fruit— about twice the amount of food anyone could eat.

Lauriol Plaza

Spanish/Mexican
★★
Moderate

Quality 72   Value B

Zone 6   Dupont Circle/
                 Adams–Morgan
1801 18th Street, NW
(202) 387-0035

Reservations:	Weekends only before 7 P.M.
When to go:	Any time
Entree range:	$5.95 − 15.95
Payment:	VISA, MC, AMEX, DC, D
Service rating:	★★½
Friendliness rating:	★★★
Parking:	Validated up to 2 hours
Bar:	Full service
Wine selection:	Fair
Dress:	Business, casual
Disabled access:	Good
Customers:	Local, ethnic
Brunch:	Sunday, 11 A.M.−3 P.M.
Lunch/Dinner:	Sunday − Thursday, 11:30 A.M.−11 P.M.;
	Friday and Saturday, 11:30 A.M.−midnight

Atmosphere/setting: Pretty but refreshingly simple, with blushing cream walls and color supplied by the china and the rich Impressionist reproductions on the walls. The sidewalk tables are much in demand.

House specialties: Steamed mussels or shrimp lavished with butter and garlic; ceviche; paella; duck with black olives; great hot bread (to sop up the shrimp or mussels).

Other recommendations: Roast pork in orange zest; grilled swordfish.

Summary & comments: The main problem here is not the meal, not at all—it's getting past the shrimp and the never-ending baskets of crusty rolls to the main course. Some people never make it, or settle for one of the lighter Mexican nibbles, such as enchiladas or quesadillas. But while the neighborhood trends may have persuaded the owners to emphasize the Tex-Mex dishes, the Spanish entrees are more striking.

Lavandou

French (Provençal)
★★½
Inexpensive

Quality 78   Value B

Zone 7   Upper Northwest
3321 Connecticut Avenue, NW
(202) 966-3002

Reservations:	Recommended
When to go:	Lunch, any time
Entree range:	$12.95−16.95
Payment:	VISA, MC, AMEX
Service rating:	★★★
Friendliness rating:	★★★
Parking:	Lot (free for first 1½ hours)
Bar:	Full service
Wine selection:	Limited but good
Dress:	Casual
Disabled access:	Difficult
Customers:	Locals
Lunch:	Monday−Friday, 11:30 A.M.−2:30 P.M.
Dinner:	Sunday−Thursday, 5−10 P.M.;
	Friday and Saturday, 5−11 P.M.

Atmosphere/setting: A plausible re-creation of a country inn, this is a cheerfully crowded storefront operation, a rough-plaster-and-beam fishhook of a room, with most of its color provided by Impressionist reproductions.

House specialties: Whatever's on the daily specials: lamb noisettes; grilled tuna; duck confit or duck breast salad; cod bouillabaisse; grouper with cilantro pesto; coarse rabbit pâté with figs (served alongside a pile of mesclun that makes the entree superfluous).

Other recommendations: Sweetbreads (call a day ahead to make sure the kitchen orders them); crisp grilled chicken; monkfish or salmon in saffron sauce; a sunny-flavored lamb stew with white beans and artichoke hearts.

Summary & comments: This is rich, hearty (mostly) Provençal fare, and the best of it is less de rigeur and more unpretentiously indulgent—the rabbit pâté, for instance, is more satisfying than the merely competent veal scaloppine in brown mustard sauce. It has trained several other fine chefs, too, notably Keo Koumtakoun of La Provence and Le Paradis. There is a $10.95 lunch special and a $14.95 early-bird dinner (5−6:30). Oddly, coffee is not a strong point here— the espresso is gritty and the American coffee weak.

Le Caprice

Zone 5   Georgetown
2348 Wisconsin Avenue, NW
(202) 337-3394

French (Alsatian)
★★★
Expensive

Quality 81   Value C

Reservations:	Recommended
When to go:	Any time; Monday for couscous
Entree range:	$13.50−22
Payment:	VISA, MC, AMEX
Service rating:	★★★
Friendliness rating:	★★★
Parking:	Street, valet (dinner only)
Bar:	Full service
Wine selection:	Good
Dress:	Dressy or informal
Disabled access:	No
Customers:	Locals
Lunch:	Monday−Friday, 11:30 A.M.−2 P.M.
Dinner:	Monday−Thursday, 6−10 P.M.;
	Friday and Saturday, 6−10:30 P.M.;
	Sunday, 6−9:30 P.M.

Atmosphere/setting: A tiny, two-story town house whose rooms suggest the parlors of a pension; in good weather tables are set on the front terrace.

House specialties: Alsatian-influenced French farm classics, notably the choucroute of sausages, smoked pork, and duck confit with fermented turnips in place of the usual sauerkraut; elegant pastry crusts over chicken dishes; puff pastry toques over crab-stuffed artichoke bottoms; smoked fish thinly sliced into salads; country-estate versions of game such as rolled leg and saddle of rabbit stuffed with rabbit mousse and served over braised cabbage; a bacon-stuffed venison roll braised in red wine. Monday's couscous can be ordered with lamb, chicken, or seafood.

Other recommendations: Puff pastry again, in a salmon tartare and mousse "napoleon"; daily fish specials; beef tenderloin poached in bouillon.

Summary & comments: This is one place where simplicity is not always a virtue, since the "ordinary" dishes seem to be handled by the kitchen staff, while the chefs are caught up in the more demanding entrees; thus, plain, fresh asparagus can be overcooked and salads sometimes over-dressed. Talents prevail, however, with silken quiche-custard tarts the size of butter pats served as complimentary appetizers; and again, the more unusual the creation, the more attention it receives. Le Caprice offers a four-course fixed-price dinner each evening for $29.50.

Le Gaulois

	French
Zone 11A Virginia suburbs	★★½
1106 King Street, Alexandria	Moderate
(703) 739-9494	Quality 79 Value C

Reservations: Recommended
When to go: Any time
Entree range: $6.75−18
Payment: VISA, MC, AMEX, CB, DC
Service rating: ★★★
Friendliness rating: ★★★
Parking: Street
Bar: Full service
Wine selection: Good
Dress: Informal
Disabled access: Fair
Customers: Locals
Open: Monday−Thursday, 11:30 A.M.−10:30 P.M.;
                      Friday and Saturday, 11:30 A.M.−11 P.M.;
                      Sunday, closed.

Atmosphere/setting: Outside, the stripped-to-the-grain columns and carved heads of helmeted medieval soldiers (meant to fit the name, but oddly like the American Express logo) gives this pleasant, exposed-brick Old Town rowhouse an eccentric distinction. Inside, its pretty simplicity and cheery fireplaces seem less classical and more kitchen-countrified.

House specialties: Hearty stews and soups and a fine pot-au-feu; sweetbreads or brains; old-fashioned pike quenelles with lobster sauce; julienned zucchini "spaghetti" topped with shrimp, scallops, and mussels in a brandy cream sauce; grilled mushrooms.

Other recommendations: Braised shanks; sweetbreads; the chef's platter of chicken liver pâté, garlic sausage, smoked salmon, and prosciutto; cassoulet; the low-cal special, a fish du jour en papillote.

Summary & comments: This is the suburban second-generation version of a long-popular downtown bourgeois bistro. Though the food is the same, and the quarters far less cramped and kibbitz-y, it seems more of a neighborhood secret, which is even odder considering its broad menu. Or maybe it's just become a matter of habit, since younger-yup Old Townies may not see the charm of such traditionally substantial offerings. Though there are cuisine minceur dishes on the list, such daintiness doesn't come naturally to the kitchen.

Le Lion d'Or

	French
Zone 6 Dupont Circle/	★ ★ ★ ½
Adams-Morgan	Expensive
1150 Connecticut Avenue, NW	
(202) 296-7972	Quality 86 Value C

Reservations:	Required
When to go:	Any time
Entree range:	$24 – 36
Payment:	VISA, MC, AMEX, CB, DC
Service rating:	★ ★ ★ ★
Friendliness rating:	★ ★ ★
Parking:	Validation for lot
Bar:	Full service
Wine selection:	Very good
Dress:	Jacket and tie required
Disabled access:	No
Customers:	Local, business, tourist
Dinner:	Monday – Saturday, 6 – 10 P.M.; Sunday, closed.

Atmosphere/setting: Old continental-style room with leather banquettes, tableside service carts, and faience platters around the walls.

House specialties: Whole lobster presented with pasta; lobster soufflé; rack of lamb; roast game birds. Daily specials are the key here—high interest for both parties.

Other recommendations: Seasonal game specials, including venison, guinea hen, hare, and so on; rolled crêpes with oysters and caviar; squab; red snapper baked in a papillote of thinly sliced potatoes.

Summary & comments: Chef/owner Jean-Pierre Goyenvalle is a Washington institution, a purveyor of the best in classic French cuisine who does not believe nouvelle is necessarily better. You might almost call him the last of an endangered species. Whole fresh fish is broiled in salt and skinned at the table; pâté is wrapped in pastry; squab and filet of lamb are pan-sautéed and simply deglazed. But classic need not be hidebound: An almost guilt-free morsel of foie gras is served in ravioli or melted over pasta. Seafood is always a fine bet.

Le Paradis

French (Provençal)
★★★
Moderate

Quality 83   Value B

Zone 10B   Maryland suburbs
347 Muddy Branch Road (Festival
  Shopping Center)
(301) 208-9493

Reservations:	Recommended
When to go:	Any time
Entree range:	$14.95−21.95
Payment:	VISA, MC, AMEX, DC, D
Service rating:	★★★
Friendliness rating:	★★★★
Parking:	Free lot
Bar:	Beer and wine only
Wine selection:	Limited
Dress:	Informal
Disabled access:	Good
Customers:	Local (meaning as far as Potomac and Bethesda)
Lunch:	Monday−Saturday, 11:30 A.M.−2:30 P.M.; Sunday, closed.
Dinner:	Monday−Saturday, 5:30−10 P.M.; Sunday, closed.

Atmosphere/setting: Just a tiny room, but somehow more convincing than you'd expect a shopping center storefront to be—a little hotel dining room with white draperies, white linen, candles, flowers, and wonderful smells.

House specialties: Bouillabaisse; a superb lobster dish with the medallions of tail and claw meat mounded over a soufflé of the body meat; rack of lamb; venison in season. Foie gras is at its best here, neither oversweet nor greasy.

Other recommendations: Seafood in general, especially the more delicate ones such as calamari or the roasted ones, monkfish or sea bass.

Entertainment & amenities: Some sidewalk dining in good weather.

Summary & comments: Although former chef-owner Keo Koumtakoun is Laotian by birth, he has worked at several popular French restaurants in Washington and Provençal-style cooking is his specialty, so he has trained his staff well. In fact, this is the kind of little joint critics hate to recommend because they prefer to keep them to themselves (which is a little safer now, since he's moved on to La Provence in Virginia: see profile). On a friendly and practical note, Le Paradis serves a prix-fixe lunch that ought to wean local workers away from the pizza joints: soup or salad, dessert, and a choice of the catch of the day, quiche, or coq au vin, all for $9.95.

LE REFUGE

	French
	★★
	Moderate
	Quality 73 Value B

Zone 11C   Virginia suburbs
127 North Washington Street,
    Alexandria
(703) 548-4661

Reservations:	Helpful
When to go:	Early dinner
Entree range:	$12−19
Payment:	VISA, MC, AMEX, DC, CB
Service rating:	★★★
Friendliness rating:	★★★
Parking:	Street
Bar:	Full service
Wine selection:	Limited
Dress:	Informal
Disabled access:	No
Customers:	Local, business
Lunch:	Monday−Saturday, 11:30 A.M.−2:30 P.M.
Dinner:	Monday−Saturday, 5−10 P.M.; Sunday, closed.

Atmosphere/setting: Brightly bistro-ish, daring to be sentimental (a few souvenir Eiffel Towers and plates) and verging on the kitschy, with flickering fake gas lamps, pink linens, cheerful prints, and bright teal pottery.

House specialties: Bouillabaisse, almost regularly offered here; venison medallions with the classic chestnut puree; leg of lamb, also a staple; veal normande; even beef Wellington (when's the last time you thought of that?).

Other recommendations: Scallops or other shellfish (often specials); duck breast.

Summary & comments: This is not haute by any standard, unless you live in a Hollywood stage set from *Moulin Rouge*, but it's hospitable, filling, and fun in a totally flagrant way. All Monday evening and before 7 P.M. the other weeknights, the chef assembles a three-course dinner for $15.95.

LEBANESE TAVERNA

	Lebanese
	★★
	Moderate
	Quality 74 Value B

Zone 6   Dupont Circle/
              Adams-Morgan
2641 Connecticut Avenue, NW
(202) 265-8681

Zone 11B   Virginia suburbs
5900 Washington Boulevard, Arlington
(703) 241-8681

Reservations:	Accepted until 6:30 P.M.
When to go:	Any time
Entree range:	$9.50−14.50
Payment:	VISA, MC, AMEX, DC, D
Service rating:	★★★★
Friendliness rating:	★★★★
Parking:	Street; free garage (D.C. only)
Bar:	Full service
Wine selection:	Limited
Dress:	Informal, casual
Disabled access:	Good
Customers:	Local, ethnic, embassy
Lunch:	*D.C.:* Monday−Friday, 11:30 A.M.−2:30 P.M.;
	Arlington: Monday−Friday, 11:30 A.M.−3 P.M.
Dinner:	*D.C.:* Monday−Thursday, 5:30−10:30 P.M.;
	Friday and Saturday, 5:30−11 P.M.;
	Sunday, 5−10 P.M.;
	Arlington: Monday−Friday, 5−10 P.M.;
	Saturday, 11:30 A.M.−10 P.M.; Sunday, 4−9 P.M.

Atmosphere/setting: A modestly fronted space made gracious and exotic by exposed-beam planters trailing ivy, carved wooden screens, palms, and country tile.

House specialties: Marinated beef and lamb, rotisserie-grilled; whole rotisserie chicken swaddled in Lebanese dough; lamb over crushed wheat bulgar and chickpeas; a mixed-grill kebab; spiced leg of lamb grilled and thinly sliced.

Other recommendations: Fattoush, the Lebanese salad of day-old bread, tomatoes, cucumbers, mint, lemon, and parsley; "Lebanese pizza."

Summary & comments: This is a dependable spot to try mezza, the assortment of appetizers served in small portions for sharing and lingering over. Among the choices: sautéed endive with coriander and caramelized onions; tangy baba gannoujh; cheese- or spinach-stuffed pastries; and the vegetarian mixes of fresh string beans and tomatoes or fava beans and garlic.

194

Legal Sea Foods

<table>
<tr><td></td><td>Seafood</td></tr>
<tr><td>Zone 4   Foggy Bottom</td><td>★★½</td></tr>
<tr><td>2020 K Street, NW</td><td>Moderate</td></tr>
<tr><td>(202) 496-1111</td><td></td></tr>
<tr><td>Zone 11A   Virginia suburbs</td><td>Quality 78   Value B</td></tr>
<tr><td>2001 International Drive (Tysons
   Galleria), McLean</td><td></td></tr>
<tr><td>(703) 827-8900</td><td></td></tr>
</table>

Reservations:	Recommended
When to go:	Early dinner
Entree range:	$12.95 – 19.95
Payment:	VISA, MC, AMEX, DC, D, CB
Service rating:	★★★
Friendliness rating:	★★★½
Parking:	Valet after 5 P.M. (downtown); valet or self-park (Virginia)
Bar:	Full service
Wine selection:	Fair
Dress:	Business, casual
Disabled access:	Good
Customers:	Business, local
Open:	*Foggy Bottom:* Monday – Thursday, 11 A.M. – 10:30 P.M.; Friday, 11 A.M. – 11 P.M.; Saturday, noon – 11 P.M.; Sunday, noon – 10 P.M.; *Tysons:* Monday – Thursday, 11 A.M. – 10 P.M.; Friday and Saturday, 11 A.M. – 10:30 P.M.; Sunday, noon – 9 P.M.

Atmosphere/setting: Both have slightly upscale takes on classic Boston style, with booths, ice-packed raw bar displays, and oversized napkins. In Tysons, two long glass walls, one downstairs overlooking the mall and one upstairs opening to the outside, make it brighter and a little more cheery.

House specialties: Smoked bluefish pâté; crab cakes; bouillabaisse; salmon in parchment; a clam chowder that was a JFK fave; steamed or crab-stuffed lobsters by weight, brushing the $70 mark; raw oysters and clams; a dozen types of fish and seafood available every day either grilled or Cajun style; crab-stuffed shrimp.

Summary & comments: Although seafood is, as they say, their middle name (and although their rigorous oyster-testing makes the first name even more appropriate), Legal Sea Foods is also steak- and sandwich-friendly, offering porterhouse and sirloin, pork and veal chops, and surf-and-turf.

Les Halles

Zone 3   Downtown
1201 Pennsylvania Avenue, NW
(202) 347-6848

Steak
★★★
Moderate
Quality 84   Value B

Reservations:	Accepted
When to go:	Any time
Entree range:	$14.50−20
Payment:	VISA, MC, AMEX, DC, D
Service rating:	★★★
Friendliness rating:	★★★½
Parking:	Valet at dinner (Tuesday−Saturday after 6:30 P.M.); pay lots
Bar:	Full service
Wine selection:	Good
Dress:	Business, informal
Disabled access:	Good
Customers:	Business, local
Open:	Every day, 11:30 A.M.−midnight

Atmosphere/setting: Considering it's in a downtown office building, Les Halles manages to create quite a bit of French brasserie atmosphere, particularly thanks to the buy-your-own meat market at the lobby entrance, the old tin ceiling, and the occasional burst of song from the maître d'. The staff is very cheery, some rather more authentic than others, but quite entertaining. There are several seating areas over three levels, with the cigar smoking segregated upstairs.

House specialties: The long, narrow cut of beef called onglet, a Parisian favorite; a classic pork loin; grilled fish of the day; a very hearty cassoulet, the stew of white beans, pork, and duck. This is the only place in town that still has steak tartare on the menu, and it's a fine, spicy version.

Other recommendations: Romantic traditional dishes such as Caesar salad and lentils with sausage; the bistro classic skillet steak with steak fries; onion soup that reminds you why soup and salad used to be a whole meal.

Entertainment & amenities: Cigar-smokers have their own room on the third floor. And, if you're lucky, the host may sing a little.

Summary & comments: Although best known for its steaks ("American beef, French style," meaning less aged and more muscular than the prime beef more familiar at a Morton's), this is really a brasserie, where you can nibble on a light meal of pâté and salad and get the same attentive service you would get if you had ordered the most expensive entree. More people are beginning to prefer the assertive flavor of the beef here.

196

Lespinasse

	Modern Continental
Zone 3 Downtown	★ ★ ★ ★
923 16th Street, NW (Carlton Hotel)	Expensive
(202) 879-6900	
	Quality 92 Value B

Reservations:	Recommended
When to go:	Any time
Entree range:	Fixed price, $65 and $110; à la carte, $28−36
Payment:	VISA, MC, AMEX, D, DC
Service rating:	★ ★ ★ ★
Friendliness rating:	★ ★ ★ ½
Parking:	Valet at dinner
Bar:	Full service
Wine selection:	Excellent
Dress:	Business, dressy; jacket required
Disabled access:	Good
Customers:	Local gourmets and food-mag trendies, business
Lunch:	Monday − Friday, 11:30 A.M.−2:30 P.M.
Dinner:	Monday − Saturday, 6 − 10 P.M.

Atmosphere/setting: One of the most beautiful rooms in Washington, rich gold and royal blue with a high, hand-painted ceiling, fleur-de-lis upholstery, broad-shouldered armchairs and plush sofas, fine china, and serious, hefty silver. The adjoining bar has also been restored to old grand-hotel splendor, with the sort of library walls and club chairs that made lobby lounges famous.

House specialties: The chef's sampler, six nominal courses (tidbits may appear at any time) for $110 or a simpler, seasonal sampling menu for $65. There is an unusually good list of wines by the glass, and if you aren't an expert, ask sommelier Vincent Ferraut, long-time wine steward at Jean-Louis.

Other recommendations: The à la carte list is fairly short—this is very labor-intensive cooking, after all, with beautiful presentations—but fine.

Summary & comments: As the closing of Jean-Louis at the Watergate (and Le Pavilion before that) demonstrates, New York − style prices are hard to get in Washington, even for New York − style quality. But if any restaurant can hold to the gold standard, it's this one. The original Lespinasse in the St. Regis in Manhattan, home of cuisine star Gray Kunz, has a Mobil five-star rating (and nobody is arguing) and the Washington chef, Troy Dupuy, has been Kunz's sous-chef for many years and knows Kunz's Asian-tinged style inside and out. If this Lespinasse continues on its current course, it will almost certainly earn five stars here, too. Pastry chef Jill Rose has her own full-sized kitchen; sometimes, even if you claim not to need another bite, a tiny palette of sweet gems will come your way.

A Little Place Called Siam

Thai/Pan Asian
★★ ½
Inexpensive

Zone 11A   Virginia suburbs
328 Elden Street, Herndon
(703) 742-8881

Quality 76   Value C

Reservations:	Accepted
When to go:	Any time
Entree range:	$9.95 – 14.95
Payment:	VISA, MC, AMEX
Service rating:	★★★
Friendliness rating:	★★★
Parking:	Free lot
Bar:	Full service
Wine selection:	House
Dress:	Casual
Disabled access:	Good
Customers:	Local, ethnic
Open:	Monday – Thursday, 11:30 A.M. – 10 P.M.; Friday, 11:30 A.M. – 10:30 P.M.; Saturday, noon – 10:30 P.M.; Sunday, noon – 9:30 P.M.

Atmosphere / setting: Of the two generations of Thai decor—the older, lavender-and-off-white style and the post-Busara/Tara Thai deep, exotic colors— this falls in between: fairly plain in the older dining room, but jazzed up with halogen lamps and mood ring paint in the bar.

House specialties: A thick coconut curry with shrimp, or shrimp and scallops cooked in a clay pot; a family-sized dish of cellophane noodles with lemongrass, shrimp, and chicken; duck with ginger.

Summary & comments: Despite the name, this suburban hideaway serves up a few Chinese, Indian, and Vietnamese dishes as well. And the farther from home the menu ranges, the less likely it is to, well, strike home. A welcome distinction here is that sticky rice, erratically available elsewhere, is always on the menu here. And dishes can be spiced up to personal taste: "American hot" is pretty darn good, but "Thai hot" is fairly marked as "for the palate that can handle almost anything."

Little Viet Garden

	Vietnamese
Zone 11B Virginia suburbs	★★½
3012 Wilson Boulevard, Clarendon	Inexpensive
(703) 522-9686	
	Quality 77 Value A

Reservations:	Accepted
When to go:	Any time
Entree range:	$5.95−12.95
Payment:	VISA, MC, AMEX, DC, D
Service rating:	★★★½
Friendliness rating:	★★★
Parking:	Free lot
Bar:	Full service
Wine selection:	Limited
Dress:	Casual, informal
Disabled access:	Good
Customers:	Local, ethnic, business
Open:	Every day, 11 A.M.−10 P.M.

Atmosphere/setting: A gay jungle of a garden room with plastic plants and twinkling holiday lights; in good weather, a terrace offers outdoor dining.

House specialties: Viet Garden steak, almost a bourguignonne with char-broiled flavor; roast quail with a black pepper vinaigrette dipping sauce; mixed seafood and vegetables with a tangy sauce in a crispy noodle basket (when available).

Other recommendations: Golden pancake, a crisp-fried crêpe stuffed with shrimp, chicken, and vegetables; marinated beef grilled in grape leaves; caramel chicken with ginger.

Entertainment & amenities: Live jazz nightly.

Summary & comments: This fairly spritely dining room in the heart of Clarendon's "Little Saigon" neighborhood labors valiantly in the shadow of better-known spots, notably the yuppie-crowded Queen Bee across the street, but it has much brighter sauces and much crispier frying than most, except for a problematic shrimp toast. It has launched two far more successful offshoots, however, the Miss Saigon restaurants in Georgetown and Adams-Morgan (see profiles).

Los Chorros

Salvadoran/Mexican

★★★

Inexpensive

Quality 82   Value B

Zone 10B   Maryland suburbs
8401 Snouffer School Rd., Gaithersburg
(301) 840-5894

Zone 10C   Maryland suburbs
2420 Blueridge Avenue, Wheaton
(301) 933-1066

Reservations:	Helpful
When to go:	Any time
Entree range:	$4.95 − 13.95
Payment:	VISA, MC, AMEX
Service rating:	★★★
Friendliness rating:	★★★
Parking:	Free lot
Bar:	Full service
Wine selection:	House
Dress:	Casual
Disabled access:	Good
Customers:	Local, ethnic
Open:	*Gaithersburg:* Sunday, 11 A.M.−11 P.M.; Monday−Saturday, 11 A.M.−midnight; *Wheaton:* Monday−Friday, 11 A.M.−11 P.M.; Saturday, 11 A.M.−midnight; Sunday, 11 A.M.−11 P.M.

Atmosphere/setting: Both of these are typical suburban shoeboxes rising above, although Wheaton's expansion has left it a little more relaxed.

House specialties: Pupusas, not surprisingly, which come in pork, cheese, or in combination; sautéed pork; grilled pork chops; marinated steak with plantains or a marinated T-bone; sautéed shrimp; a crab-and-shrimp tostada in an oversized shell. For those who like the legendary hangover-killer mondongo (tripe soup), here's a good one. There is also an unusual beef tongue−stuffed corn tortilla and broiled beef liver, for those who don't think life begins and ends with burritos.

Other recommendations: Fajitas (shrimp, beef, chicken, or combo); boiled cod right off the Spanish boat; ceviche; "green" (verde) beef enchiladas with tomatillo sauce, avocado, and melted cheese.

Summary & comments: Salvadoran food goes far beyond the Tex-Mex stereotype. Salvadoran tamales are a world away from the coarse, hard, Tex-Mex franchise things, and generally better for you, as these are corn (masa) tortillas, not wheat and lard cakes.

Louisiana Express

Zone 10A Maryland suburbs	Cajun
4921 Bethesda Avenue, Bethesda	★★½
(301) 652-6945	Inexpensive
	Quality 76 Value A

Reservations:	Not accepted
When to go:	Any time
Entree range:	$2.75 – 13.50
Payment:	VISA, MC
Service rating:	★★★
Friendliness rating:	★★★½
Parking:	Small lot, street
Bar:	Beer and wine
Wine selection:	House
Dress:	Casual
Disabled access:	No
Customers:	Locals
Breakfast:	Monday – Saturday, 7:30 – 11 A.M.
Brunch:	Sunday, 9 A.M. – 2:30 P.M.
Lunch/Dinner:	Sunday – Thursday, 11 A.M. – 10 P.M.;
	Friday and Saturday, 11 A.M. – 11 P.M.

Atmosphere/setting: This is a real New Orleans po' boy bar—just tables, chairs, a suggestion of trellises—and an order-at-the-window format. There are a few outside tables in summer.

House specialties: Fried catfish po' boy sandwich; dirty rice with chicken livers and andouille sausage; seafood creole.

Other recommendations: Catfish or redfish beignets fried in cornmeal; andouille egg rolls; cajun-spiced steak and cheese; eggs Benedict or sardou on Sunday; pralines.

Summary & comments: The menu is sort of Chinese style: Most of the dishes here—gumbos, stir-frys, étouffées and jambalayas—can be ordered with chicken, shrimp, sausage, seafood, or "the works," and are priced accordingly. Blackened redfish is homey, not in any way fancy-shmantzy. In fact, nothing here is particularly haute, it's just good-hearted. Rotisserie chicken can be cajun-rubbed, but it's not the best version around. For those who like a sugar rush in the mornings, the classic powdered-sugar beignets, three for a buck, with café au lait is the best breakfast this side of Jackson Square. The catfish beignets are the best fried bite of anything around.

Luigino

	Italian
Zone 3 Downtown	★★½
1100 New York Avenue, NW	Moderate
(12th and H)	
(202) 371-0595	Quality 79 Value B

Reservations:	Helpful
When to go:	Any time
Entree range:	$12.95−21.95
Payment:	VISA, MC, AMEX, DC
Service rating:	★★★
Friendliness rating:	★★★½
Parking:	Pay lots, meters, street
Bar:	Full service
Wine selection:	Good
Dress:	Business, informal
Disabled access:	Good
Customers:	Local, business, tourist
Lunch:	Monday−Friday, 11:30 A.M.−2:30 P.M.
Dinner:	Monday−Thursday, 5:30−10:30 P.M.;
	Friday and Saturday, 5:30−11:30 P.M.;
	Sunday, 5−9:30 P.M.

Atmosphere/setting: Without adopting the treasured Deco standards of the rehabilitated Greyhound station, Luigino's nevertheless tips its hat to the style, with sleek walls, long lines (one almost says "limbs," as if this were a young woman in an old English mystery), and sconces—crossed fetchingly with Roma-chic tile floors and rough weekendish pottery.

House specialties: Pastas, particularly daily specials and the hefty, stand-up-to-the-game rabbit and venison pappardelles (after Donna, as they used to say); any game specials; the truly comforting mushroom-polenta frittata. Pastas can be ordered in full or half-portions.

Other recommendations: Pizzas (lighter and more flavorful than the student's-best-friend crust served at the parent-restaurant, Luigi's); penne and egg-plant casserole; grilled fresh fish and shellfish.

Summary & comments: If Luigino's were a racehorse, you'd have to say it was bred for both speed and staying power: Its owners come from Luigi's, a main-stay of the quick, cheap, and plentiful school of pizza 'n' pasta; and the chef, Carmine Marzano, from the stables of Galileo, Washington's premier Italian estab-lishment. But for its uptown looks, its heart is home-style: Suckling pig may sound like a banquet dish, but it's about as lick-your-fingers as it gets.

Makoto

Zone 7 Upper Northwest	Japanese
4822 MacArthur Boulevard, NW	★★★½
(202) 298-6866	Moderate
	Quality 89 Value A

Reservations:	Recommended
When to go:	Any time
Entree range:	Fixed price, $35
Payment:	VISA, MC
Service rating:	★★★★
Friendliness rating:	★★★
Parking:	Street
Bar:	Full service
Wine selection:	House
Dress:	Business, casual
Disabled access:	No
Customers:	Ethnic, local, business
Lunch:	Tuesday – Saturday, noon – 2:30 P.M.
Dinner:	Tuesday – Sunday, 6 – 10:30 P.M.; Monday, closed.

Atmosphere/setting: A secret Japanese garden of a spot, hidden behind two wood doors (with a stone garden between where you exchange your shoes for bedroom slippers) and only two lines of diners long. The kitchen is, in effect, the decor: Slightly sunken behind what is now the sushi counter, the chefs busily stir, fry, and slice over the restaurant equivalent of a Pullman stove.

House specialties: A fixed-price omakase (chef's choice) dinner based on the market and featuring courses of two to six bites each, but extraordinarily generous for $25: up to seven courses of sashimi, sushi, grilled marinated fillet of fish (a choice), such delicate morsels as ankimo (monkfish liver) or rare duck breast with asparagus tips and sesame seeds, large bowls of wheat-noodle soup, and sherbet.

Other recommendations: Limited à la carte sushi, such as uni (sea urchin), toro, or fresh sardines; yakitori, skewer-grilled marinated chicken.

Summary & comments: This is a tiny establishment—perhaps 30 seats, even counting the new sushi bar—which explains how the chefs are able to produce such exquisite and imaginative meals. This is a form of kaiseki cuisine, the formal, Zen-derived technique that salutes both nature and art by using only fresh, seasonal ingredients and a variety of colors, textures, and cooking techniques. Be sure to show your appreciation by admiring each carefully presented dish as it arrives. Note that none of the seats have backs—they're just boxes with removable tops for storing purses, jackets, and cushion lids—and there is no separate nonsmoking area.

Market Street Bar & Grill

	Modern American
	★★½
Zone 11A Virginia suburbs	Moderate
1800 Presidents Street (Hyatt Regency), Reston	Quality 79 Value C
(703) 709-6262	

Reservations:	Recommended
When to go:	Any time
Entree range:	$10.95−22.75
Payment:	VISA, MC, AMEX, DC, D
Service rating:	★★★★
Friendliness rating:	★★★
Parking:	Street, garage
Bar:	Full service
Wine selection:	Good; all domestic
Dress:	Business, informal
Disabled access:	Good
Customers:	Local, tourist, business
Brunch:	Sunday, 10:30 A.M.−2:30 P.M.
Lunch:	Monday−Friday, 11:30 A.M.−2:30 P.M.
Dinner:	Monday−Thursday, 5:30−10 P.M.;
	Friday and Saturday, 5:30−10:30 P.M.;
	Sunday, 5:30−9:30 P.M.

Atmosphere/setting: Bright and chic, with black-and-white checks the theme (even on the staff's trousers), green marble bars, and brass trim.

House specialties: Grilled wild boar sausage with fried green tomatoes; sautéed lobster meat with grits, leeks, and mushrooms and a warm lobster salad like an updated Niçoise; saffron and squid-ink ravioli with cheese (all appetizers); a pretty toss of lemon and black-pepper linguine with seared scallops; braised lamb shank with couscous; roast pheasant with white truffle risotto.

Other recommendations: Grilled fish; squash risotto with rabbit sausage.

Entertainment & amenities: Live jazz Friday through Sunday.

Summary & comments: Having careened from too-conservative to overly ambitious and scattered, this kitchen has finally begun to find a compromise rhythm (though still paying attention to prevailing winds). This hotel restaurant provides enough trendy dishes for the pleasure diner and serves up the traditionals—prime rib, roast game hen, filet—for business diners. Seasonings are distinct without being overwhelming and the garnishes are well chosen.

204

Matuba

Zone 11B Virginia suburbs	Japanese
2915 Columbia Pike, Arlington	★★★½
(703) 521-2811	Inexpensive
Zone 10A Maryland suburbs	Quality 85 Value B
4918 Cordell Avenue, Bethesda	
(301) 652-7449	

Reservations:	Accepted
When to go:	Monday, when many menu items are $1; alternate Tuesdays for specials on sushi platters or teriyakis
Entree range:	$6.95 – 16.50
Payment:	VISA, MC, AMEX
Service rating:	★★★
Friendliness rating:	★★★★
Parking:	Street
Bar:	Beer and wine only
Wine selection:	House
Dress:	Casual, informal
Disabled access:	Fair
Customers:	Local, ethnic
Lunch:	Monday – Friday, 11:30 A.M. – 2:30 P.M.; Saturday, noon – 3 P.M.
Dinner:	Monday – Thursday, 5:30 – 10 P.M.; Friday and Saturday, 5 – 10:30 P.M.; Sunday, 5 – 9:30 P.M.

Atmosphere / setting: Small and traditional but uncomplicated, with a lot of blond wood and a few woodblock reproductions.

House specialties: Oyaku donburi, the homey chicken-and-egg (literally, "parent and child") variation on chicken and rice stew not often seen after lunch; "wedding sushi," a marriage of scallops and shrimp; soft-shell crab tempura in season.

Other recommendations: Unagi donburi; grilled teriyaki squid; sea urchin; grilled fresh fish.

Summary & comments: Matuba (pronounced "MAT-su-ba") in Arlington was one of the first Japanese restaurants in the area that Japanese patrons recommended, although being honest and dependable is not always enough to keep up in such a competitive market. It's the sort of place that rewards regular attention: For unfamiliar customers, sushi portions can be small in comparison to many other bars, though the quality is high; but known faces are treated generously. Many of the custom rolls are delicious; the Alaska roll mixes smoked salmon and scallops.

Melrose

Zone 5   Georgetown
24th and M streets, NW
(202) 955-3899

Modern American	
★★★½	
Moderate	
Quality 87	Value C

Reservations:	Recommended
When to go:	Any time
Entree range:	$21 – 28
Payment:	VISA, MC, AMEX, CB, DC, D
Service rating:	★★★
Friendliness rating:	★★½
Parking:	Valet, street
Bar:	Full service
Wine selection:	Good
Dress:	Business, informal
Disabled access:	Good
Customers:	Local, business
Breakfast:	Every day, 6:30 – 10:30 A.M.
Brunch:	Sunday, 11 A.M. – 2:30 P.M.
Lunch:	Monday – Saturday, 11 A.M. – 2:30 P.M.
Dinner:	Every day, 5:30 – 10:30 P.M.

Atmosphere/setting: At first glance, it's almost plain, but after so many overdecorated restaurants, it becomes soothing: a simple room, light and bright, with pastels, florals, marble, and magnificent flowers; glass walls along two sides allow diners to look out toward fountains, cafe-style umbrella tables, flowering shrubs, and the herb garden.

House specialties: Roasted twin medallions of pepper-crusted tuna and foie gras; poached salmon with bok choy and vanilla-and-cardamom-flavored vinaigrette; and a signature dish of steamed lobster and angelhair pasta with mascarpone sauce. Among the appetizers: house-cured gravlax stuffed with crab and crème fraîche; shrimp ravioli.

Other recommendations: Grilled seafood; duck breast with dates.

Entertainment & amenities: A quartet for dancing on Saturday nights; no corkage fee on Sunday nights.

Summary & comments: Chef Brian McBride has a light-bright attitude toward cooking that is a perfect match for the atmosphere here; he's especially good with seafood, which dominates the menu. His sauces are complements, not covers, and although the attitude is generally classic, his combinations often provide a gentle surprise. (Occasionally he wants to cover too many bases at once, but that's an explorer's risk.) The chef's choice is usually five courses for about $55.

MESKEREM

Zone 6   Dupont Circle/
          Adams-Morgan
2434 18th Street, NW
(202) 462-4100

Ethiopian
★★★½
Inexpensive
Quality 86   Value A

Reservations:	Suggested
When to go:	Any time
Entree range:	$8.50–11.95
Payment:	VISA, MC, AMEX, DC
Service rating:	★★★
Friendliness rating:	★★★
Parking:	Street
Bar:	Full service
Wine selection:	Minimal
Dress:	Casual
Disabled access:	Good
Customers:	Locals, tourists
Open:	Sunday – Thursday, noon – midnight;
	Friday and Saturday, noon – 1 A.M.

Atmosphere/setting: Simple but cheerful, with "skylight" rays painted blue and white and Ethiopian-style seating (for the limber) on leather cushions at balcony basket-weave tables.

House specialties: Kitfo (tartare with chile sauce, but it can be ordered lightly cooked, or you can have a similar hot chopped beef stew called kay watt); lamb tibbs (breast and leg meat sautéed with onions and green chiles); shrimp watt; beef or lentil and green chile sambussa (fried pastries); tikil gomen, cabbage, potatoes, and carrots in a gentle sauce.

Other recommendations: Chicken or shrimp alicha for the spice-intimidated; zilbo (lamb and collard greens); a honey-wine version of kitfo called gored-gored.

Summary & comments: There are three things novices need to know about Ethiopian food: First, it's eaten with the hands, using a spongy pancake called injera as plate, spoon, and napkin all in one; second, "alicha" is the name of the milder stew or curry preparation; and third, "watt" is the spicier one. Washington's many Ethiopian restaurants (there may be a dozen in Adams-Morgan alone) offer similar menus, in some cases without much distinction between stews, but Meskerem is one of the best. If you want a sampler—a tray-sized injera palette—order the "mesob" for $7.25. "Meskerem," incidentally, is the first month of the 13-month Ethiopian calendar, the one that corresponds to September, which in Ethiopia is the end of the rainy season and thus is akin to springtime.

Miss Saigon

Zone 6　　Dupont Circle/	Vietnamese
Adams-Morgan	★★½
1847 Columbia Road, NW	Inexpensive
(202) 667-1900	
	Quality 79　　Value B

Zone 5　　Georgetown
M Street, NW
(202) 333-5545

Reservations:	Helpful
When to go:	Any time
Entree range:	$6.95 – 11.95
Payment:	VISA, MC, AMEX, D, DC
Service rating:	★★
Friendliness rating:	★★★
Parking:	Free lot
Bar:	Full service
Wine selection:	House
Dress:	Casual
Disabled access:	Good
Customers:	Local, ethnic
Lunch/Dinner:	Monday – Thursday, 11:30 A.M. – 10:30 P.M.;
	Friday and Saturday, 11:30 A.M. – 11 P.M.;
	Sunday, noon – 10:30 P.M.

Atmosphere/setting: The Dupont Circle branch leans more toward the Franco-Viet style, with Art Deco – cafe furniture and pink and green carpeting (plus a great view of the sidewalk life), while the Georgetown branch is more like the mother shop in Arlington, with lots of greenery and wood.

House specialties: A spectacular soup with quail, shiitakes, and noodles, and topped with bits of pork fat; roast quail by itself as an appetizer; a good version of pho (without all the options available at a pure pho house); egg noodles topped with oyster sauce – flavored seafood; pumpkin in coconut-milk curry; hearty "hot pots"; beef in grape leaves.

Summary & comments: Thanks to their trendier locations, these two off-spring of Arlington's Little Viet Cafe have outstripped their parent in publicity; similarly, though the family resemblance is clear from the menu, there are some flashier dishes here. And to be frank, every new generation seems to be a little better—the Georgetown kitchen is the best. Like more and more savvy Asian restaurants, the Misses Saigon are using not only their noodles, but their mock goose and veggie duck to attract health- and animal-conscious diners.

Morrison-Clark Inn

	Modern American
	★ ★ ★
	Moderate
	Quality 83 Value B

Zone 3   Downtown
1015 L Street, NW (Massachusetts
  and 11th)
(202) 898-1200

Reservations:	Recommended
When to go:	Any time
Entree range:	$16.50−21.50
Payment:	VISA, MC, AMEX, DC, D
Service rating:	★ ★ ★
Friendliness rating:	★ ★ ★
Parking:	Valet
Bar:	Full service
Wine selection:	Good
Dress:	Business; coat and tie
Disabled access:	No
Customers:	Local, business
Brunch:	Sunday, 11:30 A.M.−2 P.M.
Lunch:	Monday−Friday, 11:30 A.M.−2 P.M.
Dinner:	Monday−Thursday, 6−9:30 P.M.;
	Friday and Saturday, 6−10 P.M.; Sunday, 6−9 P.M.

Atmosphere/setting: For many years, this was the home of a Civil War−era government supplier, and in the late 19th century it was purchased by a traveler who added a Chinese Chippendale porch and Shanghai mansard roof. In the '20s, it was the Soldiers, Sailors, Marines and Airmen's Club, and the furnishings some-how pay tribute to all that old seafaring romance—Victorian mixed with chi-noiserie that recalls the tea trade, brightened with sunny yellow wallpaper and made gracious by marble fireplaces. The combination sort of suits the menu, too, which is mostly old-fashioned but with the occasional Eastern spice.

House specialties: Loin of rabbit stuffed with greens and topped with a whiskey sauce; curry-flour-dusted catfish in tomato-sherry sauce; lemon-chive pasta with asparagus and poached salmon (lunch); calamari in fennel and orange sauce; shrimp however prepared.

Other recommendations: Hearty but not heavy meat dishes, such as mari-nated pork chop with adobe sauce or rack of lamb rubbed with balsamic vinegar.

Summary & comments: Chef Susan McCreight Lindeborg is interested in re-casting traditional foods, particularly Southern ones, in a modern light—cornmeal-fried catfish with black-eyed peas and corn relish; herb-studded biscuits with coun-try ham; chicken smothered in mustard gravy. (Obviously, "light" is not a pun here.)

Morton's of Chicago

Zone 5 Georgetown	Steak
3251 Prospect Street, NW	★★★½
(202) 342-6258	Expensive
	Quality 89 Value B

Zone 3   Downtown
Connecticut and L streets, NW
(202) 955-5997

Zone 11A   Virginia suburbs
8075 Leesburg Pike (Fairfax Square Shopping Center), Tysons Corner
(703) 883-0800

Reservations:	Recommended
When to go:	Early for prime rib
Entree range:	$19.95–49.95
Payment:	VISA, MC, AMEX, CB, DC
Service rating:	★★★
Friendliness rating:	★★★
Parking:	Valet
Bar:	Full service
Wine selection:	Good
Dress:	Business, dressy
Disabled access:	Prospect Street, fair; downtown and Leesburg Pike, good
Customers:	Business, local, tourist
Lunch:	Monday–Friday, 11:30 A.M.–2 P.M. (Virginia and downtown only)
Dinner:	Monday–Saturday, 5:30–11 P.M.; Sunday, 5–10 P.M.

Atmosphere/setting: These loud, brash gentlemen's club-cum-chophouses with LeRoy Neiman sports art and carts of raw meat rolling around are almost as much a competition as a dining experience. And, with the vigor of the bartending, waiting for a table (likely even with a reservation) is also a test of endurance.

House specialties: Porterhouse; smoked salmon; lobsters by the pound; the broiled veal chop that is becoming a steakhouse standard.

Other recommendations: Swordfish; lamb chops.

Summary & comments: This is the original cholesterol test, steak as straight as it comes, and as prime as it comes. Prime rib is one of the signature dishes here, but some people never make it in time, as it sells out early in the evening. Another

(continued)

special is the 48-ounce "double porterhouse" for couples, family groups, or *Guinness Book* aspirants. All the classics are here—New York strip, filet mignon so large it belies the name, Delmonico—and the vegetables are just as predictable: mountainous baked potatoes, spinach, tomatoes (problematic), asparagus. In classic old-boys' style, Morton's offers minicatalogs of cigars, single-malt Scotches, and more than three dozen types of martinis: After all, if you're going to hit the artery superhighway, you might as well go first-class.

Note: For disabled access at the Tysons Corner location, tell the valet to notify the dining staff that you will be using the elevator.

MRS. SIMPSON'S

	Modern American
Zone 6 Dupont Circle/	★★½
Adams-Morgan	Moderate
2915 Connecticut Avenue, NW	
(202) 332-8300	Quality 76 Value C

Reservations:	Recommended
When to go:	Any time
Entree range:	$6.95–18.95
Payment:	VISA, MC, AMEX, DC
Service rating:	★★★
Friendliness rating:	★★★
Parking:	Street
Bar:	Full service
Wine selection:	Good
Dress:	Business, informal
Disabled access:	Good
Customers:	Locals
Brunch:	Sunday, 10:30 A.M.–2:15 P.M.
Lunch/Dinner:	Sunday–Thursday, 11:30 A.M.–9:30 P.M.;
	Friday and Saturday, 11:30 A.M.–10:30 P.M.

Atmosphere/setting: Mrs. Simpson's is like the hideaway shrine of an unrequited lover, filled with photos, magazine covers, documentary memorabilia, and even children's sewing sampler coronation pillows saluting Wallis Warfield Simpson and her doting and ultimately abdicating King Edward.

House specialties: Crab cakes, whose tendency to fall apart is actually a testament to their almost pure-meat composition; "light" meat dishes, such as a seared, sliced lamb with tabbouleh and zucchini–green bean pancakes or a Chinese spice-rubbed duck breast wrapped à la moo shi in pancakes; salmon and julienned vegetables steamed in parchment; grilled salmon with pesto.

Other recommendations: Calf's liver, however garnished; grilled Belgian endive salad; a curry-spiked tomato bisque with seafood.

Summary & comments: Mrs. Simpson's is a little perplexing, in that it always seems on the verge of being a really creative restaurant but, perhaps knowing its own limitations, it clings to (a) a spicing caution; (b) an older, slightly set-in-its-ways constituency; and (c) a fair number of rich, "full-bodied" sauces. Nevertheless, it fills a prime slot as a white-linen neighborhood retreat with fine manners and dependable quality. And entrees saluting Asian or new-Italian sources can be fine indeed. The light-as-silk pâté that comes with the bread basket is almost worth the whole trip—that and the port-stewed prunes.

Mr. Yung's

Zone 3   Downtown
740 6th Street, NW
(202) 628-1098

Chinese	★★½
Inexpensive	
Quality 79	Value B

Reservations:	Helpful
When to go:	Lunch (dim sum served 11 A.M.–3 P.M. daily)
Entree range:	$6.95–24.95
Payment:	VISA, MC, AMEX, DC, D
Service rating:	★★½
Friendliness rating:	★★½
Parking:	Street, pay lots
Bar:	Full service
Wine selection:	House
Dress:	Informal, casual
Disabled access:	Fair
Customers:	Ethnic, local, tourist
Open:	Every day, 11 A.M.–midnight

Atmosphere/setting: Although the traditionally rose-colored dining room (and the rare enclosed sidewalk addition) is quite hospitable, you're apt never to notice, because during rush hour (which is most lunches) the bustle and buzz are pervasive.

House specialties: From the dim sum menu: steamed or baked roast pork buns; sweet lotus bean paste buns; black mushroom and pork dumplings; steamed stuffed bean curd; beef rice crêpe rolls. From the main menu: squid and mussels with leeks; squid with sour bok choy; baked shrimp in the shell with spiced salt; baby clams in black bean sauce; and a barbecued combination of roast duck, roast pork, and soy-glazed chicken.

Other recommendations: Daily specials, including whole fresh fish; shrimp steamed in lotus leaves; Chinese fry bread stuffed with shrimp paste; frog legs with ham.

Summary & comments: There is a particular personality quirk about Mr. Yung's, slight but sort of amusing, in that regular attendance is really rewarded. How certain dishes gear up from good to extra-good is hard to explain, but perhaps customers (at least non-Chinese ones) have to pass an informal muster. Presentations even seem to become prettier.

Music City Roadhouse

<table>
<tr><td></td><td>Southern</td></tr>
<tr><td>Zone 5   Georgetown</td><td>★★</td></tr>
<tr><td>1050 30th Street, NW</td><td>Inexpensive</td></tr>
<tr><td>(202) 337-4444</td><td></td></tr>
<tr><td></td><td>Quality 74   Value A</td></tr>
</table>

Reservations:	Accepted
When to go:	Any time
Entree range:	$8.95 – 13.95
Payment:	VISA, MC, AMEX, DC, D
Service rating:	★★★
Friendliness rating:	★★★
Parking:	Validated pay lots
Bar:	Full service
Wine selection:	House
Dress:	Business, casual
Disabled access:	Good
Customers:	Local, business
Brunch:	Sunday, 11 A.M.–2 P.M.
Dinner:	Tuesday – Saturday, 4:30 – 10 P.M.;
	Sunday, 2 P.M.– 10 P.M.; Monday, closed.

Atmosphere/setting: The busiest, brightest, and cleanest country music roadhouse ever—an airy, lofty, blasted-clean brick warehouse hung with Opry photos, beer ads, strings of lights, and so on. There's a sort of dining balcony around the dining room, views of the canal, and a "properly" dim front bar for smokers.

House specialties: An all-you-can-eat supper served family style, including soup, a choice of three meats/fish/chicken (pot roast, fried chicken, barbecued ribs, fried catfish, broiled trout, pork chops, meatloaf, etc.) plus three vegetables (greens, mashed potatoes, sweet potatoes, slaw, black-eyed peas, corn on the cob, succotash), and cornbread.

Other recommendations: À la carte ribs; the vegetable platter.

Entertainment & amenities: Live gospel music at Sunday brunch; collection of single-barrel bourbon.

Summary & comments: If you ever went to church suppers or had a big family, you might be homesick for this sort of boardinghouse-reach table service; if you're fussy and overly neat, you won't have half the fun you ought to here. Bring a big appetite. Note that the "vegetable" plate is not vegetarian; there are plenty of hocks and such in the pots. Doe's Eat Place, the Mississippi-to – Little Rock steak-and-tamale legend, has moved into the back room.

Mykonos

Zone 4   Foggy Bottom
1835 K Street, NW
(202) 331-0370

	Greek
	★★★
	Moderate
	Quality 80 Value B

Reservations:	Helpful (dinner only)
When to go:	After 1:30 or for dinner; it's a lunch-hour express
Entree range:	$9.95–18
Payment:	VISA, MC, AMEX, DC, D
Service rating:	★★★½
Friendliness rating:	★★★★
Parking:	Validated
Bar:	Full service
Wine selection:	Limited
Dress:	Business, informal
Disabled access:	No
Customers:	Ethnic, business
Lunch:	Monday–Friday, 11:30 A.M.–3:30 P.M.
Dinner:	Monday–Friday, 5:30–10:30 P.M.;
	Saturday, 5:30–11 P.M.; Sunday, closed.

Atmosphere/setting: The brightest Greek decor: lots of whitewashed "plaster" walls with marine blue accents, slate flooring, archways, and sun-drenched paintings and travel posters.

House specialties: A fine vegetarian platter featuring stuffed eggplant, spanakopita, lemon-and-parsley-drenched white beans and Greek salad, among other things; grilled salmon (a real slab, crusty and moist); spinach-and-feta-stuffed flounder and a similar chicken breast; roasted lamb or broiled chops.

Other recommendations: An appetizer of roasted, caramelized eggplant topped with tomatoes and pine nuts; lamb du jour at lunch, particularly the shanks; veal with mabrodaphne wine and mushrooms.

Summary & comments: There's not a faster way to lose those old prejudices against Greek cooking than to sample Mykonos' versions of fried squid or even stuffed grape leaves; the spanakopita, served as a complimentary appetizer, is far and away the best in town, with greens that seem too tangy and fresh to be just spinach. There are various combination platters, but for two or more the "deluxe dinner," 15 dishes served in 3 presentations for $19.95 a head, is the banquet of your dreams. Mykonos uses a fair amount of oil, but first-class olive oil it is; and the feta is delicate.

New Heights

Zone 6 Dupont Circle/	Modern American
Adams-Morgan	★★★½
2317 Calvert Street, NW	Moderate
(202) 234-4110	Quality 88 Value C

Reservations:	Recommended
When to go:	Any time
Entree range:	$17−25
Payment:	VISA, MC, AMEX, DC, D
Service rating:	★★½
Friendliness rating:	★★★
Parking:	Valet
Bar:	Full service
Wine selection:	Good
Dress:	Informal, business
Disabled access:	Fair
Customers:	Local
Brunch:	Sunday, 11 A.M.−2:30 P.M.
Dinner:	Sunday−Thursday, 5:30−10 P.M.;
	Friday and Saturday, 5:30−11 P.M.

Atmosphere/setting: A small Woodley Park town house simply Deco-rated and opened up to take advantage of the light and the glorious view down Connecticut Avenue to Dupont Circle.

House specialties: The menu changes seasonally, but typical dishes include bouillabaisse with lemongrass; Provençal brandade of salt cod with tomatoes and truffle oil; lobster flan with wild mushrooms; pan-roasted pheasant with coffee barbecue.

Other recommendations: Marlin "layered" traditional Japanese style with miso and pearl rice; poached salmon with roast mushrooms and artichokes.

Summary & comments: This is a back-to−modern basics kitchen with an Asian slant and an even bigger Mediterranean wanderlust. Even nicer, several of the entrees can be ordered in appetizer portions. Some people find its eclecticism off-putting, but currently it's strongly on track: Chef Matthew Lake was named one of the ten most promising chefs of 1996 by *Food & Wine* magazine. In fact, the owner here, Umbi Singh, has a great eye for chefs and a willingness to give them room to stretch; Lake is the fifth success story here, following Alison Swope (Sante Fe East, Stella's), Melissa Balinger (Clyde's group corporate chef), Greggory Hille (Gabriel), and Dean Winning (Red Sage, the Turning Point Inn).

NIWANO HANA

	Japanese
	★★★ ½
	Inexpensive

Zone 10B   Maryland suburbs
887 Rockville Pike (Wintergreen
    Plaza), Rockville
(301) 294-0553

Quality 87   Value B

Reservations:	Helpful
When to go:	Any time
Entree range:	$9.50−22.95
Payment:	VISA, MC, AMEX, D, DC
Service rating:	★★★
Friendliness rating:	★★★
Parking:	Free lot
Bar:	Full service
Wine selection:	House
Dress:	Casual
Disabled access:	Good
Customers:	Local, ethnic
Lunch:	Monday−Friday, 11:30 A.M.−2:30 P.M.; Saturday, 11:30 A.M.−3 P.M.
Dinner:	Monday−Saturday, 5:30−10 P.M.; Sunday, 5−9:30 P.M.

Atmosphere/setting: Traditionally styled, with polished blonde wood, a long sushi bar down one side and tables along the other, and the added interest of a partially visible kitchen.

House specialties: Sushi, the sort that has to be extremely fresh: sea urchin, live scallops, mussels, and so on; jaw of yellowtail teriyaki; soft-shell crab tempura.

Other recommendations: Be sure to read the daily specials mounted on the walls over the sushi bar and grill; toro (fatty tuna) is served generously here, and ankimo (you'll probably have to order it as monkfish liver, since they speak very little Japanese) is extremely good.

Summary & comments: Although this restaurant is actually Korean-owned (it's part of the Unification Church empire), and most of the chefs are Korean or Chinese, the sushi tends to be first-rate, oversized by traditional Japanese standards (perhaps a good two bites each), and made from high-quality seafood and well-seasoned rice. Seasonal seafood such as green mussels and Canadian scallops, as well as the now common toro, make for unusually broad variety. The staff also invents the usual multiflavored rolls such as the "alligator roll," a huge eel-and-shrimp tempura maki hooded in a half-avocado. And all the usual soups, teriyakis, and tempura combinations (including a good veggie version) are also available.

Nizam

<table>
<tr><td></td><td>Turkish</td></tr>
<tr><td>Zone 11A Virginia suburbs</td><td>★★</td></tr>
<tr><td>523 Maple Avenue West, Vienna</td><td>Moderate</td></tr>
<tr><td>(703) 938-8948</td><td>Quality 72 Value B</td></tr>
</table>

Reservations:	Recommended
When to go:	Weekends
Entree range:	$11.95 – 22.50
Payment:	VISA, MC, AMEX, D
Service rating:	★★★
Friendliness rating:	★★★
Parking:	Free lot
Bar:	Full service
Wine selection:	Limited
Dress:	Informal, casual
Disabled access:	No
Customers:	Local, ethnic
Lunch:	Monday – Friday, 11 A.M. – 2:30 P.M.
Dinner:	Tuesday – Thursday, 5 – 10 P.M.;
	Friday and Saturday, 5 – 11 P.M.; Sunday, 4 – 9 P.M.

Atmosphere/setting: A modest, pretty room filled with hanging plants and brassware tucked inside its shopping center exterior.

House specialties: Donner kebab, marinated lamb rolled, rotisserie grilled, pinwheel sliced, and served with tomato and yogurt sauce (available Tuesdays and weekends); lamb shank with eggplant; ground lamb with sautéed pita and smoked eggplant; baba ghanoush.

Other recommendations: Manti, a sort of Turkish ravioli related to the Afghani aushak; char-grilled chicken.

Summary & comments: "Kebab" is the most prominent word on Nizam's menu, and so the grilling (and marinating) is given great care. But unlike some Turkish kitchens, this one doesn't forget the little things, like seasoning the stuffed grape leaves (these are studded with pine nuts and raisins) or draining the oil from the moussaka. Some critics sniff that the donner kebab isn't as authentic as home-style, which has layers of many meats, but its admirers are louder.

NORA

Zone 6   Dupont Circle/
           Adams-Morgan
2132 Florida Avenue, NW
(202) 462-5143

Modern American
★ ★ ★
Moderate
Quality 80   Value C

Reservations:	Recommended
When to go:	Any time
Entree range:	$18.95 − 25.95
Payment:	VISA, MC
Service rating:	★ ★ ★ ½
Friendliness rating:	★ ★ ★ ★
Parking:	Street, valet
Bar:	Full service
Wine selection:	Good
Dress:	Business, casual
Disabled access:	No
Customers:	Locals
Dinner:	Monday − Thursday, 6 − 10 P.M.;
	Friday and Saturday, 6 − 10:30 P.M.;
	Sunday, closed.

Atmosphere/setting: A pretty corner town house with exposed brick walls and a gallery of handicrafts, quilt pieces, and faux naif art in the dining rooms; an enclosed greenhouse balcony in the rear is the prettiest area.

House specialties: The menu changes frequently, but look for shellfish, such as a lobster-shellfish pan roast; organ meats from additive-free animals; seared squab or tuna appetizers; home-cured gravlax or trout; veal or lamb; honey-and-spice-glazed pheasant; roasted salmon; vegetarian platters.

Summary & comments: Nora, the neighborhood hangout of the Dupont Circle A and B lists, was haute organic before organic was chic. The back of the menu, which changes daily, lists the specific farms where the meat, produce, dairy products, and eggs—naturally low in cholesterol, according to the supplier—are raised. Nora's own all-edible flower and herb garden alongside the restaurant is indicative. The cost of acquiring such specialized ingredients is passed on, but not unreasonably. Nora was also ahead of the crowd by introducing alternative grains and pastas, and it was the first restaurant to make lentils that didn't taste like a Zen penance. Its only drawback is an odd tendency to weightiness—the meals sometimes feel heartier than they taste. Now that the Clintons and Gores have been publicized dining here, it may become more of a tourist attraction.

Obelisk

Zone 6	Dupont Circle/
	Adams-Morgan
2029 P Street, NW	
(202) 872-1180	

Italian
★★★½
Expensive
Quality 89   Value B

Reservations:	Recommended
When to go:	Any time
Entree range:	Prix fixe only, about $40
Payment:	VISA, MC, DC
Service rating:	★★★
Friendliness rating:	★★★½
Parking:	Street
Bar:	Full service
Wine selection:	Good
Dress:	Business, informal
Disabled access:	No
Customers:	Local, business
Dinner:	Monday – Saturday, 6 – 10 P.M.; Sunday, closed.

Atmosphere/setting: A tiny room that's elegant and good-humored; the customers, staff, and accoutrements—not only the room's floral centerpiece and silver chest but the astonishingly light breadsticks and bottles of grappa—work intimately elbow to elbow.

House specialties: Chef Peter Pastan has figured out the cure for overlong, overrich menus—he offers a fixed-price menu, four to five courses with only two, maybe three, choices per course. Among typical antipasti: marinated anchovies and fennel; artichokes with goat cheese; caramel-soft onion and cheese tart; crostini; a thick soup; quail terrine; crispy fried cheese; polenta with Gorgonzola; potato or rice balls. The *primi* course is apt to be seafood or pasta (red pepper noodles with crab and pungent chive blossoms; gnocchi with pesto; wheat noodles with rabbit ragout) or soup; the *secondi*, veal (particularly tenderloin prepared with artichokes or chanterelles), fish (pompano with olives; black sea bass with grilled radicchio), or perhaps game bird or a mixed grill. After that comes a fine bit of cheese, with or without a dessert course following. Whatever the price—it varies with the daily menu—it's a quality bargain in this town.

Summary & comments: Pastan's hand is so deft he doesn't need to overdress anything; sauces are more like glazes, and pungent ingredients—olives, pine nuts, garlic, and greens—are perfectly proportioned to their dish. Above all, it shows the value of letting a chef who knows exactly what he likes do as he likes. Pastan, who also owns Pizzeria Paradiso next door, is co-owner of the new Blue Plate.

Occidental Grill

	Modern American
	★★½
	Moderate
	Quality 75 Value B

Zone 3   Downtown
1475 Pennsylvania Avenue, NW
(202) 783-1475

Reservations:	Recommended
When to go:	Any time
Entree range:	$13.95–19.95
Payment:	VISA, MC, AMEX, DC
Service rating:	★★★★
Friendliness rating:	★★★★
Parking:	Pay lot (validated)
Bar:	Full service
Wine selection:	Good
Dress:	Informal, business
Disabled access:	Good
Customers:	Local, business, tourist
Open:	Monday–Saturday, 11:30 A.M.–11:30 P.M.; Sunday, noon–9 P.M.

Atmosphere/setting: The best of old-club style, with a red-plush dining room upstairs and an informal corporate mess hall in white linen downstairs. Every square inch of wall space is taken up by photos of government and media vets.

House specialties: Hearty appetizers that can easily serve as light entrees (and are often a better bargain proportionately), including a signature charred rare tuna with orange and ancho chile vinaigrette; catfish strips fried in pecan flour on roasted pepper coulis; smoked trout with fennel, snow peas, and daikon sprouts in soy-anise dressing. Seafood is especially good here: marlin with banana, green peppercorns, and Myers rum, topped with mango relish; marinated fillet of salmon with napa cabbage and ginger/coriander vinaigrette; braised rockfish.

Other recommendations: Tuna au poivre; veal loin chop with shiitake and spiced pear; Cornish hen with a spanky green olive and ginger sauce.

Summary & comments: This is a courtly and comfy restaurant that treats tourists (it's within view of the White House) and hotel guests as well as its regular customers. Dishes are new-cuisine mainstream, but cleverly combined.

Old Angler's Inn

	Modern American
Zone 10B Maryland suburbs	★★★½
10801 MacArthur Boulevard, Potomac	Expensive
(301) 299-9097	Quality 89 Value C

Reservations:	Required
When to go:	Any time
Entree range:	$23−30
Payment:	VISA, MC, AMEX, DC
Service rating:	★★★
Friendliness rating:	★★★
Parking:	Free lot
Bar:	Full service
Wine selection:	Brief
Dress:	Dressy, business, jacket and tie
Disabled access:	No
Customers:	Locals
Brunch:	Sunday, noon−2:30 P.M.
Lunch:	Tuesday−Saturday, noon−2:30 P.M.
Dinner:	Tuesday−Friday, 6−10:30 P.M.;
	Saturday, 5:30−10:30 P.M.;
	Sunday, 5:30−9:30 P.M.; Monday, closed.

Atmosphere/setting: A beautiful, old-fashioned inn above the river, with a blazing fireplace in the parlor bar downstairs and a huddle of small dining rooms up a narrow iron spiral staircase (and bathrooms out of the servants' quarters). The stone terrace and gazebo levels are open in good weather.

House specialties: Ostrich and venison; lobster; buttery (but butterless) pumpkin soup or asparagus bisque with lump crabmeat; roast monkfish with macadamia crust; stuffed grilled quail or Cornish hen; rabbit sausage with couscous; shrimp with a fresh, coarse salsa; roast pheasant with spinach spaetzle.

Summary & comments: This has always been a beautiful site, but years of haphazard service and pretentious, overpriced food had nearly ruined Old Angler's reputation. (The wine list is still underconsidered.) But under chef Jeffrey Tomchek, this has settled down to a consistently satisfying, unobtrusively healthful kitchen, light on butters and creams but big on flavor and contrast. Altogether, Tomchek is pushing close on his fourth star. Improv is close to Tomchek's heart: Upon request, the kitchen will provide a much more intriguing, five-course tasting dinner for $55 a head (or seven courses for $75), which you may request with all or no seafood, red meat, etc. One all-vegetarian version included a butternut squash ravioli, potato-cheese soup, and beautifully orchestrated mixed salad with truffles.

Old Ebbitt Grill

	American
Zone 3 Downtown	★★½
675 15th Street, NW	Moderate
(202) 347-4801	
	Quality 77 Value C

Reservations:	Recommended
When to go:	Sunday brunch; after work for power-tripping
Entree range:	$9.95−14.95
Payment:	VISA, MC, AMEX, DC, D
Service rating:	★★★
Friendliness rating:	★★★
Parking:	Pay lots (validated after 6 P.M.)
Bar:	Full service
Wine selection:	Good
Dress:	Business, informal
Disabled access:	Very good (through G Street atrium)
Customers:	Business, feds, locals, tourists
Breakfast:	Monday−Friday, 7:30−11 A.M.;
	Saturday, 8−11:30 A.M.
Brunch:	Sunday, 9:30 A.M.−4 P.M.
Lunch/Dinner:	Monday−Saturday, 11 A.M.−midnight;
	Sunday, 4 P.M.−midnight

Atmosphere/setting: An updated old-boys' club, but with equal opportunity hospitality: a few horsey accoutrements (bridles, snaffles) in front, lots of greenery and etched glass dividers in the main room, and a classic oyster bar.

House specialties: Linguine with shrimp, basil, and fresh tomatoes; pork chops with homemade applesauce; black pepper−rubbed leg of lamb with papaya relish; old-fashioned pepperpot beef; steamed mussels; smoked salmon (a company signature) and smoked bluefish when available. Annually, during the brief halibut season in Alaska, the Old Ebbitt and its Clyde's cousins have a halibut celebration that is a command performance for seafood lovers. For brunch, fat old-style French toast and corned beef hash.

Entertainment & amenities: Occasional piano music at happy hour.

Summary & comments: This is one restaurant whose whole experience is somehow better than the food might indicate by itself. The Old Ebbitt—actually, the new Old Ebbitt for those who remember the fusty Back Bay−style original around the corner and its stuffed owls and scuffed bar rails—takes its White House neighborhood location seriously, but not too seriously. That is, it gives out pagers to patrons waiting for tables, but the staff democratically seats the ties and T-shirts side by side.

Old Glory

Zone 5   Georgetown
3139 M Street, NW
(202) 337-3406

Barbecue

★★½

Moderate

Quality 78   Value B

Reservations:	Parties of 6 or more only, for lunch or weekday dinner
When to go:	Afternoon
Entree range:	$6.25 – 14.95
Payment:	VISA, MC, AMEX, D, DC
Service rating:	★★½
Friendliness rating:	★★★
Parking:	Pay lots, street
Bar:	Full service
Wine selection:	Minimal
Dress:	Casual, informal
Disabled access:	Good
Customers:	Local, tourist
Brunch:	Sunday, 11 A.M.–3 P.M.
Lunch/Dinner:	Monday – Thursday, 11:30 A.M.–11:30 P.M.; Friday and Saturday, 11:30 A.M.–12:30 A.M.; Sunday, 11 A.M.–11 P.M.; late-night menu available every day, 11:30 P.M. until close

Atmosphere/setting: A chic and cheeky take on roadhouse diner decor with a sort of Six Flags theme: The state colors of Tennessee, Texas, Georgia, Kentucky, Kansas (which used to be Arkansas), and the Carolinas hang overhead, while each table is armed with bottles of six different barbecue sauces—mild, sweet, vinegary, multi-chile'd, mustardy, tomatoey—named for the same six states. A mix of old and new country and honky-tonk music plays on the PA.

House specialties: Pork ribs or beef short ribs; "pulled" (shredded rather than chopped) pork shoulder; smoked chicken; grilled summer sausages; smoked ham; and various combinations or sandwich versions thereof. Daily specials often include pit-fired steaks or fresh seafood.

Other recommendations: Pit-grilled burgers with cheddar and smoked bacon; marinated and grilled skewered vegetables; hot barbecued shrimp.

Entertainment & amenities: Live music Tuesday, Thursday, and Saturday.

Summary & comments: This trendy finger-lickers' stop is surprisingly good, particularly when it comes to the sort of Southern side dishes that rarely travel well. The biscuits are fine (the cornbread isn't) and the hoppin' John—black-eyed peas and rice—is better than authentic; it's neither mushy nor greasy.

Olney Ale House

	American (tavern fare)
Zone 10C Maryland suburbs	★★½
2000 Sandy Spring Road	Inexpensive
(Route 108), Olney	
(301) 774-6708	Quality 76 Value C

Reservations:	Not accepted
When to go:	A little after the early-bird dinner crush
Entree range:	$3.95 – 12.95
Payment:	VISA, MC, D
Service rating:	★★★
Friendliness rating:	★★★★
Parking:	Free lot
Bar:	Full service
Wine selection:	House
Dress:	Casual
Disabled access:	Good
Customers:	Locals
Lunch:	Every day, 11:30 A.M. – 2:30 P.M.
Dinner:	Sunday – Thursday, 5:30 – 10 P.M.;
	Friday and Saturday, 5:30 – 10:30 P.M.

Atmosphere/setting: Standing in the fork of the road like an old highway tollhouse, this is such a comfy combination of a good-times tavern and a good-eats roadhouse (and eco-conscious boomers) that it regularly draws three-generation family groups, whole softball and soccer teams, bikers, and businessmen, all of whom coexist quite happily. It also has something of a summer- or fishing-camp – dining-room look, all well-traveled wood, wide-window views, and a fireplace to boot.

House specialties: A famous beef stew served with a splendid loaf of home-made bread, or a veggie chili, more interesting than most; crab cakes; a roasted-red-pepper – walnut-spread sandwich with artichokes; the nightly specials, which might range from pan-fried catfish or stuffed trout to roast chicken and grilled fish.

Other recommendations: Fried chicken (free range); steamed fish (lunch only); a grilled turkey, provolone, and blue cheese sandwich with sprouts and mushrooms called the "Jose." Loaves of the bread, usually two choices a day—the house standard (molasses-oatmeal) and one other—can be bought for carryout at $2.95.

(continued)

225

Entertainment & amenities: Outdoor picnic tables (with one of those old-fashioned service windows for quick post-game beers); draft microbrews; a great jukebox.

Summary & comments: This looks like a sandwich joint, and the soups and sandwiches are a big part of its appeal; but the kitchen is comfortably ambitious, making a couple of series dinner dishes every night and turning out really fine breads and desserts. The Ale House is also popular with vegetarian and vegan diners—there are a half-dozen veggie dishes, appetizers, and a vegetarian special every Thursday night—and it makes a dairy-free rice pudding that's good enough for anyone. In fact, it's one of the few places that vegetarians can have nachos with everybody else. The house wines are organic.

Oodles Noodles

Zone 4 Foggy Bottom	Pan Asian
1120 19th Street, NW	★★½
(202) 293-3138	Inexpensive
Zone 10A Maryland suburbs	Quality 78 Value B
4907 Cordell Avenue	
(301) 986-8833	

Reservations:	Not accepted
When to go:	Any time
Entree range:	$6.95–8.95
Payment:	VISA, MC, AMEX, DC, D
Service rating:	★★★
Friendliness rating:	★★★
Parking:	Street
Bar:	Full service
Wine selection:	House
Dress:	Casual
Disabled access:	Good
Customers:	Local, ethnic
Lunch:	Every day, 11:30 A.M.–2:30 P.M.
Dinner:	Sunday–Thursday, 5:30–10 P.M.;
	Friday and Saturday, 5:30–10:30 P.M.

Atmosphere/setting: Bethesda is fairly plain, with perhaps a hint of sushi-bar style—lots of highly polished blonde wood, some lattice work, and a wall area for those waiting to sit down. The kibbitzing can be quite intense, incidentally—one of the problems of the no-reservation policy.

House specialties: Steamed pork dumplings (called "ravioli" for no obvious reason) and Japanese-style dumplings (though these and other fried dishes can be unexpectedly greasy sometimes); hot Thai drunken noodles with basil and chicken; grilled eel (downtown only); grilled chicken and noodle soup that will erase Campbell's concept from your grocery list.

Other recommendations: Nasi campur, a cross between a composed salad and a rijsttafel, with hot-and-sour shrimp, curried chicken, hard-boiled egg, dried fish, and peanuts mounded around rice; fried, stuffed dumplings with Malayish peanut dipping sauce. "Noodles on the boat," which is served in a canoe-shaped vessel, is a fairly light dish of rice vermicelli topped with lemon-grilled chicken.

(*continued*)

Summary & comments: Most of these dishes are moderately good imitations of the ethnic originals, although not to a terribly deep degree, since some of the dishes are fuzzily similar. Much more flavorful versions of nabeyaki udon, for example, are available in a half-dozen places within earshot. And the seasonings are also somewhat fuzzy, especially when it comes to heat—although the Bethesda branch, surrounded as it is by Thai and Southwestern chili-head parlors, is braver with its Thai drunken noodles. Those on low-sodium diets will have a hard time getting along here. The price and the exotic choices have made the Bethesda restaurant in particular a mixed-age hangout from teens to seniors, while the downtown shop is more business lunchers.

The Palm

<table>
<tr><td></td><td>Steak</td></tr>
<tr><td></td><td>★★½</td></tr>
<tr><td></td><td>Expensive</td></tr>
<tr><td></td><td>Quality 79   Value B</td></tr>
</table>

Zone 6   Dupont Circle/
                  Adams-Morgan
1225 19th Street, NW
(202) 293-9091

Reservations:	Recommended
When to go:	Any time
Entree range:	$14.50−29
Payment:	VISA, MC, AMEX, DC
Service rating:	★★★
Friendliness rating:	★★
Parking:	Street, valet after 6 P.M.
Bar:	Full service
Wine selection:	Good
Dress:	Business, casual
Disabled access:	Good
Customers:	Tourist, business, local power
Open:	Monday−Friday, 11:30 A.M.−10:30 P.M.;
	Saturday, 5:30−10:30 P.M.;
	Sunday, 5:30−9:30 P.M.

Atmosphere/setting: Truth in advertising—a cross between a classic white-linen steakhouse and a rogue's gallery, its walls crammed frame-to-frame with caricatures of the rich, the famous, the infamous, and the overrated but extravagantly tipping.

House specialties: New York strip; lobsters priced by the pound (and up to four pounds or so); "Palm steak," sliced sirloin with grilled sweet peppers and onions; veal and lamb chops; jumbo shrimp cocktail.

Other recommendations: Grilled fish of the day; prime rib.

Summary & comments: The Palm is just one of those places—cranky, condescending, crowded, celebrity-conscious, physically and fiscally out of control, and occasionally (albeit rarely) a disappointment—that many people love to hate. And if you're a regular, or rich enough, they'll love to let you. The Palm is now a quarter-century old, and in all fairness, has mellowed somewhat (not to mention taken a lesson from the popularity of spit-and-polish rival Sam & Harry's across the street). But the competition to see and be seen there is more unseemly than ever. Class, as in caste, takes too much attention away from quality.

Panjshir

	Afghani
	★★½
	Inexpensive
	Quality 79 Value A

Zone 11B   Virginia suburbs
924 West Broad Street, Falls Church
(703) 536-4566

Zone 11A   Virginia suburbs
224 West Maple Avenue, Vienna
(703) 281-4183

Reservations:	Accepted (Vienna only)
When to go:	Any time
Entree range:	$9.95 – 13.95
Payment:	VISA, MC, AMEX, D
Service rating:	★★★
Friendliness rating:	★★★
Parking:	Small lot
Bar:	Full service
Wine selection:	House
Dress:	Informal, casual
Disabled access:	Vienna only
Customers:	Local, business, ethnic
Lunch:	Monday – Friday, 11:30 A.M. – 2 P.M.
Dinner:	Every day, 5 – 10 P.M.

Atmosphere/setting: A surprisingly comfortable shopping strip storefront made bright by embroidered pillows and fringe—a sink-back-and-relax sort of place.

House specialties: Zardack palow, sliced carrots, prunes, chickpeas, and walnuts tossed with lamb and rice (available without meat); quorma-e-seib, apples baked with tomato sauce, prunes, walnuts, split peas, and lamb; shalgram, turnips with brown sugar, ginger, and onion served as a vegetarian dish or with lamb.

Other recommendations: Aushak, the Afghan ravioli in which the scallions are on the inside and the ground meat is on the outside; a combination kebab of beef, lamb chops, chicken, and lamb; beef and chickpea-stuffed sambosays.

Summary & comments: Panjshir uses only soybean oil, and unusually little of that; the use of mint and coriander is generous and rice is pasta-smooth. Remember, however, that "relaxing" is a key word here, and the service is sometimes leisurely, too.

Paolo's

<table>
<tr><td></td><td>Italian</td></tr>
<tr><td>Zone 5   Georgetown</td><td>★★½</td></tr>
<tr><td>1303 Wisconsin Avenue, NW</td><td>Moderate</td></tr>
<tr><td>(202) 333-7353</td><td></td></tr>
<tr><td>Zone 11A   Virginia suburbs</td><td>Quality 76   Value B</td></tr>
<tr><td>Market and Fountain streets, Reston</td><td></td></tr>
<tr><td>(703) 318-8920</td><td></td></tr>
</table>

Reservations:	Lunch and brunch only
When to go:	Happy hour, early dinner
Entree range:	$11–17
Payment:	VISA, MC, AMEX, DC, D
Service rating:	★★★½
Friendliness rating:	★★★
Parking:	Pay lots (Reston free)
Bar:	Full service
Wine selection:	Fair
Dress:	Casual
Disabled access:	Good
Customers:	Local, business
Brunch:	*Georgetown:* Saturday and Sunday, 11 A.M.–4 P.M.; *Reston:* Sunday, 11 A.M.–3 P.M.
Lunch/Dinner:	*Georgetown:* Monday–Thursday, 11:30 A.M.–midnight; Friday, 11:30–12:30 A.M.; Saturday, 11–12:30 A.M.; Sunday, 11 A.M.–midnight; *Reston:* Sunday–Thursday, 11 A.M.–midnight; Friday and Saturday, 11–12:30 A.M.

Atmosphere/setting: This local mini-chain has a sharp but not swaggering young-designer feel, with lots of dark marble, polished wood columns, and mirrors; the signature uniform cloth, a black-blue-white, Jackson Pollack dash and splash, sums up its crispness and non-traditional flair.

House specialties: Wood-grilled pizzas (including an indulgent but erratic lobster version and a great grilled chicken, pesto, and goat cheese version); a number of heart-healthy dishes, such as a pot-roasted chicken with peppers and potatoes and a grilled chicken–black pepper pasta; a rich Gorgonzola and pesto tortellini with roasted tomato sauce; fettuccine with fennel-spiked sausage.

Summary & comments: Like the Old Ebbitt, Paolo's overall effect is better than the sum of its parts; and the quality of employees is one of those "parts" that keeps Paolo's in the listings.

Paradise

Zone 10A   Maryland suburbs
7141 Wisconsin Avenue, Bethesda
(301) 907-7500

Reservations:	Accepted
When to go:	Lunch buffet
Entree range:	$7.95−13.95
Payment:	VISA, MC, AMEX, DC
Service rating:	★★★
Friendliness rating:	★★½
Parking:	Free lot after 5; street
Bar:	Full service
Wine selection:	House
Dress:	Informal, casual
Disabled access:	No
Customers:	Local, business
Open:	Monday−Friday, noon−10 P.M.;
	Saturday and Sunday, noon−11 P.M.

Atmosphere/setting: Non-specifically elegant, with mirrored walls and linen, except for a small area up front with ethnic paintings.

House specialties: Qormeh Sabzi, a "green stew" of beef and beans cooked in coriander, scallions, parsley, and leeks; shirin polo, a slightly sweet rice dish with chicken in almonds, orange peel, and saffron; aushak, the Afghan ground meat and yogurt ravioli, with particularly light dough.

Other recommendations: Vegetarian versions of eggplant, mushroom, pumpkin, and spinach sautées; lamb kebab marinated in mustard; grilled chicken.

Summary & comments: Paradise uses no lard, pork, or alcohol in its cooking, but like many Middle Eastern kitchens, it's generous with its oil; ask for the creamy kashk-e bademjan, an eggplant−sour cream spread, without the added oil. Rice is intriguingly crisp here.

Paul Kee

	Chinese
	★★
	Inexpensive
	Quality 71 Value A

Zone 10C   Maryland suburbs
11305-B Georgia Avenue, Wheaton
(301) 933-6886

Reservations: Accepted
When to go: During soft-shell crab season, early in the evening
Entree range: $10–22
Payment: VISA, MC
Service rating: ★★★
Friendliness rating: ★★★★
Parking: Free lot
Bar: Beer and wine
Wine selection: House
Dress: Informal, casual
Disabled access: Good
Customers: Ethnic, local
Open: Sunday–Thursday, 11 A.M.–1 A.M.;
                          Friday and Saturday, 11 A.M.–2 A.M.

Atmosphere/setting: This is almost a family kitchen, with no attempt to disguise its storefront location, but with delicious-looking roasted ducks and chickens hanging from their necks in the back and a real mom-and-pop staff, complete with small children.

House specialties: Stir-fried squid (or tripe) with sour cabbage; scallops with black pepper; steamed flounder with ginger and scallion sauce; thinly sliced pork kidneys and livers with ginger sauce; both beef and pork tripe; cold shredded jellyfish; and for the adventurous (or British), a sort of Cantonese black pudding called duck blood, dressed with pig's skin or with ginger and scallions.

Other recommendations: Peking-style chicken with both a tang of peppers and the more common mushroom and vegetable garnish; lamb with dry bean curd; roast pork with oysters.

Summary & comments: Though it easily and warmly accommodates the most pedestrian of American tastes—an Hispanic neighbor's order of carryout sweet-and-sour pork, moo goo gai pan, and beef with broccoli was greeted with the same courtesy as a tripe with sour cabbage—it also offers some of the real Hong Kong dishes Wheaton's vigorous Chinese community misses: Hong Kong–style wonton soup, with the soft, shrimp-stuffed dumplings rather than the overfried noodles often passed off as wontons; Singapore-style noodles and sea cucumber with duck's feet.

PEKING EASTERN HOUSE

	Chinese
	★★½
	Inexpensive
	Quality 79 Value A

Zone 10B   Maryland suburbs
16041 Frederick Road, Rockville
(301) 527-8558

Reservations:	Helpful
When to go:	Any time
Entree range:	$5.95 – 21.95
Payment:	VISA, MC
Service rating:	★★★
Friendliness rating:	★★★½
Parking:	Free lot
Bar:	None
Wine selection:	None
Dress:	Casual
Disabled access:	Very good
Customers:	Local, ethnic
Open:	Every day, 11:30 A.M. – 10 P.M.

Atmosphere / setting: This is the kind of description you almost fill in as "not applicable"—a few hand-painted Chinese verses on the wall and a picture or two—but it's clean, bright, and down-to-business. Most of the larger tables have lazy Susans in the center, which hints at the preponderance of the large family and church groups who eat here (vans are common in the parking lot).

House specialties: Lamb moo shu; five-spice chicken; spicy shredded beef with noodles; long, tortilla-sized, lamb pot stickers; a light, braised, baby bok choy and shiitakes.

Other recommendations: Veggie dumplings, both steamed and fried, rich in greens and tofu; barbecued lamb, like a kebab; huge bowls of soup and noodles; for kids especially, the beef shian bing, not inappropriately called "Chinese hamburgers" on the menu—seasoned ground beef patties in five-inch dough wrappers, like beef in a blanket.

Summary & comments: This is a Muslim establishment, so there are no pork dishes, but there is a wealth of unusual lamb and organ meats such as tripe (on the menu in various forms but also available stir-fried with ginger and scallions by request). And it's a genuinely helpful place; if you come a couple of times, they will be delighted to see you and to help you explore the menu.

234

PERRY'S

Zone 6 Dupont Circle/	Fusion
Adams-Morgan	★★½
1811 Columbia Road, NW	Moderate
(202) 234-6218	Quality 79 Value B

Reservations:	Helpful
When to go:	Sunday drag brunch; late night; early evening
Entree range:	$7.95−16
Payment:	VISA, MC, AMEX, D, DC
Service rating:	★★★
Friendliness rating:	★★★
Parking:	Street
Bar:	Full service
Wine selection:	Fair
Dress:	Casual
Disabled access:	No
Customers:	Local, gay, hip
Brunch:	Sunday, 11:30 A.M.−3 P.M.
Lunch:	Every day, 11:30 A.M.−2:30 P.M.
Dinner:	Sunday−Thursday, 5:30−10 P.M.;
	Friday and Saturday, 5:30−10:30 P.M.

Atmosphere/setting: Depending on whether you're inside or not, you might be in an opium den, a disco, a garden party, or a slightly decadent and intentionally over-the-top cocktail lounge—all of which are equally fun.

House specialties: Both Perry's and its half-sibling Xing Kuba have fusion on the brain, but fun fusion—duck-ginger dumplings with a red curry−coconut dipping sauce and wild boar rubbed with orange and chiles. Light dishes, especially seafood preparations, are good bets. The sushi bar is extremely popular, although as often the case, the seafood is far better than the rice it rides in on.

Summary & comments: After blowing its initially good reputation by getting not merely sloppy but somehow slatternly, this hilariously high-spirited nightspot is getting its kitchen act together under chef Melissa Horowitz (if managing sushi, pizza, tapas, and game all at the same time can even be called a single act). Two of the more amazing special attractions are the Sunday drag brunch, which is fine so long as you don't mind rubbing elbows with Carol Channing, and the pretheater menu: three courses of at least three seasonal choices for $12.95 or $15.95 with a glass of the house wine. Since the early menus change as often as once a week, you can easily get into the habit of dropping in straight from the office.

PESCE

Zone 6   Dupont Circle/
           Adams–Morgan
2016 P Street, NW
(202) 466-3474

Seafood
★★★½
Moderate
Quality 86   Value B

Reservations:	Helpful
When to go:	Lunch; early or late dinner
Entree range:	$12.50−17.50
Payment:	VISA, MC, AMEX, D, DC
Service rating:	★★★
Friendliness rating:	★★★
Parking:	Street, pay lots
Bar:	Full service
Wine selection:	Good
Dress:	Business, casual
Disabled access:	Good
Customers:	Local
Lunch:	Monday−Saturday, 11:30 A.M.−2:30 P.M.
Dinner:	Monday−Thursday, 5:30−10 P.M.;
	Friday and Saturday, 5:30−10:30 P.M.;
	Sunday, 5−9:30 P.M.

Atmosphere/setting: This is a classic, Dupont Circle row house–cum-cafe, with exposed brick, woodwork trim, cheeky wooden fish-market fish, and a bistro-style sandwich board on the sidewalk chalked up with the day's offering. It's always busy, as is the bar-waiting area, but has a congenial air that recalls the best European cafes.

House specialties: Seafood stews that are far more complex (and more solid) than the usual shellfish-in-a-broth dish, often involving roasted fish and vegetables or beds of braised greens; consistently complementary sauces of Asian or Mediterranean flavors; seafood pastas and risottos.

Other recommendations: For straight seafood lovers, a daily range of grilled and sometimes poached fish or steamed shellfish; soft-shell crabs in season.

Summary & comments: The menu at every meal is a matter of market freshness and kitchen fancy, which makes it hard to predict, perhaps, but also consistently fascinating. And, although it's listed as moderately priced, for its location, innovation, variety, and cachet (the joint jewel and idea of haute chefs Roberto Donna and Jean-Louis Palladin, though on-site chef David Craig is fully on his own here), it should almost be described as inexpensive. It's definitely a bargain.

Pho Cali/The Quality Seafood Place

Vietnamese
★★½
Inexpensive
Quality 79   Value A

Zone 11B   Virginia suburbs
1621 South Walter Reed Drive (at
  Glebe Road), Arlington
(703) 920-9500

Reservations:	Accepted for 7 or more
When to go:	Any time
Entree range:	$6.95 – 12.95
Payment:	VISA, MC, AMEX, D
Service rating:	★★★★
Friendliness rating:	★★★★
Parking:	Small lot, street
Bar:	Beer and wine
Wine selection:	Minimal
Dress:	Casual, informal
Disabled access:	Fair
Customers:	Local, international
Open:	Sunday – Thursday, 10:30 A.M. – 10 P.M.; Friday and Saturday, 10 A.M. – 11 P.M.

Atmosphere/setting: A smallish room made cheery with the plastic plants and miniature lights that appear to be a Viet-decor cliché; a much nicer wooden patio outside offers seating in good weather.

House specialties: Whole steamed fish (usually red snapper or flounder, sometimes rockfish) with either scallions or black bean sauce; buttered sweet roast quail with lemon – black pepper dipping sauce; weirdly dignified whole fried fish.

Other recommendations: Fried soft-shell crabs in season; pho, the now ubiquitous Vietnamese noodle soup with an assortment of beef cuts or tripe as topping; seafood fondue (sea anemone, shrimp, clams, jellyfish, scallops, etc.) for two.

Summary & comments: This is not just a friendly place; the staff is so helpful it's nigh on to garrulous. And it can be very generous: As in several other Vietnamese restaurants, the appetizer-sized roast quail is as big as the entree, but here that's three whole birds; and extra rice is included free with leftovers packages. The kitchen rightly believes a little tang is good for the soul, and the blandest of the dishes — mixed seafood hot pots or a starchy rice-noodle bird's nest — are the least impressive. Seafood is tenderly handled, with the exception of squid, which can be disappointingly chewy. Fresh crabs are especially good. There are also several multicourse dinners offered for two, four, or six people — the last, at $59.95, a real bargain. Not quite as great as the $4.95 large pho pot, though.

Pho 75

Vietnamese

★★½

Inexpensive

Quality 79   Value A

Zone 11B   Virginia suburbs
1711 Wilson Boulevard, Arlington
(703) 525-7355

Zone 10D   Maryland suburbs
1510 University Boulevard East,
   Langley Park
(301) 434-7844

Zone 11B   Virginia suburbs
3103 Graham Road, Falls Church
(703) 204-1490

Zone 10B   Maryland suburbs
771 Hungerford Drive, Rockville
(301) 309-8873

Reservations:	Not accepted
When to go:	Any time
Entree range:	$4.25 − 5.95
Payment:	Cash only
Service rating:	★★★
Friendliness rating:	★★★
Parking:	Free lot
Bar:	None
Wine selection:	None
Dress:	Casual
Disabled access:	Good
Customers:	Ethnic, local
Open:	Every day, 9 A.M.−8 P.M.

Atmosphere / setting: These are perfect examples of the maxim that if you do one thing and do it well, you don't need to do anything more. These are simple, nearly unadorned, no-nonsense dining halls—literally, soup kitchens.

House specialties: Pho in 16 beef combinations (including tendons and tripe), all at $1 a topping. The basic bowl of star-anise broth and noodles comes in two sizes with add-to-taste bowls of peppers, fresh mint, and bean sprouts; the meat toppings are stirred in at the table and "fondue'd" right in the bowl.

Other recommendations: Real Vietnamese-style coffee, brewed espresso-thick into the cup and then mixed with sweetened condensed milk; tapioca and a corn/coconut milk custard.

Summary & comments: Pho is to Vietnamese cuisine as rice is to Japanese—not just a staple, but an honored and reassuring old friend. It's also their equivalent of a fast-food hamburger, so while group eating can be a social event at a pho kitchen, it can also be a pretty brisk atmosphere, with customers slurping noodles and devouring Vietnamese-language newspapers simultaneously.

Pizza de Resistance

	Pizza
Zone 11B Virginia suburbs	★★½
2300 Clarendon Boulevard, Arlington	Inexpensive
(703) 351-5680	
	Quality 75 Value B

Reservations:	Accepted
When to go:	Any time
Entree range:	$6.95–11.95
Payment:	VISA, MC, AMEX, DC
Service rating:	★★★
Friendliness rating:	★★★
Parking:	Free after 5 P.M.
Bar:	Full service
Wine selection:	Good
Dress:	Business, casual
Disabled access:	Good
Customers:	Local, business
Open:	Monday, 11:30 A.M.–9:30 P.M.;
	Tuesday–Thursday, 11:30 A.M.–10 P.M.;
	Friday, 11:30 A.M.–11 P.M.; Saturday, 4–11 P.M.;
	Sunday, 4–9:30 P.M.

Atmosphere/setting: Chicly post-modern, Pizza de Resistance is full of visual puns on the pizzeria business—stone tabletops and great rounded walls and bar—and some courtyard tables near the fountains.

House specialties: Puck-ish toppings such as mesquite-grilled chicken; seafood and pesto with sun-dried tomatoes; spinach, shiitakes, and goat cheese over whole wheat; ground andouille, Creole shrimp, smoked mozzarella, and rémoulade sauce on a tomato–black pepper crust.

Other recommendations: Chicken and asparagus in double black pepper crust; grilled shrimp and roasted pepper on dill crust; a veggie calzone primavera.

Summary & comments: PdR has one big gimmick—five crusts, including a blue cornmeal dough, sourdough, whole wheat, and one studded with black pepper and sun-dried tomatoes—and a bunch of little ones: the toppings. PdR also offers pasta by personal design: pick a pasta, then a sauce, then a topping. In the pizza business, as in burlesque, you gotta have a gimmick, but if you don't have the goods, the curtain falls fast. Pizza de Resistance delivers.

Pizzeria Paradiso

Zone 6   Dupont Circle/
           Adams–Morgan
2029 P Street, NW
(202) 223-1245

Pizza	
★★★	
Inexpensive	
Quality 83	Value A

Reservations:	Not accepted
When to go:	Any time except about 8 – 10 P.M.
Entree range:	$5.50 – 15.95
Payment:	VISA, MC, DC
Service rating:	★★★
Friendliness rating:	★★★
Parking:	Street
Bar:	Beer and wine
Wine selection:	Limited
Dress:	Casual
Disabled access:	No
Customers:	Local, tourist, student
Open:	Monday – Thursday, 11 A.M.–11 P.M.;
	Friday and Saturday, 11 A.M.–midnight;
	Sunday, noon – 10 P.M.

Atmosphere/setting: As tiny as this upper room is, it's hilariously decorated, with trompe l'oeil stone walls opening at the "ruined roof" to a blue sky; columns with capitals of papier-mâché veggies; a wood-burning stove painted like a smokestack; and semi-impressionistic painted cardboard pizzas like Amish hexes around the walls (a sly comment on the mass-market competition, perhaps?).

House specialties: Pizzas with four cheeses or "the atomica," with salami, black olives, and hot peppers; zucchini, eggplant, peppers, and fresh buffalo mozzarella; mussels (surprisingly, yes); and potato with pesto sauce and Parmesan.

Other recommendations: Thick sandwiches made with focaccia, including roast lamb and roasted veggies, as well as multimeat Italian subs and pork with hot peppers.

Summary & comments: It may seem extravagant to give such high marks to a pizzeria, but pizza this good—shoveled in and out of the deep oven, with a splash of extra-virgin olive oil and a handful of cheese tossed on at the last moment—makes most American takeout blush. It's almost a redefinition of pizza. This restaurant also has real attitude—not commercial camp, just an irresistible New Wave nonchalance. No larger than its next-door sibling, Obelisk, Pizzeria Paradiso shoehorns them in and rolls them out at an astonishing but validating rate.

Prime Rib

Zone 4   Foggy Bottom
2020 K Street, NW
(202) 466-8811

Steak	
★★★½	
Expensive	
Quality 88	Value B

Reservations:	Recommended
When to go:	Lunch
Entree range:	$19−29
Payment:	VISA, MC, AMEX, CB, DC
Service rating:	★★★★
Friendliness rating:	★★★½
Parking:	Street, lot, valet (dinner only)
Bar:	Full service
Wine selection:	Good
Dress:	Jacket and tie required
Disabled access:	Good
Customers:	Business, local
Lunch:	Monday−Friday, 11:30 A.M.−3 P.M.
Dinner:	Monday−Thursday, 5−11 P.M.;
	Friday and Saturday, 5−11:30 P.M.;
	Sunday, closed.

Atmosphere/setting: The presence up front of the Lucite grand piano makes a strange, slightly disco first impression, backed up by the leopard-print carpet; but this black-and-gold room is veddy veddy civilized.

House specialties: Prime rib; lobster; crab imperial that is this establishment's second nickname.

Other recommendations: Calf's liver; grilled fish; great potato skins.

Summary & comments: If Morton's is a red meat marathon, and Sam & Harry's a pinstripe convention (see profiles), the Prime Rib is a strategy session — a little more reasonable in price and without the brand-your-own-beef attitude. It's a power-lunchers' paradise (a bit more attentive to women than some steakhouses), and worth every penny of it; at night the bar does a surprisingly busy singles business — but again, very civilized.

Primi Piatti

Zone 4 Foggy Bottom	Italian
2013 I Street, NW	★★½
(202) 223-3600	Expensive
Zone 11A Virginia suburbs	Quality 77 Value C
8045 Leesburg Pike, Tysons Corner	
(703) 893-0300	

Reservations:	Helpful
When to go:	Any time
Entree range:	$10.95 – 19.95
Payment:	VISA, MC, AMEX, DC
Service rating:	★★½
Friendliness rating:	★★★
Parking:	Valet (Virginia only); pay lots (D.C.)
Bar:	Full service
Wine selection:	Good
Dress:	Business, informal
Disabled access:	Good
Customers:	Local, business, tourist
Lunch:	Monday – Friday, 11:30 A.M. – 2:30 P.M.
Dinner:	D.C.: Monday – Thursday, 5:30 – 11 P.M.;
	Friday, 5:30 – 11:30 P.M.; Saturday, 5 – 11:30 P.M.;
	Sunday, 5 – 9 P.M.;
	Virginia: Monday – Thursday, 5:30 – 10 P.M.;
	Friday and Saturday, 5:30 – 10:30 P.M.

Atmosphere/setting: Prettily understated, the D.C. restaurant effects a villa manner with pale terra-cotta paint and marble. Tysons Corner is similar, but darker and more self-satisfied; after all, it's in the platinum card shopping neighborhood.

House specialties: Grilled pears over polenta and Gorgonzola; veal stuffed with a mustardy chutney and sausages; new-era pizzas from the wood oven; daily specials such as filet of beef stuffed with goat cheese and a wood-grilled veal chop; chicken breast rolled around spinach, sausage, and chopped egg; risotto.

Summary & comments: Primi Piatti made a big splash when it first opened, then began to pale in comparison as i Ricchi, Galileo, and Obelisk leaped forward. Now settled into a confident but not conservative middle age — and willing to learn from the above-mentioned, judging from the menu — Primi Piatti is a dependable and often satisfying, if occasionally theatrical, trattoria. After all, owner Savio Racino is an ambitious and market-savvy restaurateur; he's a partner with celebrity chef Yannick Cam in Coco Loco and the new El Catalan.

PROVENCE

Zone 6	Dupont Circle/
	Adams-Morgan
2401 Pennsylvania Avenue, NW	
(202) 296-1166	

French (Provençal)
★★★½
Moderate

Quality 87   Value C

Reservations:	Recommended
When to go:	Lunch
Entree range:	$18.95 – 29.95
Payment:	VISA, MC, AMEX, DC, CB
Service rating:	★★½
Friendliness rating:	★★★
Parking:	Pay lot, valet at dinner
Bar:	Full service
Wine selection:	Good
Dress:	Business, informal
Disabled access:	Good
Customers:	Local, business, tourist
Lunch:	Monday – Friday, noon – 2 P.M.
Dinner:	Monday – Thursday, 6 – 10 P.M.;
	Friday and Saturday, 5:30 – 11:30 P.M.;
	Sunday, 5:30 – 9:30 P.M.

Atmosphere/setting: Aristo-rustic, with huge windows, flagstone flooring, dried flowers, artfully weathered hutches, iron trellises, shutters, and trompe l'oeil stonework—a sunny French South villa of a fashion magazine's dreams.

House specialties: Grilled langoustines (appetizer), squid stuffed with lavender or wild mushrooms, hare-stuffed ravioli, grilled monkfish with anchovies, grilled squab with capers, grilled lobsters with truffle oil, pheasant with figs, rolled stuffed loin of rabbit, stewed veal tongue, whole fish with fennel seed. Daily specials are particularly good, but can be extremely pricey, too.

Summary & comments: This Provençal haven is the creation of local star chef Yannick Cam, first of the cutting-edge nouvelle French, Le Pavillion, and now co-owner of the Brazilian Coco Loco and the regional Spanish El Catalan. Unfortunately, such intellectual and culinary restlessness means that Cam doesn't keep his finger in the sauce as often as might be desired. But in most ways, this is truly an indulgent experience. Its heavy reliance on grilling, aromatic herbs, chard, figs, and citrus is evidence of the close relationship between Tuscan and Provençal cooking. If you like real hearty, garlicky seafood dishes, Cam has a bourride for you, a seafood stew with aïoli. Execution is somewhat erratic, and service can be wildly condescending, but when it's good, it's very, very good.

243

QUEEN BEE

Zone 11B Virginia suburbs	Vietnamese
3181 Wilson Boulevard, Arlington	★★½
(703) 527-3444	Inexpensive
	Quality 76 Value B

Reservations:	Recommended
When to go:	Soft-shell crab season
Entree range:	$4.95–8.50
Payment:	VISA, MC, AMEX
Service rating:	★★½
Friendliness rating:	★★★
Parking:	Street
Bar:	Beer and wine
Wine selection:	House
Dress:	Informal, casual
Disabled access:	Fair
Customers:	Locals
Open:	Every day, 11:15 A.M.–10 P.M.

Atmosphere/setting: A small, bustling storefront in the Little Saigon area of Arlington, Queen Bee has only a smattering of decor, and in fact looks more like the old amorphous Chinese establishments, with red flocking and plastic placemats; but it is very hospitable.

House specialties: Grilled pork, which tastes more Korean than typically Vietnamese in its marinade, but is served with traditional lettuce wrappings and dipping sauce; roast quail or duck, which can be ordered here as appetizers, entrees (the same size), or as deluxe toppings for noodle soup; papaya and jerky salad; daily fish specials, crispy fried (with a choice of toppings: the hot sauce is better than the sweet).

Other recommendations: Grilled jumbo shrimp; Saigon pancake, which is sort of like a spring roll chopped up and fried all together rather than rolled up; pho, the national noodle soup.

Summary & comments: For many years, Queen Bee earned its name as the premiere all-round Vietnamese restaurant, and it still gets almost automatic kudos, even on days when the food and the service seem a little slapdash. Still, the portions are fairly large and many old regulars are still happy—there just doesn't seem a whole lot of reason to stand in line anymore when there are a half-dozen other good Vietnamese places within eyeshot. The upside is, the increasing market power of these other cafes has forced the old dowager to brush up on her performance.

Rabieng

Zone 11B   Virginia suburbs
5892 Leesburg Pike, Baileys Crossroads
(703) 671-4222

	Thai
	★★½
	Inexpensive
	Quality 79 Value B

Reservations:	Helpful
When to go:	Any time
Entree range:	$7.95−16.95
Payment:	VISA, MC, AMEX, DC
Service rating:	★★★
Friendliness rating:	★★★
Parking:	Free lot
Bar:	Full service
Wine selection:	House
Dress:	Casual
Disabled access:	Yes
Customers:	Local, ethnic
Open:	Sunday−Thursday, 11:30 A.M.−10 P.M.;
	Friday and Saturday, 11:30 A.M.−10:30 P.M.

Atmosphere/setting: Outside, it looks like a carpet warehouse. Inside, it's super-sleek, cream-colored table tops; lacquer-smooth cream columns; and touches of dark, polished wood. The mezzanine is all wood, almost clubby.

House specialties: "Country-style" curries (usually referring to the northern or northeastern area where coconut milk is not used) and "esan" dishes, referring to the same region and usually, though not always, denoting serious chiles, such as esan sausage and a fine chopped catfish with lemongrass and chiles (both appetizers) or mustard green soup; a richer but also hot southern-style shrimp; grilled quail served with sticky rice (also chicken, whole or half); fried beef or pork with fried garlic.

Other recommendations: Panang (a phrase usually indicating curry paste) chicken with roasted peanuts; wild boar stir-fried with basil and chiles and the similarly prepared standard squid.

Summary & comments: You could learn a lot about real regional Thai cooking just by hanging out with this neighborhood restaurant group: Asian street food at Bangkok Street Grill, French-tinged court cuisine at Duangrat, and down-home chow here, including such "country favorites" as sticky rice and "farmer's" green vegetable curry. Actually, since the menu lists both Bangkok and "provincial" favorites (another French imperial touch, presumably), you could get some good contrasts here alone, and you'd be in more serious dining company than at the other, trendier two. Use the chile-pod meter in the menu.

Raku: An Asian Grill

Zone 6	Dupont Circle/
	Adams-Morgan
1900 Q Street, NW	
(202) 265-7258	
Zone 10A	Maryland suburbs
7240 Woodmont Avenue, Bethesda	
(301) 718-8680	

> Pan Asian
> ★★★½
> Inexpensive
>
> Quality 84   Value A

Reservations:	Not accepted
When to go:	Any time
Entree range:	$6.50−8.75
Payment:	VISA, MC
Service rating:	★★★
Friendliness rating:	★★★
Parking:	Street, lot
Bar:	Wine, beer, and Japanese saké
Wine selection:	Limited
Dress:	Business, casual
Disabled access:	Good
Customers:	Hip local, tourist
Open:	*D.C.:* Monday−Thursday, 11:30 A.M.−11 P.M.;
	Friday and Saturday, 11:30 A.M.−midnight;
	Sunday 11:30 A.M.−10 P.M.;
	Bethesda: Sunday−Thursday, 11:30 A.M.−10 P.M.;
	Friday and Saturday, 11:30 A.M.−11 P.M.

Atmosphere/setting: A very lively, loud crowd in a chic, cheeky, modern Asian mix, with bamboo shades, Asian music and videos, slate floors, all-exhibition cooking on grills, and dumpling steamers imported from Japan. Some tables are communal (i.e., family style) as they are in Japan; or you can sit at the "bar" right across from the grill. Glass walls slide back for deck-style sidewalk dining in Dupont Circle.

House specialties: "Peking duck" dumplings, wrapped in Vietnamese rice papers instead of moo shi pancakes; gyoza, dumplings simultaneously steamed and griddled; a very light and cooling mound of organic soba noodles with dipping sauce; Indonesian satays; noodle soups.

Other recommendations: Korean chile-fired strips of beef in broth and, for the fat-fearless, coconut curries and shrimp-paste "lollipops" on sugar cane.

Entertainment & amenities: Sidewalk cafe seating in Dupont Circle.

(continued)

Summary & comments: Creator Mark Miller of Coyote Cafe fame calls these first of a projected national chain (outlets in New York and San Francisco so far) alternatives to business delis and carryouts, with "fast, fun, and flavorful foods." Nothing will take more than five minutes to prepare, and the entire menu is nondairy and low-fat except for deep-fried foods, which are even made with low-saturated oil. The menu is divided into five food groups: noodle dishes, "wrapped" dishes, skewered foods, fried foods, and desserts. And three broths, one traditional pork and chicken, one seaweed, and one coconut, allow vegans, vegetarians, and carnivores to dine together.

Red Hot & Blue

Barbecue	
★★½	
Inexpensive	
Quality 79	Value B

Zone 11B   Virginia suburbs
1600 Wilson Boulevard, Clarendon
(703) 276-7427

Zone 10B   Maryland suburbs
16811 Crabbs Branch Way (Grove
  Shopping Center), Gaithersburg
(301) 948-7333

Zone 11B   Virginia suburbs
208 Elden Street, Herndon
(703) 318-7427

Reservations:	Not accepted
When to go:	Weekdays
Entree range:	$4.75–11.95
Payment:	VISA, MC
Service rating:	★★½
Friendliness rating:	★★★
Parking:	Street (free lot, Gaithersburg)
Bar:	Full service
Wine selection:	Limited
Dress:	Casual
Disabled access:	Good
Customers:	Local, tourist
Open:	Every day, roughly 11 A.M.–10 P.M.; call individual franchises for exact times.

Atmosphere/setting: These are get-down-to-it diners with crowds to spare but, fortunately, usually with a rowdy-friendly bar to wait in.

House specialties: Wet (rubbed and sauced) or dry (smoked and rubbed) pork ribs in half or full "slabs"; pulled chicken and pork shoulder sandwiches.

Other recommendations: The Tennessee Triple, your choice of three meats (though not wet and dry together) with slaw, beans, and bread; smoked beef brisket chili; smoked chicken nachos.

Summary & comments: Although there are burgers, ham and home-smoked turkey sandwiches, and salads on the menu, the ribs are this Memphis transplant's raison d'être (and frankly, their transplanted popularity is a puzzle). Barbecue is, of course, a source of constant bickering among adherents; these ribs can be overdone and the meat chewy, but they remain stand-in-line popular. There's a carryout branch at 3014 Wilson Boulevard in Arlington (phone (703) 243-1510), plus branches in Annapolis, Frederick, Manassas, and Laurel.

Red Sage

Zone 3   Downtown
605 14th Street, NW
(202) 638-4444

New Southwestern
★★★★
Expensive

Quality 94   Value B

Reservations: Essential for dining room; not accepted in chili bar
When to go: Any time
Entree range: $19–36
Payment: VISA, MC, AMEX, DC, D
Service rating: ★★★
Friendliness rating: ★★★
Parking: Pay lots (validated)
Bar: Full service
Wine selection: Good
Dress: Dressy, informal
Disabled access: Excellent
Customers: Local, tourist, gourmet mag groupies
Lunch: Monday–Friday, 11:30 A.M.–2:15 P.M.;
                       Chili bar: Monday–Friday, 11:30 A.M.–11:30 P.M.
Dinner: Monday–Thursday, 5:30–9:45 P.M.;
                       Friday and Saturday, 5:30–10:30 P.M.;
                       Sunday, 5–9:45 P.M.;
                       Chili bar: Saturday, 5:30–midnight;
                       Sunday, 4:30–11:30 P.M.

Atmosphere/setting: A fun and funny $5-million-plus New Wave slant on Santa Fe chic, with cast-iron lizard door handles, plaster clouds with "lightning" in the chili bar, and $100,000 worth of glass etched with campfires and broncos.

House specialties: Wild mushroom–Swiss chard ravioli; cinnamon-smoked or roasted quail with pecans and ham; wood-roasted duck; house-smoked salmon or tuna carpaccio with habanero pesto; bourbon rabbit; a vegetarian plate with poblano tamales and wood-roasted mushrooms; sausage of the day (venison, duck, rabbit, even wild boar); venison chili in the chili bar.

Other recommendations: The Cubana Torta, griddled pork loin with ham and cheese; blue cornmeal oysters. At lunch, the upstairs cafe has a choice of fascinating salads, small chic pizzas, four flavors of rotisserie chicken, etc.

Summary & comments: After the biggest preopening ballyhoo of the decade, and the inevitable deflation, Red Sage has found its feet, and its heat, gloriously. The roasted-chiles cuisine made famous by owner Mark Miller is a pungent panoply rather than a painful blur; each dish is seasoned with just the right flavor of pepper and to just the right degree, so that you are constantly astonished by the nuances. All meats and game are steroid-free.

249

Rio Grande Cafe

Zone 10A   Maryland suburbs
4919 Fairmont Avenue, Bethesda
(301) 656-2981

Zone 11B   Virginia suburbs
4301 North Fairfax Drive, Ballston
(703) 528-3131

Zone 11B   Virginia suburbs
1827 Library Street (Reston Town Center), Reston
(703) 904-0703

Reservations:	Not accepted
When to go:	Thursday for goat; early or late dinner
Entree range:	$7.25 − 16.50
Payment:	VISA, MC, AMEX, CB, DC, D
Service rating:	★★½
Friendliness rating:	★★★½
Parking:	Street
Bar:	Full service
Wine selection:	House
Dress:	Casual
Disabled access:	Good
Customers:	Local, tourist
Open:	Monday − Thursday, 11 A.M. − 10:30 P.M.;
	Friday, 11 A.M. − 11:30 P.M.;
	Saturday, 11:30 A.M. − 11:30 P.M.;
	Sunday, 11:30 A.M. − 10:30 P.M.

Atmosphere / setting: Cheeky tortilla warehouse with crates of Southwestern beer on the floor, exposed industrial ducts overhead, jokey "native" art (and even jokier graffiti on the bright walls, which is unfortunately reminiscent of South of the Border billboards), and an improbably torturous Rube Goldberg of a tortilla machine grinding out the pancakes.

House specialties: Cabrito, barbecued baby goat and goat ribs, available only on Thursdays; grilled quail; chiles rellenos.

Other recommendations: Frog legs; grilled shrimp; enchiladas.

Summary & comments: Rio Grande may not have invented the frozen-margarita-in-a-machine technique, but they perfected it and got a pretty good recipe going, too. You almost never have to wait for a refill—which is a good thing, since you may be waiting for a table. On the other hand, it may make you feel as if you're drinking on an assembly line.

Rocklands

Barbecue

★★★

Inexpensive

Quality 80   Value C

Zone 5   Georgetown
2418 Wisconsin Avenue, NW
(202) 333-2558

Zone 11B   Virginia suburbs
4000 North Fairfax Drive, Arlington
(703) 528-9663

Reservations:	Not accepted
When to go:	Afternoon, late dinner
Entree range:	$3.95−15.75
Payment:	AMEX
Service rating:	★★½
Friendliness rating:	★★★
Parking:	Limited street meters
Bar:	None
Wine selection:	None
Dress:	Casual
Disabled access:	No
Customers:	Locals
Open:	*Georgetown:* Monday−Saturday, 11:30 A.M.−10 P.M.; Sunday, 11 A.M.−9 P.M.; *Arlington:* Monday and Tuesday, 11:30 A.M.−9 P.M.; Wednesday, 11:30 A.M.−10 P.M.; Thursday, 11:30 A.M.−11 P.M.; Friday, 11:30 A.M.−midnight; Saturday, 11 A.M.−11 P.M.; Sunday, 11 A.M.−9 P.M.

Atmosphere/setting: Its small storefront size, and the fact that most of the room is taken up by pit space, kitchen, and grill, means that this is authentically a stand-up or bolt-and-carryout spot; there's only one communal service table and six or eight stools at the window counter, and the food is served in burger-shop paper dishes. The primary decor is supplied by the two wall cabinets of trendy pepper and super-hot chile sauces, chutneys, etc. The Arlington branch is really the kitchen partner of an auto dealership-turned−billiard parlor called, appropriately, the Car Pool.

House specialties: Chopped-pork sandwiches (actually almost everything, including the marinated sliced lamb loin, trout, and catfish, except the ribs and

(continued)

chicken wings, is served as a sandwich); racks in quarter, half, and full sizes; and frequently "exotic" meats or fresh fish such as salmon and swordfish.

Other recommendations: Most of the old-style side dishes, such as the greens (mustard, turnip, etc., available in pints and quarts), potato salad, slaw, fresh green beans, and red beans and rice are very good. The corn pudding is more like Stovetop Stuffing, although there are those who swear by the Caesar salad. A yuppie-ish side dish, perhaps, and one that seems to go strangely with the crew, but hey, this is Glover Park, after all.

Summary & comments: Amid the tidal wave of authentic (and only "authentic-style") pit barbecue, Rocklands might be considered a nouveau-retro meat counter, attracting both barbecue heads and food trendies. Owner John Snedden not only stocks a huge selection of super-hot chile sauces—and sets out several at a time for taste-testing—but he also likes to serve up meats more interesting than the usual pig. He's experimented with elk, boar, venison, and ostrich, and he often throws out a whole carcass (of whatever) as happy-hour fare.

R.T.'s

Zone 11C   Virginia suburbs
3804 Mount Vernon Avenue,
    Alexandria
(703) 684-6010

Cajun
★★
Moderate

Quality 73   Value B

Reservations:	Helpful but not always helpful enough
When to go:	Any time
Entree range:	$11.95−18.95
Payment:	VISA, MC, AMEX, CB, DC, D
Service rating:	★★½
Friendliness rating:	★★★
Parking:	Street
Bar:	Full service
Wine selection:	Limited but good
Dress:	Casual
Disabled access:	Good
Customers:	Locals
Lunch:	Monday−Saturday, 11 A.M.−5 P.M.
Dinner:	Monday−Thursday, 5−10:30 P.M.; Friday and Saturday, 5−11 P.M.; Sunday, 4−9 P.M.

Atmosphere/setting: A neighborhood tavern in a blue-collar neighborhood, best-known for its proximity to the Birchmere Club and for the occasional patronage of Al and Tipper Gore.

House specialties: Butter-barbecued Tabasco-lemon shrimp; crab imperial; shrimp and crab in a creamy Jack Daniel's−meets−Welsh rarebit sauce; cornmeal-fried calamari with rémoulade; crawfish étouffé; penne with roast pork, shrimp, and sausage.

Other recommendations: Pecan-flour-fried catfish or chicken topped with crabmeat; seafood linguine; blackened redfish; veal "Mardi Gras" with crabmeat.

Summary & comments: This is fun, finger-licking food, but it's definitely not for the cholesterol-conscious. Fried, heavily creamed, buttered, and proud of it, it's the sort of food New Orleans restaurants were famous for before Paul Prudhomme discovered his toes. You can get your seafood plain here, but it doesn't come naturally, and isn't always of the same-day freshness seafood purists are used to. Besides, why bother? Either go with the house's strength, or go elsewhere.

Russia House

<table>
<tr><td></td><td>Russian</td></tr>
<tr><td>Zone 11B   Virginia suburbs</td><td>★★½</td></tr>
<tr><td>790 Station Street, Herndon</td><td>Moderate</td></tr>
<tr><td>(703) 787-8880</td><td></td></tr>
<tr><td></td><td>Quality 79   Value B</td></tr>
</table>

Reservations:	Required
When to go:	Any time
Entree range:	$16.95 − 22.95
Payment:	VISA, MC, AMEX, D, DC
Service rating:	★★★
Friendliness rating:	★★★
Parking:	Street
Bar:	Full service
Wine selection:	House
Dress:	Casual
Disabled access:	Good
Customers:	Locals
Lunch:	Monday − Friday, 11:30 A.M.− 2:30 P.M.
Dinner:	Monday − Friday, 5:30 − 10 P.M.;
	Saturday, 5:30 − 10:30 P.M.; Sunday, 5 − 9 P.M.

Atmosphere/setting: Not terribly evocative—an émigré's cafe; if anything, just sort of generic restaurant—but with some funny murals and those painted wood dolls. And for area diners sick of franchised fare, this is a godsend.

House specialties: Beef-stuffed pelmeni dumplings; a good version of kulebiaka, a layered casserole of rice and vegetables, but here made with lamb instead of the usual salmon; steak tartare; duck with sour cherries or, more intriguingly, with rinsed sauerkraut; "Georgian-style" (meaning classic Black Sea/Middle Eastern) lemon-sautéed chicken; a cheesy pork and lamb casserole; a rich fettuccine with sour cream and salmon caviar that will make you forsake Alfredo forever.

Other recommendations: A good but not unforgettable traditional beef stroganov; a not-so-traditional scallops with sun-dried tomatoes; stuffed cabbage leaves.

Summary & comments: This is a fun spot, although not so over-the-top dramatic as the better-known Serbian Crown. And the cooking can be more erratic, although less so as time goes on. If you'd like to linger, make a meal of vodka and various zakuski, the forerunners of French hors d'oeuvres, such as caviar, snails, pâté, shrimp flambé, smoked salmon, and meat-and-cabbage-stuffed piroshki.

Sabang

Zone 10B Maryland suburbs	Indonesian
2504 Ennalls Avenue, Wheaton	★★½
(301) 942-7859	Inexpensive
	Quality 75 Value B

Reservations:	Helpful
When to go:	Any time
Entree range:	$7−12
Payment:	VISA, MC, AMEX
Service rating:	★★★
Friendliness rating:	★★★
Parking:	Street
Bar:	Full service
Wine selection:	Minimal
Dress:	Informal, casual
Disabled access:	Good
Customers:	Local, ethnic
Open:	Monday−Thursday, 11 A.M.−10 P.M.; Friday, 11 A.M.−11 P.M.; Saturday, noon−11 P.M.; Sunday, noon−10 P.M.

Atmosphere/setting: An elaborately distracting room with splendidly carved animals, huge peacock fans, statuary, and the ornate, oversized umbrella shades of Indonesia stuck around the room.

House specialties: Various fish—red snapper and grouper among them—offered in sauces ranging from a light curry to a tangy but not really challenging chile-tomato sauce; anything (beef, fish, pork) in kalio sauce, a delicious coconut-coriander potion.

Other recommendations: Vegetarian dishes; pork or beef satay with either sweet or hot dipping sauces.

Entertainment & amenities: Thickly cushioned seats and the intriguing offer to sell ten of the carved wooden napkin holders, which are fish or frogs or shrimp turned on themselves, for $6.

Summary & comments: A fun way to sample Sabang's kitchen is to order a rijsttafel, the Dutch-style "rice table" of numerous small portions. There are four types here, ranging from the vegetarian to the "super" seafood version, priced from $27 to $55 for two and involving 15 to 17 dishes. Some dishes admittedly get repetitious, particularly in the vegetarian version, but the fish dishes are remarkable.

SAM & HARRY'S

Zone 6	Dupont Circle/
	Adams-Morgan
1200 19th Street, NW	
(202) 296-4333	

Steak
★★★
Expensive

Quality 84   Value C

Reservations:	Recommended
When to go:	Any time
Entree range:	$19–31.95
Payment:	VISA, MC, AMEX, CB, DC, D
Service rating:	★★★★
Friendliness rating:	★★★★
Parking:	Street, lot, valet (dinner only)
Bar:	Full service
Wine selection:	Very good
Dress:	Business, dressy
Disabled access:	Good
Customers:	Business, local
Lunch:	Monday–Friday, 11:30 A.M.–2:30 P.M.
Dinner:	Monday–Saturday, 5:30–10:30 P.M.;
	Sunday, closed.

Atmosphere/setting: Dark columns and woodwork pun on (or provide protective camouflage for) the silk-stocking law and lobby firms that surround this expense-account parlor; glass and French doors make seating flexible.

House specialties: The signature steak is a two-inch-thick New York strip, and there is also a two-pound Delmonico house favorite; also, prime rib, lobsters in the three- to four-pound range, and crab cakes. Sam & Harry's has an amazing special between Fourth of July and Labor Day. Every bottle of wine in the cellar is half-price on Friday and Saturday nights.

Other recommendations: Veal T-bones; shrimp and scallop salad (lunch only).

Entertainment & amenities: The adjoining Evening Star Jazz Bar offers live music and light entrees every evening.

Summary & comments: Modeled on Morton's of Chicago, where one of the owners once worked, Sam & Harry's serves everything in giant portions, including triple-sized salads and baked potatoes the size of small pets. The staff is so used to splitting meals, even those potatoes, that they sometimes bring extra plates without waiting for you to ask—and you'll still need a doggie bag. Potatoes are offered in six or seven versions. Salads offer a little variety, too; one features goat cheese, apples, pecans, and endive. Play to the kitchen's strength; don't expect too much of the fish here.

Sam Woo

Korean
★★★
Moderate

Quality 81   Value B

Zone 10B   Maryland suburbs
1054 Rockville Pike, Rockville
(301) 424-0495

Reservations:	Accepted
When to go:	Any time
Entree range:	$10−20
Payment:	VISA, MC, AMEX, DC
Service rating:	★★★
Friendliness rating:	★★★
Parking:	Free lot
Bar:	Beer and wine
Wine selection:	House
Dress:	Casual
Disabled access:	Good
Customers:	Local, ethnic, business
Open:	Every day, 11:30 A.M.−10:30 p.m

Atmosphere / setting: Rather simple, with varnished wood; sushi bar and Japanese banners to one side.

House specialties: Monkfish stew, spicy shredded beef, and rice soup; yook hwe bibimbag (raw beef with vegetables and rice); a sort of sashimi version of raw fish and vegetables with noodles; bulgoki (sweet-soy marinated Korean barbecue); tripe stew (for two).

Other recommendations: Sushi; spicy squid or octopus in a skillet; flounder with chile sauce; tempura.

Summary & comments: This is the best example of a long-underrated cuisine finally getting its due—and not having to pull its spice punches anymore. Grill-topped tables offer Korean-style barbecuing applied to homey dishes, such as beef tongue, as well as chicken or pork. The all-you-can-eat lunch buffet for $6.95 draws big crowds and offers both Korean- and Japanese-style dishes.

Santa Fe East

Zone 11C   Virginia suburbs
110 South Pitt Street
(703) 548-6900

New Southwestern
★★★
Moderate

Quality 80   Value B

Reservations:	Recommended
When to go:	Weekdays before 7:30
Entree range:	$12−18
Payment:	VISA, MC, AMEX, DC
Service rating:	★★½
Friendliness rating:	★★★
Parking:	Street; validated nearby garage after 5 P.M.
Bar:	Full service
Wine selection:	Limited but good
Dress:	Informal, casual
Disabled access:	Good
Customers:	Local, tourist
Open:	Sunday − Thursday, 11:30 A.M.−10 P.M.;
	Friday and Saturday, 11:30 A.M.−11 P.M.

Atmosphere/setting: Unquestionably one of the prettiest restaurants in this area, with exposed brick and wood planking, trompe l'oeil windows, cigar store Indian carvings and artifacts, and a lovely enclosed courtyard.

House specialties: A sort of fusion empanada stuffed with shrimp, hearts of palm and mushrooms, tequila-splashed shrimp, or goat cheese-stuffed poblano peppers fried in blue cornmeal and topped with green pork chile (appetizers); salmon marinated in coconut milk and seared on the griddle; a traditional paella; roast monkfish and lump crab with Pommery sauce; duck leg confit and grilled duck breast with pumpkin seed mole. Daily specials, especially game, are the most interesting here, although they hew pretty closely to the new-Southwest creed of turning both chic: An "apache-style" braise of buffalo ribs was dressed with green chiles and a merlot reduction, which might have surprised the abstemious tribe a little; but there was plenty of Wild West romance in a mixed grill with veal tenderloin, wild boar loin, and semi-boneless quail stuffed with chorizo and served with a green pepper−corn whiskey sauce.

Summary & comments: This kitchen is fighting hard to retain its reputation for inventive and amusing cooking under Alison Swope (now gone to Stella's) and it's had to learn the hard way what is fresh and what is merely frantic. A smoked duck and black bean quesadilla with melted Brie seemed only cute; but such missteps are occurring less often. Note that a 17% gratuity is added to bills for eight or more diners.

SARINAH SATAY HOUSE

Zone 5   Georgetown
~~1338 Wisconsin Avenue, NW~~
~~(202) 337-2955~~

Indonesian	
★★½	
Inexpensive	
Quality 77	Value C

Reservations:	Accepted
When to go:	Any time
Entree range:	$7.95 − 14.95
Payment:	VISA, MC, AMEX, DC, D
Service rating:	★★
Friendliness rating:	★★★
Parking:	Street
Bar:	Full service
Wine selection:	House
Dress:	Casual, informal
Disabled access:	No
Customers:	Locals
Lunch:	Tuesday − Saturday, noon − 3 P.M.
Dinner:	Tuesday − Sunday, 6 − 10:30 P.M.; Monday, closed.

Atmosphere/setting: This is a clandestine lovers' dream spot. A mysterious hallway opens up into a secret garden, a courtyard glassed over but with tree trunks still protruding from its stone flooring, carved zoological imps, and obliging waiters in batik.

House specialties: Spring rolls with chile-spiked dipping sauce; chicken with a darker peanut dip; a combination plate of coconut chicken, skewered beef, and spicy, crisp green beans.

Other recommendations: Potato croquettes with nuggets of meat; seafood dumplings; a firestorm beef stew.

Summary & comments: Although Wheaton's Sabang is better known and more theatrical, Sarinah has more punch for the penny and more personalized service. This is a good place to put together a sampler dinner of your own design; rijsttafel here is a dozen dishes long, but for $22.95 a couple, its dishes don't range far from the standard menu.

SEA CATCH

Zone 5   Georgetown
1054 31st Street, NW
(202) 337-8855

Seafood	
★★★	
Moderate	
Quality 83	Value B

Reservations:	Recommended
When to go:	Early
Entree range:	$15.75−23
Payment:	VISA, MC, AMEX, DC, D
Service rating:	★★★
Friendliness rating:	★★½
Parking:	Valet
Bar:	Full service
Wine selection:	Good
Dress:	Casual, business
Disabled access:	Good
Customers:	Local, business
Lunch:	Monday−Saturday, noon−3 P.M.
Dinner:	Monday−Saturday, 5:30−10:30 P.M.; Sunday, closed.

Atmosphere/setting: Sleekly elegant, with a white marble raw bar, polished-wood dining room with fireplace and, in good weather, a balcony overlooking the Chesapeake and Ohio Canal.

House specialties: House-smoked salmon and big-eye tuna; lobster specials, such as medallions over fettuccine or steamed lobster, mussels, oysters, clams, and shrimp; shrimp with saffron; soft-shell crabs with pesto; scallops with black olive and tomato tapenade; the low-fat, catfish-flavored Amazon fish called pirarucu.

Other recommendations: The four-course prix fixe special showcasing "Riviera"—meaning primarily southern French—fare; trout with sun-dried tomatoes; crab cakes. A personal "off the menu" favorite is the lobster sashimi, which is only available when the raw bar isn't too busy.

Summary & comments: This is an underrated seafood establishment particularly ideal for people who suffer from fear of frying. The key here is balance: The kitchen likes to play with its presentations, but not to the point where the quality or texture of the shellfish is obscured. Those who prefer the straighter stuff may order lobster steamed, grilled, broiled, baked, or poached; a variety of fresh fish (there is no freezer in the kitchen, proof of the chef's dedication to freshness) brushed with oil and grilled; or an updated surf-and-turf of tenderloin and crab-stuffed mushrooms. However, for dedicated carnivores, the Thai-marinated roast chicken or the steaks are very dependable. There is also a pretheater menu for $18.95.

Seasons

Zone 5 Georgetown	Modern American
2800 Pennsylvania Avenue	★★★★
(Four Seasons Hotel)	Expensive
(202) 944-2000	Quality 93 Value B

Reservations:	Recommended
When to go:	Any time
Entree range:	$19.97 − 34
Payment:	VISA, MC, AMEX, DC
Service rating:	★★★★
Friendliness rating:	★★★
Parking:	Valet (validated)
Bar:	Full service
Wine selection:	Very good
Dress:	Business, informal
Disabled access:	Good
Customers:	Business, tourist, local
Breakfast:	Monday − Friday, 7 − 11 a.m;
	Saturday and Sunday, 8 − noon
Lunch:	Monday − Friday, noon − 2:30 P.M.
Dinner:	Daily, 6 − 10:30 P.M.

Atmosphere / setting: A classic grand-hotel dining room as far as service and setting is concerned, but with lots of plants to up the intimacy level.

House specialties: The menu changes almost constantly, but characteristic dishes include wild mushroom ravioli, carpaccio with sun-dried tomato tapenade, duck foie gras with apple and grape compotes, mushroom and barley-stuffed quail or richly colored grilled vegetable terrine (all appetizers); loin of rabbit with braised endive and tangerines; loin of venison with porcini risotto; crispy oriental duck with ginger − stir fried vegetables; grilled Chilean bass with tapenade.

Summary & comments: It's almost incomprehensible that chef Doug Mc-Neill, who can maintain a suitably MOR hotel menu while investing it with so much interest, could be so under-celebrated in his own city except by his industry peers. (He's so admired by some more critically acclaimed chefs, in fact, that it recalls the old saying, "Plagiarism is the sincerest form of flattery.") It's also hard to imagine a place that has introduced more consumer-friendly ideas, such as the long list of moderately priced good wines by the glass, the business-oriented "$19.97 express lunch," and really good vegetarian and low-cal/low-fat/low-sodium dishes. In fact, this was one of the first restaurants in Washington to put any real thought into alternative cuisine. The chef's tasting dinner for $55 is a must.

Serbian Crown

Zone 11A Virginia suburbs	Russian
1141 Walker Road, Great Falls	★★★
(703) 759-4150	Expensive
	Quality 80 Value B

Reservations:	Helpful
When to go:	Any time
Entree range:	$16–24
Payment:	VISA, MC, AMEX, D, DC
Service rating:	★★★
Friendliness rating:	★★★½
Parking:	Free lot
Bar:	Full service
Wine selection:	Fair
Dress:	Business, informal
Disabled access:	Good
Customers:	Locals
Lunch:	Thursday and Friday, 11:30 A.M.–2:30 P.M.
Dinner:	Monday–Thursday, 5:30–8:30 P.M.;
	Friday and Saturday, 5:30 P.M.–1:30 A.M.;
	Sunday, 4–8:30 P.M.

Atmosphere/setting: Although the outside has a certain A-frame ski resort look, inside is a kitschy cross between a Romanov hunting lodge and a comfortable Southern house of ill repute—going for baroque, but in a nice way: wine-red walls, somewhat garish paintings hung frame-to-frame, carved wood trim, and a huge glass-topped piano in the bar for singalongs. In fact, it's hard to imagine a weirder good-time evening, especially in this residential and somewhat restrained neighborhood, than tossing back vodka in the bar.

House specialties: Kulebiaka, the classic salmon in pastry (served for two); marinated wild boar and game specials, especially venison; chicken Kiev (breast meat pocketed with butter, rolled in breadcrumbs, and sautéed in more butter); cold lobster; and, of course, stroganov.

Other recommendations: Piroshki, little meat dumplings, or a mixed appetizer zakuski platter with smoked fish and pâté; skewered pork, veal, or lamb (reminders of the Tartar connection).

Summary & comments: This second-generation site (it was for many years atop Tenleytown) is a little less hoity-toity than in the old days, and a little more gypsy-violin theatrical, but with the boom in Russian nostalgia, it may rise again.

SESTO SENSO

Zone 6 Dupont Circle/	Italian
Adams-Morgan	★★★
1214 18th Street, NW	Moderate
(202) 785-9525	Quality 82 Value B

Reservations:	Recommended
When to go:	Lunch, early dinner (unless you dance)
Entree range:	$7–21
Payment:	VISA, MC, AMEX, DC
Service rating:	★★★
Friendliness rating:	★★★
Parking:	Valet (dinner only), street, garage
Bar:	Full service
Wine selection:	Good
Dress:	Business, informal
Disabled access:	Good
Customers:	Local, business, hip
Lunch:	Monday–Friday, 11:30 A.M.–3 P.M.
Dinner:	Monday–Saturday, 5:30–10:30 P.M.;
	Sunday, closed.

Atmosphere/setting: Tuscan gold and easy to eat in, this is one of those restaurants that goes Eurotrash disco after dinner and edges into a serious singles scene. Dress to impress.

House specialties: Really intriguing pastas, ranging from spinach tagliolini with eggplant and plum tomatoes to pappardelle with braised artichokes; from shrimp-stuffed capellacchi to tricolor stacchi with sautéed cabbage, pancetta, and potatoes; and one of the finest vegan dishes in town, an eggless strozzapreti with artichokes, mushrooms, and fresh tomato concassé. There are usually a couple of "meat" dishes—by which we mean stewed baby octopus, scallops, or some other seafood and probably a steak—that are good, but do not play to the kitchen's strength. In fact, it's a place you might want to have a full-sized pasta and an appetizer meat, such as the marinated sliced veal with sweet-and-sour shallots.

Other recommendations: Comforting antipasti-sized dishes of carpaccio, grilled veggies, grilled calamari, etc. (or a combo); '90s pizzas, topped with calamari and zukes, prosciutto and mushrooms, baby artichokes, etc.

Summary & comments: If all pasta-and-poseur places were this good at what they did, we'd all be wearing Armani. Or rather, if they were as good as this one is on its good days; undependability remains the major bugaboo.

701

Zone 3 Downtown	Modern American
701 Pennsylvania Avenue, NW	★★½
(202) 393-0701	Moderate
	Quality 79 Value C

Reservations:	Recommended
When to go:	Any time
Entree range:	$14.50−22.50
Payment:	VISA, MC, AMEX, DC
Service rating:	★★★★
Friendliness rating:	★★★
Parking:	Valet (dinner only), street
Bar:	Full service
Wine selection:	Very good
Dress:	Dressy, business, informal
Disabled access:	Excellent
Customers:	Business, local, tourist
Lunch:	Monday−Friday, 11:30 A.M.−3 P.M.
Dinner:	Monday−Thursday, 5:30−11 P.M.;
	Friday and Saturday, 5:30 P.M.−midnight;
	Sunday, 5:30−9:30 P.M.

Atmosphere/setting: Elegant, sweeping, Deco curves with striking modern art and bright window expanses.

House specialties: Caviar and vodka from the caviar bar; tapas, served at lunch and all evening, including mussels in chervil, squid in beer, marinated eggplant, and quail; charred giant rib steak in cracked white pepper; "alternative cuisine" vegetarian dishes.

Other recommendations: Oysters on the half shell with shrimp salsa; shrimp-ricotta ravioli; ginger and soy-flavored spaghetti squash; polenta with wilted greens.

Entertainment & amenities: Live jazz nightly.

Summary & comments: 701 offers a broad range of fun-fancy dining, from a whole night of caviar or tapas to cassoulets and pastas. If anything, such versatility may be its only weakness; sometimes a few of the entrees seem not quite finished (or, alternatively, overdone). But this ambitious restaurant improves every month, and its romance quotient is very high. 701 also offers a generous, three-course pretheater meal, available 5:30 to 7 P.M., for $19.95.

Seven Seas

Zone 10B   Maryland suburbs
1776 East Jefferson Street (1776 Plaza
    Shopping Center), Rockville
(301) 770-5020

	Chinese
	★★★½
	Moderate
Quality 85	Value B

Reservations:	Only for 5 or more
When to go:	Early on weekends
Entree range:	$9.95 – 25
Payment:	VISA, MC, AMEX, D
Service rating:	★★★
Friendliness rating:	★★½
Parking:	Free lot
Bar:	Full service
Wine selection:	House
Dress:	Informal, casual
Disabled access:	No
Customers:	Ethnic, local
Open:	Every day, 11 A.M. – 1 A.M.

Atmosphere/setting: A large, bustling series of rooms divided by oriental archways and a few paintings; sushi bar and bar to one side.

House specialties: Fresh seafood and fish, particularly blue and Dungeness crabs available in your choice of spicy black bean, ginger, or mild Cantonese sauce; tiny Manila or giant razorback clams; live Pacific scallops looking and tasting more like mild oysters and topped with julienned scallions and ginger; steamed whole fish, particularly the slightly fatty black cod (it stays moist and the fatty layer drops away), simmered at the table in light ginger and soy broth.

Other recommendations: Jumbo shrimp in ginger sauce; squid in black bean sauce; wrap-it-yourself lettuce rolls with minced seafood and water chestnut filling; lovely delicate bok choy with mushrooms. On weekends, some dim sum.

Summary & comments: The first thing you see in this Shanghai palace is the tanks of live lobsters, crabs, and shellfish and the menu board of seafood specials: pink scallops; green-shelled mussels; Manila clams; Ice Island cod; and red, blue, and Dungeness crabs among them. Take that as a strong hint: Although this is a full-range Chinese restaurant, seafood is what they do best. Beef or pork dishes are better elsewhere. There are also Japanese items on the menu, but stick to sashimi: The cold, pasty, and poorly seasoned sushi rice doesn't pass muster.

1789

Zone 5   Georgetown
1226 36th Street, NW
(202) 965-1789

Modern American
★★★
Expensive
Quality 83   Value C

Reservations:	Recommended
When to go:	Any time
Entree range:	$18−29
Payment:	VISA, MC, AMEX, DC, D
Service rating:	★★★
Friendliness rating:	★★★
Parking:	Valet
Bar:	Full service
Wine selection:	Good
Dress:	Jacket required
Disabled access:	No
Customers:	Local, business, tourist
Dinner:	Sunday−Thursday, 6−10 P.M.; Friday, 6−11 P.M.; Saturday, 5−11 P.M.

Atmosphere/setting: A meticulously maintained Federal town house with blazing fireplaces, polished silver, and historic poise; a certain formality is implied rather than expressed.

House specialties: Pan-roasted lobster with ginger and cilantro; rockfish with carrots and fennel; grilled barbecued duck breast with greens; venison medallions with black trumpet mushrooms.

Other recommendations: Rack of lamb with polenta; lobster risotto; three-way salmon appetizers (smoked, salt-cured, and tartare); pan-seared salmon with cherries.

Summary & comments: This menu, inspired by seasonal availability, showcases regional game and seafood with care and respect. The kitchen aims to re-create and reclaim classic dishes—grilled quail with oysters and bacon, venison medallions, rack of lamb—and update them rather than invent novel treatments. In other words, it's more of a culinary tender of the flame than an innovator, which suits its old-money clientele. However, under the direction of chef Ris Lacoste, the kitchen is moving with increasing confidence into a middle ground, still classic but fresh. Vegetarian options are especially intriguing.

Star of Siam

Zone 6   Dupont Circle/
          Adams-Morgan
1136 19th Street, NW
(202) 785-2838

Zone 6   Dupont Circle/
          Adams-Morgan
2446 18th Street, NW
(202) 986-4133

Thai
★★★
Inexpensive
Quality 80   Value A

Reservations:	Accepted
When to go:	Any time
Entree range:	$7.95−12.95
Payment:	VISA, MC, AMEX, DC, D
Service rating:	★★★
Friendliness rating:	★★★
Parking:	Street
Bar:	Full service
Wine selection:	House
Dress:	Casual
Disabled access:	No
Customers:	Locals
Lunch/Dinner:	*19th Street:* Monday − Saturday, 11:30 A.M.−11 P.M.
Dinner:	*18th Street:* Monday − Friday, 5−11 P.M.;
	Saturday, noon−11 P.M.; Sunday, noon−10 P.M.;
	19th Street: Sunday, 5−10 P.M.

Atmosphere/setting: Both are in bright town houses, the 19th Street one predominantly lavender and horticulture, the 18th Street site with a traditional seating area of multicolored cushion-chairs in a vast loft.

House specialties: Fried whole fish with chiles; shrimp and scallops with basil and chiles; red curry with duck, pineapple, and coconut; green curry of chicken with eggplant.

Other recommendations: Spicy rice noodles with beef and basil; roast duck salad; Thai-style sweet-and-sour pork; shrimp, scallops, and squid with onions, chiles, and basil.

Summary & comments: Flavors come in colors here: green, red, yellow, and even a pale pink, tinted by basils and chiles and coconut milk. Since Thai kitchens in general became freer with the chiles, Star of Siam has stopped pulling its punches and the food can be had extremely hot if you ask specifically.

Straits of Malaya

Zone 6   Dupont Circle/
           Adams-Morgan
1836 18th Street, NW
(202) 483-1483

Indonesian	
★★	
Inexpensive	
Quality 71	Value C

Reservations:	Accepted
When to go:	Any time
Entree range:	$9.95−14.95
Payment:	VISA, MC, AMEX
Service rating:	★★½
Friendliness rating:	★★★½
Parking:	Street, parking lot
Bar:	Full service
Wine selection:	House
Dress:	Casual
Disabled access:	No
Customers:	Locals
Lunch:	Monday−Friday, noon−2 P.M.
Dinner:	Sunday−Thursday, 5:30−10 P.M.;
	Friday and Saturday, 5:30−11 P.M.

Atmosphere/setting: An exotic theme inside—lots of batik fabrics, grass-look wallpaper—and bustly/yuppie up on the roof deck.

House specialties: Fat rice noodles with chile and chicken; moderately spicy Indonesian beef curry; spicy eggplant curry with chicken; five-spice roll; laksa, a meal-sized soup.

Other recommendations: Coconut-milk shrimp; satays; whole chile flounder; scallion-flavored shrimp crêpes with hot dipping sauce.

Summary & comments: This is a perfect microcosm of Singapore culture: a little Indian, a lot of Chinese, a touch of Japanese, and some happily hybrid spicing—and almost any dish can be ordered in vegetarian form. If you want something really hot, it's best to ask, although the natural blend here is tangy to just fleetingly sweaty. Service is better when the room is busier, for some reason.

Sushi Kappo Kawasaki

Zone 6	Dupont Circle/
	Adams-Morgan
1140 19th Street, NW	
(202) 466-3798	

Japanese
★★★
Expensive

Quality 84   Value D

Reservations:	Recommended
When to go:	Any time
Entree range:	$12−30
Payment:	VISA, MC, AMEX, DC
Service rating:	★★★
Friendliness rating:	★★★
Parking:	Street
Bar:	Limited liquor
Wine selection:	House
Dress:	Business, informal
Disabled access:	No
Customers:	Ethnic, local, business
Lunch:	Monday−Friday, noon−2:30 P.M.
Dinner:	Monday−Saturday, 5:30−10 P.M.; Sunday, closed.

Atmosphere/setting: A natty, varnished wood hideaway in the English basement of a modern, charcoal-grey office building, divided into a corridor of small dining areas, with three tatami rooms in the rear.

House specialties: Sushi; tempura.

Other recommendations: Broiled eel; nabeyaki udon, a soup with fat noodles, seafood, and shrimp.

Summary & comments: This is an offshoot of an earlier sushi bar that catered primarily to Japanese businessmen with expense accounts. The clientele is much the same and so are the prices: at least 25% higher and in some cases as much as twice as expensive as most other sushi bars in town, although the quality is very high and the pieces quite large, particularly of the fatty tuna delicacy known as toro. To preserve its freshness, however, Sushi Kappo keeps the temperature of its sushi bar rather low, and the fish occasionally loses a bit of its flavor, so it's a toss-up. The tempura here is the best in town—light, greaseless, and crisp. Service depends to some degree on a customer's familiarity with the staff and food (or language). Sushi Kappo also offers a kaiseki dinner (see the profile for Makoto) for $60 and up.

Sushi-Ko

Zone 5   Georgetown
2309 Wisconsin Avenue, NW
(202) 333-4187

Japanese
★★★★
Moderate

Quality 92   Value B

Reservations:	Recommended on weekends
When to go:	Any time
Entree range:	$8.50−18.50
Payment:	VISA, MC, AMEX
Service rating:	★★★
Friendliness rating:	★★★
Parking:	Street, valet (dinner only)
Bar:	Full service
Wine selection:	House
Dress:	Business, casual
Disabled access:	No
Customers:	Local, ethnic
Lunch:	Tuesday−Friday, noon−2:30 P.M.
Dinner:	Monday−Friday, 6−10:30 P.M.;
	Saturday, 5−10:30 P.M.; Sunday, 5−10 P.M.

Atmosphere/setting: Sushi bar to the max: a simple but natty, samurai-print-and-varnished-wood, two-story establishment with the sushi bar in the rear.

House specialties: Sushi, especially seasonal dishes such as ankimo (monk-fish liver) and toro (fatty tuna); and any of head chef Kaz Okochi's original recipes, such as a "Napoleon" of chopped sea trout layered in fried wontons and smoked ankimo over mesclun with purple potato vinaigrette. These are usually chalked up on a board near the sushi bar.

Other recommendations: Broiled eel; soft-shell crabs; octopus salad; grilled fish.

Summary & comments: Thanks to its upper Georgetown location, an early jump on the sushi bandwagon and smart, selective pampering, Sushi-Ko attracts a broad, generally knowledgeable and fairly affluent crowd. This has made it possible for owner Daisuke Utagawa and Okochi to offer a more flexible style of cooking, both traditional and improvisational—that is, based on market availability and traditional seasonal factors. However, while the "ordinary" sushi is reasonable, those specials can make dinner somewhat more pricey than a meal at most other sushi bars, so don't waste it on someone who's happy with grocery-store California roll. Utagawa is also intrigued with the notion of matching Japanese food to wines, and with offering higher quality sakés.

Tabard Inn

Zone 6   Dupont Circle/
Adams-Morgan
1739 N Street, NW
(202) 833-2668

Modern American
★★½
Moderate
Quality 77   Value B

Reservations:	Recommended
When to go:	Any time
Entree range:	$15−22
Payment:	VISA, MC
Service rating:	★★½
Friendliness rating:	★★★
Parking:	Street
Bar:	Full service
Wine selection:	Limited
Dress:	Informal
Disabled access:	No
Customers:	Locals, power women
Breakfast:	Every day, 7−10 A.M.
Brunch:	Saturday and Sunday, 11 A.M.−2:30 P.M.
Lunch:	Monday−Friday, 11:30 A.M.−2:30 P.M.
Dinner:	Sunday and Monday, 6−10 P.M.;
	Tuesday−Saturday, 6−10:30 P.M.

Atmosphere/setting: This almost anachronistic English-rural inn has a series of dining rooms, some really parlors; brick terrace for good weather; and a wood-lined library with fireplace for evening cocktails.

House specialties: Vegetarian platters; home-smoked bluefish or trout; seafood salads and pastas; blini (buckwheat waffles) and salmon; chicken with ever-shifting seasonings; grilled game birds.

Other recommendations: Vegetable salads; daily specials; Asian-spiced calamari or eggplant; smoked salmon and cheese Napoleons; house-peppered vodka.

Summary & comments: The Tabard likes to use its own additive-free farm produce whenever possible, so spring and summer veggies and herbs are particularly good. The menu hopes to cover most of the bases every day, so there's usually at least one chicken, one pasta, one veggie special, etc. The menu always commands interest, though the success of each dish may vary.

Taberna del Alabardero

Zone 3   Downtown
1776 I Street, NW (entrance on 18th
    Street)
(202) 429-2200

Spanish
★★★½
Expensive

Quality 88   Value C

Reservations:	Recommended
When to go:	Any time for tapas; lunch for fixed-price meals
Entree range:	$18−25
Payment:	VISA, MC, AMEX, DC, D
Service rating:	★★★★
Friendliness rating:	★★★
Parking:	Free next door
Bar:	Full service
Wine selection:	Very good
Dress:	Jacket and tie suggested
Disabled access:	Good
Customers:	Local, embassy, ethnic
Lunch:	Monday−Friday, 11:30 A.M.−2:30 P.M.
Dinner:	Monday−Thursday, 6−10 P.M.;
	Friday and Saturday, 6−11 P.M.; Sunday, closed.

Atmosphere/setting: Lace curtain and velvet Old-World elegance, with ornate moldings and a magnificent private room (like a chapel) in the center.

House specialties: Lobster paella at night, as well as traditional paella and the pasta version called fideua (there is a variety of versions at lunch); venison; rabbit casserole or boneless rabbit and lobster medallions dealt alternately on the plate; duck confit; stuffed squid in ink; sweetbreads.

Other recommendations: Daily specials, particularly game, and at least a half-dozen seafood specials every day; quail or pheasant; halibut with mussels.

Summary & comments: This is a very Old-World-style restaurant and quite dignified; some people may find it weighty as well. One alternative is to dabble in Taberna's riches via the tapas menu, a selection of a dozen smaller-sized dishes, including a serving of the paella, for $3.50 to $6.50 apiece (and you can linger as long as you like). Other choices include artichoke bottoms baked with ham; empanadas; grilled chorizo; poached calamari in a salad of sweet peppers. There is also a list of a dozen sherries by the glass and red or white sangria. Taverna now offers ten set lunch menus, ranging from $28−38, making it a little quicker, if not less expensive. And it's also getting into the special-events trend, with wine dinners and imported guest chefs.

Tachibana

<table>
<tr><td>

Zone 11A   Virginia suburbs
6715 Lowell Avenue, McLean
(703) 847-1771

</td><td>

Japanese
★★★½
Moderate

Quality 88   Value B

</td></tr>
</table>

Reservations:	Recommended on weekends
When to go:	Any time
Entree range:	$8.95 – 25
Payment:	VISA, MC, AMEX, DC, D
Service rating:	★★★
Friendliness rating:	★★★
Parking:	Large lot
Bar:	Full service
Wine selection:	House
Dress:	Informal, casual
Disabled access:	Good
Customers:	Local, ethnic
Lunch:	Monday – Friday, 11:30 A.M. – 2 P.M.
Dinner:	Monday – Thursday, 5 – 10 P.M.; Friday and Saturday, 5 – 10:30 P.M.

Atmosphere/setting: A sophisticated though not particularly traditional room: slightly split-level, mostly dark green and polished wood, but with two separate sushi bars. The larger front one is a sleek lacquer-like curve and the second, in the back room, is smaller and simpler, with two slabs of what appear to be polished driftwood hanging overhead instead of the usual cloth flags.

House specialties: Teriyaki jaw of yellowtail; squid tempura; shabu shabu (requires 24 hours' notice); soft-shell crabs in season.

Other recommendations: One-pot meals such as nabeyaki or sukiyaki, available in vegetarian versions; traditional grilled salmon over rice with green tea poured over it.

Summary & comments: This may not be one of the grandest sushi bars in the area, but it's one of the best. Although some of the high-quality sushi here has American names, it tends to be authentic under the seaweed skin: "Washington roll," for example, is broiled eel with scallions and shiso, the basil-like Japanese herb. Tachibana's seafood is fresh and generously sliced, and the teriyaki jaw of yellowtail enormous. The homier soups and stews, not available in more trend-minded shops, are not only fine bargains but real comfort food; after all, Japanese mothers have been making nabemono as long as Jewish mothers have been making chicken soup.

273

Tako Grill

Zone 10A   Maryland suburbs
7756 Wisconsin Avenue, Bethesda
(301) 652-7030

Japanese	
★★★★	
Moderate	
Quality 92	Value B

Reservations:	Not accepted
When to go:	Before 7
Entree range:	$7.50−16.50
Payment:	VISA, MC, AMEX
Service rating:	★★★★
Friendliness rating:	★★★
Parking:	Street, public garages, free lot (dinner only)
Bar:	Wine and beer
Wine selection:	House
Dress:	Casual, informal
Disabled access:	Very good
Customers:	Local, business
Lunch:	Monday−Friday, 11:30 A.M.−2 P.M.
Dinner:	Monday−Thursday, 5:30−10 P.M.;
	Friday and Saturday, 5:30−10:30 P.M.;
	Sunday, 5−9:30 P.M.

Atmosphere/setting: A cool, hip, very '90s-Tokyo room, a study in white, black, and scarlet, but with deft artistic touches (the flower arrangements) and almost hallucinatory "script" versions of Japanese verses hung on the walls. (The chefs, particularly the younger ones, are very Tokyo-stylish, too—check out the bleached and reddened hair.)

House specialties: Grilled jaw of yellowtail; ankimo, a monkfish liver pâté; soft-shell crabs tempura-fried and chopped into hand rolls.

Other recommendations: Grilled whole red snapper or rainbow trout; glazed grilled eel; tiny candied whole octopus.

Summary & comments: Of the three best Japanese restaurants in the area, each has a different slant: Makoto's classic; Sushi-Ko's cutting-edge; and Tako's cool. In addition to some of the best and freshest sushi and sashimi in the area, Tako has a hot-stone grill called a robotai, on which whole fish, large shrimp, and a variety of fresh vegetables are cooked. The line of customers waiting to get in— the recent expansion notwithstanding—is the surest evidence of Tako's quality. Weekday lunches are a business special: soup, salad, rice, and a daily entree (orange roughy, chicken teriyaki, pork cutlet), plus six pieces of rolled sushi for $5.95. And since several of the waitresses are vegetarian or vegan, Tako is especially well-equipped to satisfy customers with special diets.

Tara Thai

Zone 11A Virginia suburbs	Thai
226 Maple Avenue West, Vienna	★★★½
(703) 255-2467	Moderate
Zone 10A Maryland suburbs	Quality 85 Value A
4828 Bethesda Avenue, Bethesda	
(301) 657-0488	

Reservations: Helpful
When to go: Weekdays
Entree range: $7.95 – 12.95
Payment: VISA, MC, AMEX, DC, D
Service rating: ★★★
Friendliness rating: ★★★½
Parking: Free lot
Bar: Full service
Wine selection: House
Dress: Informal, casual
Disabled access: Fair
Customers: Ethnic, local
Lunch: Monday – Friday, 11:30 A.M. – 3 P.M.;
                       Saturday and Sunday, noon – 3:30 P.M.
Dinner: Sunday – Thursday, 5 – 10 P.M.;
                       Friday and Saturday, 5 – 11 P.M.

Atmosphere/setting: "Tara" has nothing to do with the old South. It means "blue," and these charming restaurants are marine blue and swimming in fantastical creatures and lacquered tables. The original Vienna branch is quite small, but so friendly that it seems cheerfully crowded rather than annoyingly so. The Bethesda branch draws a more mixed 20- and 30-something crowd to its cheeky murals, window-box bar, and chrome touches.

House specialties: Whole fish, either fried with chile sauce or steamed in banana leaves with black mushrooms and ginger; soft-shell crabs; "wild" lamb curry; red curry beef; green eggplant curry with chicken.

Other recommendations: Nua sawan, thin, dried but tender beef, fried and served with slaw—sort of Thai barbecue; honey-glazed duck. For a light meal or shared appetizer, try the "heavenly wings," chicken drumettes scraped back into rattle shapes, stuffed with crab and green onion, then battered and fried.

Summary & comments: These cheerful in-circle kitchens (the staff began at the equally cerulean Busara) have quickly become area favorites; the food is extremely fresh and clean-tasting, with a variety of sauces and heat levels.

Taste of Casablanca

Zone 11B   Virginia suburbs
3211 North Washington Boulevard,
   Arlington
(703) 527-7468

Moroccan	
★★½	
Inexpensive	
Quality 79	Value A

Reservations:	Helpful
When to go:	Any time
Entree range:	$8.95−14.95
Payment:	VISA, MC, AMEX
Service rating:	★★★
Friendliness rating:	★★★★
Parking:	Street
Bar:	Full service
Wine selection:	House
Dress:	Casual
Disabled access:	Good
Customers:	Local, ethnic
Lunch:	Monday−Friday, 11:30 A.M.−2:30 P.M.
Dinner:	Sunday−Thursday, 5:30−10 P.M.;
	Friday and Saturday, 5:30−11:30 P.M.

Atmosphere/setting: One of Clarendon Row's shoebox dining rooms, but not unpleasant, with whitewashed walls, travel posters of Morocco, small prayer rugs as tapestries, and the great Bogart in cinematic splendor.

House specialties: A "royal" couscous piling lamb, chicken, and the spicy Moroccan sausages called merguez over the grains; an unusual number of tajines, incuding a lamb tajine with dried prunes and saffron and a very traditional chicken version with olives and preserved lemon.

Other recommendations: An uncommon (and slightly less sweet) seafood bastilla, with shrimp, squid, and red snapper; harrira, a spicy lentil garbanzo soup; a good lentil dish with butternut squash and hot sauce.

Entertainment and amenities: Belly dancing on weekends.

Summary & comments: There are four major food groups in North African cuisine: kebabs, tajines, bastillas, and couscous. Tajines are meat or poultry stews flavored with citrus or fruit; bastillas are cinnamon/sugar-dusted pastry pies most commonly stuffed with chicken, almonds, and egg; and couscous (the "national dish") is a semolina pasta topped with stewed meats and vegetables. Perhaps the best way to experience this restaurant is to go native, so to speak: Order one of three multicourse "package" dinners ($29.95 or $39.95 for two) and get to taste three or four dishes at once.

Taste of Saigon

Zone 10B   Maryland suburbs
410 Hungerford Drive, Rockville
(301) 424-7222

Zone 11A   Virginia suburbs
8201 Greensboro Drive, McLean
(703) 790-0700

Vietnamese	
★★★½	
Moderate	
Quality 86	Value A

Reservations:	Accepted
When to go:	Any time
Entree range:	$8–13
Payment:	VISA, MC, AMEX, CB, DC, D
Service rating:	★★★
Friendliness rating:	★★★★
Parking:	Free lot
Bar:	Full service
Wine selection:	Limited
Dress:	Informal
Disabled access:	Good
Customers:	Local, business, ethnic
Open:	Monday–Thursday, 11 A.M.–10 P.M.;
	Friday and Saturday, 11 A.M.–11 P.M.;
	Sunday, 11 A.M.–9:30 P.M.

Atmosphere/setting: An intriguingly angular, sleek, grey-and-black lacquer room slyly tucked into the back of a plain office building.

House specialties: Stuffed baby squid; steamed whole rockfish served with rice crêpes and vegetables for rolling up; grilled pork meatballs, also served with crêpes and dipping sauce; caramelized soft-shell crabs (in season) with black beans; choice of seafoods—lobster, soft shells, scallops, or shrimp—in a house special black pepper sauce.

Other recommendations: Cornish hen stuffed with pork; boneless roast quail; grilled pork with mushrooms, peanuts, and cellophane noodles; pho and other noodle soups in appetizer or entree sizes; rich venison curry; pork-stuffed Cornish hen.

Entertainment & amenities: Patio dining in good weather.

Summary & comments: The specials here are interesting dishes; it's as if the kitchen were as intrigued as the diners. The beef dishes are only fair, but the seafood and game bird entrees are particularly good. Some of the sauces are quite heavy, but if you stick to the steamed fish or bountiful soup choices, Vietnamese dinner can be a dieter's dream.

Thai Sa-Mai

Thai	
★★	
Inexpensive	
Quality 74	Value A

Zone 10B   Maryland suburbs
8371 Snouffer School Road,
    Gaithersburg
(301) 963-1800

Reservations:	Accepted
When to go:	Any time
Entree range:	$5.95 − 8.95
Payment:	VISA, MC
Service rating:	★★★
Friendliness rating:	★★★½
Parking:	Free lot
Bar:	Beer and wine
Wine selection:	House
Dress:	Casual
Disabled access:	Good
Customers:	Local, ethnic
Lunch:	Tuesday − Thursday, 11:30 A.M. − 3 P.M.;
	Friday, 11 A.M. − 3 P.M.
Dinner:	Tuesday − Thursday, 5 − 9:30 P.M.;
	Friday, 5 − 11:30 P.M.; Saturday, 4 − 10:30 P.M.;
	Sunday, 5 − 9 P.M.

Atmosphere / setting: A small, pastel room with meticulous, almost microscopically precise ethnic paintings and portraits of Thai royalty.

House specialties: Shrimp with lemongrass and hot chile; squid done the same way (not on the menu, but ask); duck with ginger in black bean sauce; fish, scallops, shrimp, and crab in chile-coconut sauce.

Other recommendations: Green or yellow coconut curries for beef, pork, or chicken; shrimp with lemongrass soup; fried squid with cashews.

Summary & comments: This mom-and-pop operation has more than willingness going for it—it has fearlessness. Parties of mixed chile tolerance will be happy here, since spiciness is measured in eight degrees, from mild/medium/hot to five stars. (Four stars is translated, "How long were you in Thailand?") Beef and pork dishes are respectable if unremarkable renditions and duck is sometimes greasy, but the squid and fish are first-rate. Portions are generous. The original staff has dispersed and perhaps the food has lost half a star, but it's still a find. In mid-winter, it tends to close on Sundays and even Monday; call ahead.

Thai Tavern

Zone 10B   Maryland suburbs
4011-E Norbeck Road (in the
   Norbeck Center), Rockville
(301) 924-1592

	Thai
	★★½
	Inexpensive
	Quality 76 Value A

Reservations:	Accepted
When to go:	Any time
Entree range:	$5.25−8.25
Payment:	VISA, MC, AMEX, D
Service rating:	★★★
Friendliness rating:	★★★
Parking:	Free lot
Bar:	Beer and wine
Wine selection:	House
Dress:	Casual
Disabled access:	Good
Customers:	Local, ethnic
Lunch:	Monday and Wednesday, 11:30 A.M.−3 P.M.
Lunch/Dinner:	Tuesday, Thursday−Saturday, 11:30 A.M.−10 P.M.
Dinner:	Monday and Wednesday, 5−10 P.M.;
	Sunday, 4−9 P.M.

Atmosphere/setting: Despite its cookie-cutter strip-mall exterior and shoe-box space, it's simple and pleasant, with the inevitable mauve and orchid walls; chalked-up daily specials sprout on the walls.

House specialties: "Country-style" yums, shredded meats, seafoods, bean threads, or even Chinese sausages served over Thai salads tanged with chiles and lemon juice; kang som, a "Thai-style bouillabaisse" with fish, shrimp, scallops, and squid in a spicy lemon sauce and wrapped in foil; whole bluefish steamed with ginger; seafoods sautéed in red curry sauce, or sometimes a whole rainbow trout baked in it; shrimp baked in oyster sauce with cellophane noodles, dry mushrooms, bacon, and ginger; duck with green curry and coconut milk.

Other recommendations: Pad thai offered with a whole range of toppings, including pork with black bean sauce, broccoli and seafood, and a pure vegetarian version (like most Asian restaurants, Thai Tavern has plenty for non−meat eaters); steamed whole snapper, sea bass, rainbow trout, or flounder.

Summary & comments: This is one of those amazing little walk-ins that makes you think the proliferation of pre-fab shopping strips in America might not be such a bad idea. It's totally unfrilly, absolutely clean, and surprisingly good, whether you prefer spice (you are welcome to discuss the degree of heat you wish) or simplicity.

That's Amore

Zone 10B   Maryland suburbs
15201 Shady Grove Road, Rockville
(301) 670-9666

Zone 11A   Virginia suburbs
150 Branch Road, SE, Vienna
(703) 281-7777

Zone 7   Upper Northwest
5225 Wisconsin Avenue, NW, Chevy Chase
(202) 237-7800

Reservations:	Accepted for 6 or more
When to go:	Any time
Entree range:	$12−44, all for double portions
Payment:	VISA, MC, AMEX, DC, D
Service rating:	★★½
Friendliness rating:	★★★½
Parking:	Free lot; valet in Chevy Chase
Bar:	Full service
Wine selection:	Average
Dress:	Business, informal
Disabled access:	Good
Customers:	Local, business
Lunch/Dinner:	*Maryland, Chevy Chase, and Virginia:* Monday−Thursday, 11:30 A.M.−10:30 P.M.; Friday, 11:30 A.M.−midnight; *Chevy Chase:* Saturday, 11:30−midnight; Sunday, 11:30−9:30 P.M.
Dinner:	*Maryland and Virginia:* Saturday, 4 P.M.−midnight; Sunday, 4−9:30 P.M.

Atmosphere/setting: Although it's intended to suggest your Sicilian grandmother's kitchen on a Sunday evening, it somehow comes closer to evoking your Sicilian godfather's steakhouse: dark polished walnut, etched glass, a truly gorgeous old, pressed-tin ceiling and hundreds of old immigrant-ancestor photos (most donated by friends of the owners). The Chevy Chase restaurant, the renovated Hamburger Hamlet, has patio seating.

House specialties: Grilled calamari; mussels with pesto (an addict's portion); mixed seafood over fettuccine; clams in a white—really seafood broth and wine, not cream—sauce; chicken cacciatore, really the way Mamma made it.

(continued)

Other recommendations: Fresh fish specials, such as rockfish with clams, mussels, and fresh tomato sauce; Caesar salad; almost any pasta; braised escarole; sausages, veal chops, and even steaks—the porterhouse is of a heft to give Morton's fans pause, and offered in four versions.

Entertainment & amenities: Free mouthwash in the rest rooms for the garlic-wary.

Summary & comments: If the way to the heart is through the stomach, the name is an understatement: These load-it-up restaurants might as well have been called "That's Abondanza." Every dish here is intended to be split, and a lot of them would serve three easily, so they're best enjoyed in a group. A mixed seafood pasta plays like an episode of "Little Mermaid's Neighborhood." Since the dishes, with the exception of a few meatball types, will be too "straight" for the kids, this is a good place for two or three couples to meet, or at least for two weekend jocks to carb up. No wonder they do such a big business in doggie bags. (That's Amore has recently, and under heavy lobbying from neighboring offices, agreed to offer single-serving sizes at lunch.) That's Amore has also gone heavily into the wine-dinner trend, offering one just about every month. There are also branches in Towson, Maryland, and Cascades, Virginia.

TIA QUETA

Zone 10A   Maryland suburbs
4839 DelRay Avenue, Bethesda
(301) 654-4443

Mexican	
★★½	
Moderate	
Quality 75	Value B

Reservations:	Accepted
When to go:	Late evening for sidewalk dining
Entree range:	$10−17
Payment:	VISA, MC, AMEX
Service rating:	★★½
Friendliness rating:	★★★
Parking:	Valet (dinner only), street
Bar:	Full service
Wine selection:	House
Dress:	Casual
Disabled access:	Good
Customers:	Locals
Open:	Monday−Thursday, 11:30 A.M.−10 P.M.; Friday and Saturday, 11:30 A.M.−11 P.M.; Sunday, 2−10 P.M.

Atmosphere/setting: A pretty little villa of white plaster, wood, and the occasional bit of bright porcelain; the outdoor tables are very popular with the afterwork margarita crowd.

House specialties: A chicken mole worth driving for, redolent of bittersweet chocolate and cinnamon but somehow not sweet, and an even better green chile mole.

Other recommendations: Cuban-style roast pork with mixed spices; poached flounder (sometimes red snapper).

Summary & comments: Despite the boom in "new" Tex-Mex, with its slushee-machine drinks and neo-Southwest indigenous red bean cuisine, this homey standby knows its niche—hearty ranchers' food—and sticks to it.

Tony Cheng's Mongolian Restaurant

	Chinese
	★★½
Zone 3 Downtown	Inexpensive
619 H Street, NW	
(202) 842-8669	Quality 75 Value A

Reservations:	Accepted
When to go:	Any time
Entree range:	$8.50–13.95
Payment:	VISA, MC, AMEX
Service rating:	★★½
Friendliness rating:	★★★
Parking:	Street
Bar:	Full service
Wine selection:	House
Dress:	Informal, casual
Disabled access:	Fair
Customers:	Local, tourist, ethnic
Open:	Sunday–Thursday, 11 A.M.–11 P.M.;
	Friday and Saturday, 11 A.M.–midnight

Atmosphere/setting: A big, bright, open room with woven chairs and a giant iron grill in the center surrounded by coolers.

House specialties: Mongolian hot pot, a stockpot of broth with vegetables and noodles to which one adds more ingredients—clams, squid, oysters, chicken, even tripe—at $1.95 to $3.95 per ingredient plus $5 for the pot; or the all-you-can-eat Mongolian barbecue, a sort of similar pick-your-flavor arrangement, but cooked on the grill, for $13.95.

Other recommendations: None—it's a two-item menu, in effect.

Summary & comments: The barbecue is the more fun choice: Customers fill a serving bowl with meats, seafood, or vegetables from the cooler trays, then hand it over to the chef, who dumps the whole plateful onto the grill and stir-fries it—the Mongolian version of Benihana. The cooked dish is flavored with soy sauce, ginger, rice wine, garlic, or chile oil and eaten at the table by stuffing it into little sesame rolls. Tony Cheng's has become an all-you-can-eat indulgence for dieters, especially the hot pot. A good seafood restaurant is upstairs, incidentally, which serves not only a variety of set-price lunches or dinners for parties of four or more and a very serious broad Chinese menu, but dim sum daily from 11 to 3.

TRUMPETS

Zone 6   Dupont Circle/
          Adams-Morgan
1603 17th Street, NW
(202) 232-4141

	Modern American
	★★½
	Moderate
	Quality 79 Value B

Reservations:	Helpful
When to go:	Any time
Entree range:	$9.95−19.95
Payment:	VISA, MC, AMEX, D, DC
Service rating:	★★★
Friendliness rating:	★★★
Parking:	Street
Bar:	Full service
Wine selection:	Good
Dress:	Business, casual
Disabled access:	Good
Customers:	Local, hip
Brunch:	Sunday, 11 A.M.−3 P.M.
Dinner:	Daily, 5:30−11 P.M.

Atmosphere/setting: This funky, not forward, hideaway restaurant began as a gay-lesbian hangout, but anyone who's reluctant to try its good-humored skewering of home cooking because of uncertainty about the comfort level should immediately make tracks. Trumpets is a casual delight; Sunday brunch is evidence of its familiarity with the community.

House specialties: Gratin of lump crab with fresh corn; artichoke ravioli with lemon pesto. And, on top of all that, you can always get a real hamburger.

Summary & comments: David Hagedorn is one of those chefs who doesn't like to be bored, which guarantees that his patrons aren't apt to be either. The menu shifts every several months and is trend- and audience-savvy, but he's not a fashion victim. For instance, last summer the menu tweaked the Dupont Circle body-conscious (and the new, more conservative gay crowd) by dividing dishes between the low-fat recipes, complete with nutritional analyses, and the don't ask/don't tell lists. He likes to play with his food, so to speak, calling a mozzarella-layered portobello cap a mushroom "pizzeto" (mini-pizza) or calling sea bass tempura with rémoulade sauce a "Cajun fish and chips." If suddenly everyone is talking new Southern cuisine or Mediterranean meze, he can do it better and funnier: corn flake-crusted pork chops with Tabasco, cheese grits, and fried okra, straight from his home town of Gadsden, Alabama; roasty baba ghanoush and marinated chèvre with pita, and so on. But the flavor's no joke.

284

Two Quail

Zone 2 Capitol Hill	Modern American
320 Massachusetts Avenue, NE	★★½
(202) 543-8030	Moderate
	Quality 79 Value C

Reservations:	Recommended
When to go:	Early evening
Entree range:	$11−19.50
Payment:	VISA, MC, AMEX, DC, CB, D
Service rating:	★★½
Friendliness rating:	★★★½
Parking:	Street
Bar:	Full service
Wine selection:	Limited
Dress:	Business, informal
Disabled access:	No
Customers:	Business, local, tourist
Lunch:	Monday − Friday, 11:30 A.M.−2:30 P.M.
Dinner:	Monday − Thursday, 5 − 10:30 P.M.;
	Friday and Saturday, 5 − 11 P.M.;
	Sunday, 5 − 10 P.M.

Atmosphere/setting: A classic Hill rowhouse done up like one of those literary-boudoir retreats that show up every once in a while in travel magazines: old-fashioned, flowery wallpaper, lace-trimmed linen over floral tablecloths, a little stained glass, a few old daguerrotypes and such. Either you find it lushly romantic or fussy and over-Ashley.

House specialties: The "house signature" of quail stuffed with walnuts, apples, herbed cheese, and artichoke sauce; scallops, pancetta, and tomatoes over linguine; ravioli stuffed with asparagus and tossed with a marinara sauce lightly "creamed" with Boursin cheese.

Other recommendations: Smoked peppered bluefish; pork chops stuffed with apricots and sausage, a longtime favorite; spicy veggie quesadillas and cornbread-stuffed chicken.

Summary & comments: This is a popular spot for the go-with-the-conservative-flow power women who lunch: lobbyists and lawyers and Hill aides who want to indulge in newish but not nouvelle cuisine—that is, chic enough to match a fashionable outfit but not too heavy and not too cutting-edge. The menu stays reasonably small but varied; it's kind of trend-lite, but in a good way for such a neighborhood standard. And smartly, it's in no hurry to overbroaden its appeal. At night, its intimate little booths are in high date demand.

Vegetable Garden

Zone 10B   Maryland suburbs
11618 Rockville Pike (White Flint
   Station Shopping Center), Rockville
(301) 468-9301

Chinese (vegetarian)
★★★
Moderate

Quality 80   Value B

Reservations:	Accepted
When to go:	Any time
Entree range:	$6.75−12.95
Payment:	VISA, MC, AMEX
Service rating:	★★½
Friendliness rating:	★★★
Parking:	Free lot
Bar:	Full service
Wine selection:	House
Dress:	Casual
Disabled access:	Good
Customers:	Local, ethnic
Lunch:	Monday−Friday, 11:30 A.M.−2:30 P.M.
Dinner:	Sunday−Thursday, 5−10 P.M.;
	Friday and Saturday, 5−10:30 P.M.

Atmosphere/setting: Light suburban Asian, with pink walls, pink and green carpeting and floral upholstery, and nice poster art of the chain-gallery variety.

House specialties: A really good "vegi-goose" dish, thin soy crêpes wrapped around minced vegetables and mushrooms; crunchy sesame "chicken" nuggets (all the meats are soy foods, with slightly differing textures); carved shiitake mushrooms with asparagus and a little chile bite; spinach-stuffed tofu-skin rolls fried with asparagus and sweet-and-sour sauce.

Other recommendations: Crispy (fried) spicy eggplant or braised eggplant in hot sauce; and noodle choices of soba, rice noodles, and lo mein. There are also a variety of appetizers, such as steamed or pan-fried dumplings, spinach "knishes" and "latkes" (this is Rockville, after all), and spaghetti squash patties.

Summary & comments: The Vegetable Garden is beginning to be noticed by national magazines catering not only to vegetarians and vegans but young, nutrition-conscious women. Nothing is really strong-tasting, even the dishes marked spicy (unless you make a point of it), but it's surprisingly soothing—a different concept of comfort food. And much, though not all, is low-cal, as a fringe benefit. The menu follows Buddhist rules, so it eliminates dairy foods entirely; if you ask, the staff will even tell you which dishes are made with only organic ingredients. You also have a choice of brown or white rice.

286

Vidalia

Zone 6	Dupont Circle/	Modern American
	Adams-Morgan	★★★★
1990 M Street, NW		Expensive
(202) 659-1990		Quality 93 Value B

Reservations:	Recommended
When to go:	Any time
Entree range:	$19−22
Payment:	VISA, MC, AMEX, D
Service rating:	★★★★
Friendliness rating:	★★★
Parking:	Street, garage, valet (dinner only)
Bar:	Full service
Wine selection:	Very good
Dress:	Business, dressy, casual
Disabled access:	Good
Customers:	Business, local, tourist
Lunch:	Monday−Friday, 11:30 A.M.−2:30 P.M.
Dinner:	Monday−Thursday, 5:30−10 P.M.;
	Friday and Saturday, 5:30−10:30 P.M.;
	Sunday, 5−9:30 P.M.

Atmosphere/setting: Although this is actually a below-stairs establishment (disabled access is through the office lobby elevators), it's remarkably bright for a basement and as new−Southern Revival as a Martha Stewart magazine: sponged buttercup walls (the chef's wife's handiwork), dried flower wreaths, stripped-wood banisters and dowels.

House specialties: Roasted sweetbreads with morels and a tang of bacon and chard; salmon seared in a fennel-seed crust; fried squid with blackened fennel; a Provençal-style round-bone lamb steak with artichokes, olives, and roast garlic; double "porterhouse" pork chop with pears and currants at dinner and a cornbread-and-sausage-stuffed chop at lunch.

Other recommendations: Monkfish roasted in a mushroom crust; a lunchtime steak salad with arugula, fennel, and shiitakes; breast of duck with duck confit; a seared but rare salmon appetizer with marinated scallops and Southwestern spices. For light fare, go into the Onion Bar and check out the $4 tapas.

Summary & comments: Jeff Buben is another of those chefs who delights in native American ingredients based on sheer flavor rather than tradition. His luxuriant sauces aren't low-cal but he serves them with a light touch. Particularly if you dally over the big, first-course salads and the scones, Vidalia can be a bargain.

Vincenzo al Sole

		Italian
Zone 6	Dupont Circle/	★★★
	Adams-Morgan	Expensive
1606 20th Street, NW		
(202) 667-0047		Quality 82 Value C

Reservations:	Recommended
When to go:	Any time
Entree range:	$15.75−21.75
Payment:	VISA, MC, AMEX, DC, CB
Service rating:	★★★
Friendliness rating:	★★½
Parking:	Street, valet (dinner only)
Bar:	Full service
Wine selection:	Good but limited
Dress:	Casual, business
Disabled access:	Good
Customers:	Local, business, tourist
Lunch:	Monday−Friday, noon−2 P.M.
Dinner:	Monday−Saturday, 6−10 P.M.; Sunday, closed.

Atmosphere/setting: An elegant old Dupont Circle mansion whose small, intimate rooms are given unusual warmth by huge floral arrangements and the glassed-in patio-cum-conservatory. The casual place settings make it seem like your rich uncle's country estate.

House specialties: Although seafood is no longer the only choice, it's still the best: antipasto di mare with marinated shrimp, steamed clams, and fried squid; sea bass with olives; shrimp fried with fennel; squid with Swiss chard. The next best choice is pasta. Among meats, sweet-and-sour rabbit with polenta; braised veal.

Other recommendations: Daily specials; grilled mackerel.

Summary & comments: Once D.C.'s best Italian seafood specialist, Vincenzo had slipped from its longtime prominence with the influx of showier Italian restaurants; and a couple of ill-conceived image retoolings—not only of the menu but a bewildering merry-go-round of names and levels of formality—had confused and even alienated some of its clientele. So it is gradually doing what it probably should have done the first time—gotten back to its basics. It still conveys an odd sense of ambivalence, however: The kitchen alternates between a sort of brash confidence and a longing for security, which results in first-rate food one night, merely satisfying fare another. Disabled access is through the rear.

Willard Room

	Modern Continental
	★★★
	Expensive
	Quality 82 Value B

Zone 3   Downtown
1401 Pennsylvania Avenue, NW
   (Willard Hotel)
(202) 637-7440

Reservations:	Recommended
When to go:	Any time
Entree range:	$18.50−29
Payment:	VISA, MC, AMEX, D, DC
Service rating:	★★★
Friendliness rating:	★★★
Parking:	Valet (dinner only), free lot
Bar:	Full service
Wine selection:	House
Dress:	Jacket and tie recommended
Disabled access:	Good
Customers:	Local, business
Breakfast:	Monday−Friday, 7:30−10 A.M.
Lunch:	Monday−Friday, 11:30 A.M.−2 P.M.
Dinner:	Daily, 6−10 P.M.

Atmosphere / setting: An old-style grand hotel room restored to full (and for some, overwhelming) grandeur, with plush crimson damask draperies, ornate carved columns, gilded touches, and fine china and silver.

House specialties: Roast "loin" of tuna in phyllo with spinach and black olives; venison loin with chestnuts and vegetables in pastry; duck foie gras and confit with honeyed turnips or marinated fresh sardines with green onion and horseradish cream (both appetizers); roast pheasant with red cabbage.

Other recommendations: Shad roe with morels; beef with eggplant "caviar" and portobellos; poached halibut with clams; nightly specials, particularly of game, such as a baked rack of elk with winter squash.

Entertainment and amenities: Piano music nightly, 6:30 to 10:30.

Summary & comments: This is rich stuff, both to the eye and on the palate. Executive chef Guy Reinbolt is Alsatian, but he's also worked in New Orleans, France, Germany, and even Memphis, and there's a little of all that, plus a leftover touch o' fusion Thai from another stint, in his cooking. This is a good place to settle back and order the chef's tasting menu—three courses for $33 or four courses for $42—which is apt to have the more interesting specials. The Willard Room is also open from 2 to 4 on weekends for high tea.

Woo Lae Oak

Zone 11B   Virginia suburbs
1500 South Joyce Street, Arlington
(703) 521-3706

Korean
★★★
Moderate
Quality 82   Value A

Reservations:	Accepted, suggested on weekends
When to go:	Any time
Entree range:	$8.50−15
Payment:	VISA, MC, AMEX, DC
Service rating:	★★★★
Friendliness rating:	★★★
Parking:	Free lot
Bar:	Full service
Wine selection:	Fair
Dress:	Casual, informal
Disabled access:	No
Customers:	Ethnic, local
Open:	Daily, 11:30 A.M.−10:30 P.M.

Atmosphere/setting: California Asian, this freestanding section of an apartment complex is a big curving slice of a room on stilts, with modernized versions of traditional wood-slat-and-rice-paper decor. All tables have barbecue grills built in.

House specialties: Shin sun ro, a fancy hot pot (Korean shabu shabu) that requires 24-hours' notice; saeng sun jun, battered and grilled fish; bulgoki, the familiar sweet-soy beef barbecue; spicy fish stew in a pot; yook hwe bibimbap, marinated raw sirloin strips with spinach, bean sprouts, zucchini, etc., in sesame oil; boneless short rib cubes.

Other recommendations: Beef liver, heart, tongue, and tripe for the more intrepid barbecuers; broiled salmon; sliced raw fish, cut in generous, steak-fry-sized pieces, not the thin Japanese layers. Modum yori, a combination grill platter, including a whole fish, shrimp, chicken, and beef, is a huge family meal, but requires a day's advance notice.

Summary & comments: This is not food to eat alone. The fun is barbecuing (or in the case of the many hot-pot dishes, dipping) with friends. Besides, many of the dishes are made for two, and the sashimi appetizer is so big—about 24 pieces, and cut Korean-style, meaning large—that it's either a meal or a first course for several. Many dishes cost less at lunch. The one real disappointment about this restaurant for non-Asian diners is that staffers frequently doubt that you know what you're ordering, or don't take it seriously; for example, even with the 24 hours' notice, it can be hit-or-miss if you get your shin sun ro.

Wurzburg Haus

Zone 10B Maryland suburbs	German
7236 Muncaster Mill Road (Red Mill	★★★
Shopping Center), Rockville	Moderate
(301) 330-0402	Quality 80 Value B

Reservations:	Not accepted
When to go:	Any time
Entree range:	$8–15
Payment:	VISA, MC, AMEX, D, DC
Service rating:	★★★
Friendliness rating:	★★★
Parking:	Free lot
Bar:	Beer and wine
Wine selection:	Limited
Dress:	Casual
Disabled access:	Good
Customers:	Locals
Open:	Monday–Thursday, 11:30 A.M.–9 P.M.;
	Friday, 11:30 A.M.–10 P.M.;
	Saturday, noon–10 P.M.; Sunday, noon–9 P.M.

Atmosphere/setting: Just a strip mall storefront, but tangibly hospitable and beer-hall chummy with lots of chalet-pointed wood accents and travel posters.

House specialties: Four kinds of veal schnitzel, two predictably breaded, but all, particularly the unbreaded version in paprika sauce, surprisingly moist; the smoked pork brauerwurst and the veal weisswurst; herring in sour cream; a fine sauerbraten with red cabbage and potato pancakes; roast duckling; occasional game specials such as venison.

Other recommendations: Black Forest chicken with Bing cherries; boneless trout; for sausage fans, a sampler platter of four.

Entertainment & amenities: A strolling accordianist performs polka music Friday and Saturday evenings. And the homemade breads are for sale.

Summary & comments: There are a couple of hard-to-find German beers on tap here and a dozen others in bottles. This is a good place to remember why German food is such comfort food, though maybe not such a good place to pursue a diet. "Hearty" is almost a pun here for "straight to your heart." You could hold the line for dessert by ordering the trout broiled and the pork chop baked, but why bother?

Yijo

Zone 10D   Maryland suburbs
9137 Baltimore Avenue/Route 1 (in
    the Days Inn), College Park
(301) 345-6500

Korean	
★★½	
Inexpensive	
Quality 78	Value B

Reservations:	Accepted
When to go:	Any time
Entree range:	$7.95−21.95
Payment:	VISA, MC, AMEX
Service rating:	★½
Friendliness rating:	★★½
Parking:	Free lot
Bar:	Full service
Wine selection:	House
Dress:	Casual
Disabled access:	Fair
Customers:	Ethnic
Open:	Every day, 10:30 A.M.−10:30 P.M.

Atmosphere/setting: "Atmosphere" is almost inapplicable here, unless perhaps you get a seat by the windows overlooking the motel pool, in which case you may have some informal entertainment. Otherwise, it's just about as plain a room as can be, considering the stainless-steel hoods and fire dousers hanging overhead. Most tables have small, built-in barbecue grills in the top (which are generally employed for Korean diners—the rest of us get food grilled in the kitchen).

House specialties: Poached seasoned salmon steak or king mackerel; braised small octopus or squid in spicy sauce; a generous and high-quality yook hwe bibimbap, the sesame-oiled steak tartare (although they keep it so cold for hand chopping that occasionally it's still icy); homey pot dishes such as sliced beef and vegetables over buckwheat noodles; monkfish casserole.

Other recommendations: Korean barbecues, including tongue, beef kidney, and pork roast; a "Korean scallion pancake with seafood" (called pajyun) which is a cross between a giant-sized, thin-crust pizza and a seafood quesadilla.

Summary & comments: This little joint is so thoroughly ethnic (as is its clientele) that even the items usually identified by their Japanese names, such as saké, sashimi, and tempura, are listed in Korean. The service is a little absentminded—close to standoffish, in fact—and you may have to flag somebody down to get a second drink. They don't explain much about Korean dining—for instance, that the plate of large lettuce leaves is for wrapping bulgoki and condiments to eat by hand—but you can always watch for hints at other tables.

YokoHAMA

Korean/Japanese
★★½
Moderate
Quality 79   Value A

Zone 10B   Maryland suburbs
11300-B Georgia Avenue, Wheaton
(301) 949-7403

Reservations:	Accepted
When to go:	Any time
Entree range:	$8.95 – 13.95
Payment:	VISA, MC, AMEX
Service rating:	★★★
Friendliness rating:	★★★★
Parking:	Small lot, street
Bar:	Full service
Wine selection:	House
Dress:	Informal
Disabled access:	Fair
Customers:	Ethnic, local
Open:	Tuesday – Thursday, 11:30 A.M. – 10:30 P.M.;
	Friday and Saturday, 11:30 A.M. – 11 P.M.;
	Sunday, noon – 10:30 P.M.; Monday, closed.

Atmosphere / setting: An island of surprising quiet in the heart of Wheaton's flourishing restaurant boomtown, Yokohama is traditional in its plain wood-and-screen decor, with partitions that confer surprising privacy for smaller groups; larger groups use the central tables. Only a few stools are at the sushi bar itself.

House specialties: From the Korean menu, a spectacular (and jumbo-sized) version of spicy julienned squid marinated and sautéed with sweet and hot peppers and onions; beef dumpling soup; pajyun, the Korean-style pancake with beef, oysters, and shrimp; hwai dupbap, a typically Korean take on chirashi sushi with the raw fish and rice topped with chile sauce; and the classic marinated and grilled beef, chicken, or pork. From the Japanese menu, salmon teriyaki, various combinations of sushi and sashimi, and broiled sweet-water eel.

Other recommendations: Tripe-noodle casserole, here offered for one instead of only two (but for $20); vegetarian offerings of tempura or cold buckwheat noodles; noodles in "black sauce" and diced pork.

Summary & comments: A less well-known but striking contender in a booming field, Yokohama is generous both in the size of its portions and in its complimentary tastes of sushi (usually California rolls, delivered with the drinks). And it has faith in Americans' penchant for chile sauces. Although the chef/owner was born in Seoul, his family is Japanese. This is probably why Yokohama is one of the better-balanced mixed-menu shops.

Zed's

Zone 5 Georgetown	Ethiopian
3318 M Street, NW	★★½
(202) 333-4710	Inexpensive
	Quality 79 Value B

Reservations:	Accepted for parties of 5 or more
When to go:	Any time
Entree range:	$7−12.50
Payment:	VISA, MC, AMEX, DC, D
Service rating:	★★★
Friendliness rating:	★★★
Parking:	Street, lot
Bar:	Full service
Wine selection:	House
Dress:	Informal
Disabled access:	No
Customers:	Local, tourist, ethnic
Open:	Every day, 11 A.M.−11 P.M.

Atmosphere/setting: Rent is high in Georgetown, and Zed's doesn't try to compete on decor, which, considering its two narrow shoebox levels, would be tough anyway. The atmosphere sort of depends on the "kindness of strangers" effect, and the decor consists of a few framed travel posters advertising Ethiopia's "13 Months of Sunshine" and a handful of handicrafts.

House specialties: Bozena shuro, a spicy stew of yellow split peas with beef; cauliflower, bean, and carrot stew; chicken strips in red pepper sauce; broiled beef short ribs.

Other recommendations: Red lentil watt; mild lamb alicha; beef stewed with collard greens.

Summary & comments: Although prices are slightly higher at Zed's than at most Ethiopian restaurants, the quality of the injera, made here with a lighter millet dough, and the few unusual dishes make Zed's notable. And accustomed as they are to student and tourist traffic, the staff is very tolerant. For explanations on eating Ethiopian (i.e., with your hands), see the profile of Meskerem.

Zio's

Zone 10B   Maryland suburbs
9083 Gaither Road, Gaithersburg
(301) 977-6300

Reservations:	Not accepted
When to go:	Any time
Entree range:	$5.75 − 12.95
Payment:	VISA, MC, AMEX, DC
Service rating:	★ ★ ★
Friendliness rating:	★ ★ ★
Parking:	Free lot, street
Bar:	Beer and wine
Wine selection:	House
Dress:	Casual
Disabled access:	Fair
Customers:	Local, business
Lunch/Dinner:	Monday − Friday, 11 A.M.− 10 P.M.; Saturday, noon − 10 P.M.
Dinner:	Sunday, 3 − 9 P.M.

Atmosphere/setting: Traditional suburban pizzeria, but smarter—green walls trimmed with black-and-white checkerboard, ivy stenciling, and neo-Deco posters.

House specialties: Pizza and calzone; stuffed eggplant and eggplant Parmesan; cold cut subs; fried calamari.

Other recommendations: Lasagna; chicken cacciatore; old-fashioned ravioli with ground meat or cheese. Surprisingly, their souvlaki salad, with a skewer of marinated beef and feta over a large plate of greens, is pretty good.

Summary & comments: The entrees are pretty good, and generous—a pasta with mussels comes with easily three dozen (pre-shelled; this is a simple place) mussels—but in truth, Zio's pizza dough, which is also used for the calzones, is so incredibly good that it's hard to pass up. Chewy but not heavy, brushed ever so lightly with olive oil, it's like the best hearth bread you can imagine. The salad and fresh fruit bar isn't large, but the ingredients aren't left to age as they are too often elsewhere.

Eclectic Gourmet Guide to Washington, D.C.
Reader Survey

If you would like to express your opinion about your Washington dining experiences or this guidebook, complete the following survey and mail it to:

> Eclectic Gourmet Guide Reader Survey
> P.O. Box 43059
> Birmingham, AL 35243

	Diner 1	Diner 2	Diner 3	Diner 4	Diner 5
Gender (M or F)	_____	_____	_____	_____	_____
Age	_____	_____	_____	_____	_____
Hometown	_____	_____	_____	_____	_____

Tell us about the restaurants you've visited . . . .

You're overall experience:

Restaurant

Comments you'd like to share with other diners: